Team Suzuki

Riders

I remember the amount of time Ray spent at Suzuki researching his book. I wa̶ ̶ whether Ray ever actually did any work for Suzuki. He and I would pore over the photos ̶ ̶ght back from Hamamatsu to include in his book. I still have a copy.

Graeme Crosby
1st TT F1 World Championship 1980 and 1981
1st Suzuka 8-Hour Endurance Race 1980
8th 500cc World Championship 1980
1st Daytona Superbikes
1st 500cc Isle of Man TT (Senior 1980 and TT F1 1981)
5th 500cc World Championship 1981
1st 500cc British Championship
2nd 500cc World Championship 1982
1st Daytona 200 1982
1st Imola 200 1982

Ray's book is far and away the most comprehensive and authoritative book on the motorcycles and people who made Suzuki one of today's most famous motorcycles. It's packed full of very interesting information and photography from beginning to end. Ray did some promotional writing for me during the days when Barry Sheene, Kenny Roberts and I battled it out for the GP World Championship

Pat Hennen
The First American to win a 500cc Grand Prix (Finnish GP 1976)
1st Marlboro Series (New Zealand) 1974–75, 1975–76 and 1976–77
3rd 500cc World Championship 1976
Texaco Heron Team Suzuki rider 1977–78
3rd 500cc World Championship 1977
6th 500cc World Championship 1978
Member of the AMA Motorcycle Hall of Fame

TEAM
SUZUKI

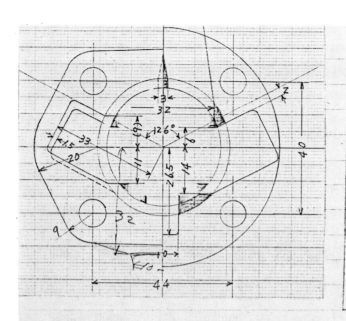

参考 RK64の各ポートのタイミング
全ストロークの割合　ストローク 30

Ex ポート 16

$$\frac{1600}{30} = 53.3\%$$

Se ポート 22.5

$$\frac{2250}{30} = 75\%$$

Ex タイミング　　$31.5 \times 53 = \underline{16.695}$

Se タイミング　　$31.5 \times 75 = \underline{23.625}$

Im タイミング　　45～70 (45～80)

動力伝達方式

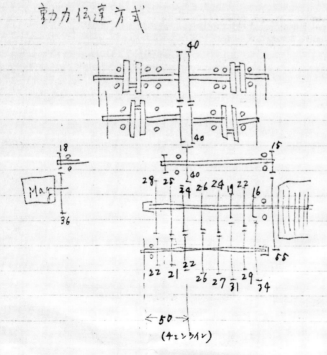

(チェンライン)

←50→

目標　16,000 rpm

210 km/h

Top の変速比 = 0.786 (RT63)

12 とれば

= 二次 = 2.83 とし

$$V = \frac{N \times 3\pi D}{50\alpha} \qquad \pi D = 1.836$$

(2.50-13)

$$\alpha = \frac{16000 \times 3 \times 1.836}{50 \times 210} = 8.4$$

$$一次 = \frac{8.4}{2.83 \times 0.786} = 3.77$$

一次は　$55/15 = 3.66$

に決定する

TEAM
SUZUKI

A definitive analysis of the
FACTORY'S ROADRACING MOTORCYCLES

RAY BATTERSBY

PARKER
HOUSE

for
John Wilkinson

ISBN-13: 978-0-9796891-5-4
ISBN-10: 0-9796891-5-5

Book design Gwyn Lewis
Cover design Chris Fayers via Gwyn Lewis
Manufactured in China

10 9 8 7 6 5 4 3 2 1

First published in 1982 by Osprey Publishing Ltd., London, UK
This edition in 2008 by Parker House Publishing Inc.

Page 1
Chasing the championship, Lucchinelli (2) and Mamola at the 1980 British GP. Both machines are XR34Ms but 'Lucky' is using a 16 inch front wheel *MCW*

Page 2
From the notebook of racing designer Seichi Suzuki: this is the RS65 125 cc square four two stroke tested in 1965. The four separate cranks and 8-speed transmission are shown, with calculations for port timing and gearing. (See also p 199) *Archives*

Parker House Publishing Inc.
PO Box 756
1826 Tower Drive
Stillwater, MN 55082, USA

www.parkerhousepublishing.com

Contents

Acknowledgements

Without the Suzuki Motor Company, *Team Suzuki* would not exist; Suzuki not only provided the subject, but gave me much-valued assistance in its research. For this I am deeply grateful, and in particular to Ryosuki Matsuki, Susumu Saito, Tadaomi Shigenoya, Sakuhiro Ikemoto and Takashi Nakamura, who with Yoshikiyo Suzuki, Seichi Suzuki, Tadao Matsui and Mitsuru Okamato provided material and offered me a regular translation service.

Suzuki's photographic files were opened to me by Mr Hashimoto and Mr Miyazaki, whilst Mr H Uchiyama, Suzuki's engineering director, kindly gave me the run of the factory racing department, allowing me to photograph hitherto secret racing machines. I also appreciated the opportunity of talking with racing personnel Etsuo Yokouchi, Makoto Hase, Yasunori Kamiya and especially Masazumi Ishikawa who made a major contribution to this book by imparting his 'full knowledge' and by offering me his private photographic collection. I extend to him my sincere thanks for this and for writing the preface.

Having scoured the world for Jimmy Matsumiya, he surfaced in Gerrard's Cross and I am grateful for his hospitality and stamina. Much assistance was gained from Lew Ellis, Ernst Degner, Frank Perris, Hans-Georg Anscheidt, Bertie Schneider and Stuart Graham, many of whom loaned me their valuable scrap books and photographs.

In tracing these key figures, I was pleased to be helped by my friends, John Van de Water of Holland and Manfred Kugler of Suzuki Deutschland whose racing contacts seemed to span at least two generations! New Zealand's Rod Coleman kindly put me in contact with Hugh Anderson and both filled in many gaps, I am indebted to them for much material assistance and advice.

I leaned heavily on Merv Wright's first hand experience and through him, I met Dick Hammer, Shoji Tanaka, Bud Wilson and Jody Nicholas. Merv also hosted me during my Los Angeles visit, a journey made possible by the generosity of Peter Agg, Heron Suzuki GB's chairman, and he introduced me to Allan Girdler, *Cycle World*'s editor who approved my eight hour rummage through his vast photographic library.

Great help was afforded me by Mick Woollet of *Motor Cycle Weekly* who gave me free rein within its records and who, like *MCN*'s editor, Bob Berry, loaned me many photographs. Others were provided by Graeme Crosby, Vic Willoughby, Rex White, 'Brandmark', *Cycle*, and the Dutch magazine *Motor*, but perhaps I am most thakful to Wolfgang Gruber with whom I spent many hours selecting photographs from his 30,000-strong collection.

My Heron Suzuki GB involvement simplified the task but a special thank you is needed for my friends Rex and Jackie White for their valuable contributions to 'Battle of Britain'. Countless hours were spent talking with Mike Sinclair, Frans VandenBroek, George Vukmanovich, Chip Hennen, Bill Buchka, and Bob White about technicalities, but in particular, I am indebted to Martyn Ogborne who provided many facts and checked the accuracy of Appendix 4 — a daunting task.

Pat Hennen, John Newbold, Graeme Crosby and Randy Mamola freely gave me their candid thoughts between their racing commitments when perhaps they preferred to be doing other things. Similarly, during the hectic 1980 TT week, Pops Yoshimura gave me valuable insight into his philosophy and tuning methods.

A special mention of my editor, Tim Parker is necessary. From our first meeting, I benefited from his unflagging support and enthusiasm for our joint project. Without his perseverance and encouragement, *Team Suzuki* would never have appeared.

For permission to quote material, I extend my gratitude to *Motocourse* and Studio Publications, whilst for his welcome guidance during times of stress, I thank friend and author Roy Bacon.

To those other un-named helpers I offer my sincere thanks, and finally, my family. Cynthia has not only typed the manuscript through its three or four drafts, she also transcribed over 70 hours of recorded interviews and tackled the indexing. And as far as my role as husband and father goes, I am ashamed to admit that in most instances of conflicting interests, *Team Suzuki* came first. During its writing, my daughter Jane has been transformed from a little girl into a young lady and sadly, I missed it all. I can only hope she feels that *Team Suzuki* was worth the sacrifice....

Ray Battersby
1 June 1982

Author's note to this new edition

Over the years many Suzuki fans have contacted me asking me to help them find a copy of *Team Suzuki* even though I, too, have problems finding copies for myself. So there's been a demand.

And then, thanks to eBay, I've seen First Edition books fetching up to ten, sometimes 20 times the original cover price that was itself pushing the boundaries in 1982. So when I caught up once again with my friend and now publisher, Tim Parker, we persuaded each other to republish the book. OK. There's a different dust jacket and I've corrected the known typos within the text but the book is otherwise the same. Maybe one day, somebody will have the stamina to write the sequel that brings the story up to date.

Ray Battersby
14 May 2008

Author's note

Throughout *Team Suzuki*, references to Suzuki racing machines are made by using their official factory codes and not their more familiar names. For example, the factory racer commonly referred to as the 'RG500' has in reality, been produced to six different specifications—discounting the 'production' RG500.

The use of the factory codes avoids confusion since, in the main, each new version was allocated a new code. Taking the 'RG500' again, on announcement in 1974 it was the XR14 whilst in 1978 it became the XR22, the XR27B (1979), XR34H and XR34M (1980) and in 1981, the XR35. These are the codes used and I have compiled a detailed analysis of them in Appendix 2.

Preface

It is my great honour to write a preface to Ray Battersby's painstaking work.

I became acquainted with Ray in June 1977. Since then, he has pursued me incessantly in order to obtain material for this book because I was engaged in the Suzuki road racing team from 1961 to 1967 and the motocross team from 1968 to 1973.

I, myself, have longed to put all material of Suzuki racing activities in order, but have wasted time, not knowing how to use it and regretfully my memories are growing faint and the material hoarded is gradually being scattered.

Upon learning of his ambition, I tried to support Ray with my full knowledge and offer him all the material in my hands.

I was amazed at his ceaseless and aggressive effort and admire the splendid masterpiece it produced. Bravo Ray!

I really thank him for his work which offers readers a pleasant and personal understanding of Suzuki racing activities.

石川 正純

M. Ishikawa

Masazumi Ishikawa
Hamamatsu, Japan
Team Suzuki Manager 1961 to 1967

Introduction

Researching and writing *Team Suzuki* has been an exciting task; my original intention was to cover only the 1970s. But there were always links with the past and I was drawn—not unwillingly—into covering the earlier period. Then, even earlier Suzuki lore appeared; many Team members of the sixties had been involved with Suzuki's Mounts Fuji and Asama exploits. I finally reached back to 1953 when Suzuki first entered a motorcycle competition and began my researches from that point.

From the outset I determined to obtain first-hand information wherever possible. My researches commenced by reading all available 'Suzuki' literature; some popular and some obscure to the English reader. The long hours spent reading proved invaluable in short-listing my future interviewees. But the task of locating these people was daunting. I travelled widely in applying the dogma of authentic comment and met many generous people who provided more than their recollections; most furnished me with previously unpublished photographs. I travelled to three continents including two visits to Japan, and a week in the USA. My most concentrated period of research was spent on the European Continent where I met Ernst Degner, the man who laid Suzuki's strong racing foundation.

Another principle I adopted was that *Team Suzuki* should concern itself only with genuine factory or 'works' machines; it was tempting to include the history of Suzuki's *production* racing equipment. Indeed, I wasted much time interviewing riders of 'factory' Suzukis only to learn during our discussions that I was dealing with a production racing machine. However, there are occasional lapses where the story would have been otherwise incomplete.

It was never my intention to write just 'another book about racing'. *Team Suzuki* is about the *Team* and how they survived half-a-world away from Japan. What was really happening behind the scenes during the hectic sixties? How much did it all cost? Here is a peep behind the veil of secrecy that will always surround factory racing teams. The environment—hostile grand prix territory—resulted in quantum leaps of technology that were essential if the two stroke engine was to overcome the prevailing four strokes. In the early sixties, race pundits opined that a two stroke would never vanquish the might of the MV, Morini and Honda four strokes. Twenty years later, Honda were openly concerned at the ability of their four stroke NR500 to out-perform the two strokes of their Japanese rivals and have now produced a two stroke racer.

To fully understand the Japanese mentality is to be Japanese! Many recent historical events are comprehensible when one considers that only in 1868 was feudalism abolished and the monarchy restored in Japan. The indoctrinated

loyalty originally extended by the Japanese to the Shoguns—the feudal lords—
has been diverted into patriotism, and more recently, toward their employers. In
common with their Japanese rivals, the Suzuki company enjoys this deeply-felt
loyalty—which extends in both directions—and which was essential to their
impressive racing achievements. Racing for Suzuki was truly a *team* effort, with
ability and unswerving devotion the only prerequisites for Team membership.

Shell sponsored the 1955
Asama Plains races where a
competitor struggles up the
volcano under the eyes of the
locals *Archives*

1   The route to Mount Fuji: the road to Asama (1953 to 1959)

In 1902, Michio Suzuki was just 15 years old. He had grown up among the crude farm implements used in his family's cotton-farming business at Hamamatsu in Japan's Shizuoka Prefecture, and now he had decided to embark upon a seven year apprenticeship in the weaving industry. In his childhood he had developed a mechanical understanding and when his apprenticeship ended he formed his own company, the Suzuki Loom Works.

Within 11 years, his company had expanded into a major exporting business and it was renamed the Suzuki Loom Manufacturing Company. By then, Michio was already married, and when the eldest of his three daughters married Shunzo, Shunzo adopted the Suzuki surname as Japanese tradition required, and was treated as Michio's son. Together, Michio and Shunzo developed the company. In 1937, Shunzo suggested that Suzuki should diversify into the automobile business and built a prototype vehicle based on the Austin Seven. One year later, the Japanese economy was on a war-footing following the outbreak of war with China and the project was shelved.

For the next decade, Suzuki's factory produced many items including armaments, but by 1952, they were producing their first motorised bicycle—the 'Power Free'—of 36 cc capacity, which was shortly increased to a full 50 cc. In the early part of 1953, a new 60 cc machine was unveiled, the 'Diamond Free', basically another 'clip-on' pedal-cycle engine. It was to publicise the 'Diamond Free' that Suzuki first entered a motorcycle competition on 12 July 1953.

The Suzuki 36 cc Power Free
Archives

Motorcycle racing had begun in 1907 in Japan, but the lack of any suitable Japanese manufacturers meant that competitors raced imported machines such as Harley-Davidson, Indian, Triumph, Norton and Sunbeam. In order to accelerate postwar motorcycle development and trade, a group of motorcycle dealers formed the Tokyo Motorcycle Race Association. Their first event was to be staged on the slopes of Mount Fuji and with nationalistic pride, imported machines were excluded. Two classes were listed: 150 cc four strokes and 90 cc two strokes, to race concurrently as a handicap event. Small modifications were allowed by the rules which referred to the entries as 'racers'. Suzuki's Diamond Free entry was complete with patented pedalling equipment, but to suit the difficult conditions a modified air cleaner and stronger chassis were fitted.

In 1953, over 40 Hamamatsu manufacturers were vying for a share of the motorcycle market, and Suzuki were determined to prove their product at Mount Fuji. Midway between Hamamatsu and the capital, Mount Fuji was ideally suited for both manufacturers and spectators who would be drawn to the event in large numbers. Pre-race build-up had been given by the event's sponsors, *Mainichi Shimbun*—literally, *Everyday Newspaper*.

The course consisted of dirt roads—compacted volcanic ash—deeply wheel-rutted and with grass growing along their crowns. It meandered through small hamlets emerging at the summit near the lip of the crater, before returning by a different route to the start; a total distance of $16\frac{3}{4}$ miles (27 Km). On dry days, these roads became enveloped in a volcanic-ash 'smog', whilst on wet days, the road was a sticky quagmire. The choice of dates was therefore critical; whilst January has the least rainfall, it is also very cold. Conversely, in July, temperatures reach 25 degrees Centigrade but are accompanied by heavy rainfall, and high humidity is the result. A July date was fixed for the first Mount Fuji Climbing Races. Suzuki's company had by then been renamed—Suzuki Jidosha Kogyo (Suzuki Automobile Company)—and the SJK Diamond Free was specially prepared by Yoshichika Maruyama and his engineers. Success at Mount Fuji became more significant as the latest economic recession bit deep and Suzuki's Hamamatsu rivals fought for survival. Suzuki's economic success hinged on Mount Fuji.

Mr Maruyama, with a small band of helpers, attended the Saturday training period and Rysaku Yamashita—Suzuki's first 'factory' rider—helped to optimise the carburettor settings to cope with the changes in course altitude. At last all was ready; the course had been decorated with huge brightly-coloured banners and flags, contrasting well with the dark green backdrop formed by Fuji's wooded slopes. At the start-finish area, the Asama Shrine stood behind the podium on which the officials would stand the following day.

On race-day, dawn broke dull and overcast. The 99 entries lined up at the start ready to commence their ascent at intervals. The weather didn't deter the hundreds of spectators lining the route where they could safely watch the riders in the cuttings below them. During the event, Yamashita had to use the pedals to supplement the 2 ft lb maximum torque of the little two stroke engine, but rumours that he carried the Diamond Free over the more arduous sections can be discounted. The focus of attention were the 150 cc four stroke machines, and although Yamashita didn't win the 90 cc class, he was recognised officially as the only rider of a cycle-based machine to finish the course in under one hour. The winner was Nagaoka-San whose Auto-Bit finished in 36 m 14 s, an average speed of 27 mph. Suzuki officials were pleased with the result; they hadn't won the event, but had proved that the Diamond Free was capable of finishing the tough course despite a 30 cc handicap.

The 1954 event was run with a slight change of rules: there were two individual 90 cc and 250 cc classes and both two and four strokes were considered equal. Meanwhile, Suzuki had again been renamed the Suzuki Motor Company, so that company registration abroad was simplified, but in Japan, products were still sold with an SJK brand-name.

During the previous year, many motorcycle manufacturers had closed down, and Suzuki's main rivals were now Honda and Tohatsu. To meet this challenge, Suzuki introduced a new motorcycle, the Colleda CO, powered by a side-valve 4 bhp engine of 90 cc, with a three-speed gearbox. To simplify maintenance, an oil filter was incorporated and the magneto ignition used contact points mounted *outside* the flywheel. The power-unit was mounted in a pressed-steel channel frame, the suspension being plunger-type at the rear and telescopic at the front. For sporting riders, the Colleda CO was available with a lightweight tubular

Toshio Matsumoto astride the 1959 Colleda RB outside the original race shop. Compare the engine—especially the cylinder—with the following photograph *Archives*

chassis, and it was this model that formed the basis of SJK's 1954 Mount Fuji machine. 'Colleda' was a corruption of the Japanese expression, 'Kore da!'— 'This one!'—and Suzuki hoped it would assist initial sales. Mr Maruyama, Masanao Shimizu, and the rider—again Yamashita—set off for Mount Fuji, accompanied by other factory personnel.

The total entry was 97 machines; 63 were 250 cc, the remainder in the 90 cc class. For the race, the weather was identical to that of the previous year, and again, a 250 cc Monarch won the event outright, crossing the line after the gruelling $16\frac{3}{4}$ (27 Km) mile course in just 29 m 44.5 s, an average speed of about 34 mph. About 12 minutes later, the first 90 cc machine crossed the line, the SJK Colleda, averaging 24 mph—unheard of even on the regular Japanese roads of that time. Suzuki were elated at winning the title for their class and were determined to continue entering competitive events although it was obvious that to remain in contention, more research would be needed.

The 1955 Mount Fuji Climbing Race was won by Yamaha's new 125 cc YA1 at record-breaking speed, but Suzuki were absent: their attention had been drawn towards another event to be held that year, the Asama Plains races.

During the early months of 1955, the major Japanese manufacturers as opposed to dealers, including Suzuki, formed a new group; the Nippon Motorcycle Race Association—the NMRA—whose stated policy was to introduce all-out racing to Japan. The NMRA was a powerful organisation and had soon lobbied the Japan Light Vehicle Manufacturers Association into supporting their first event. The objectives of the NMRA were clear: the domestic motorcycle market was limited, and manufacturers looked enviously towards their European rivals who had expanded their sales into far-flung markets, including Japan. The *world* was *their* oyster, whilst the Japanese manufacturers with their inferior products, were unable to compete. To remedy this situation the Asama regulations disqualified motorcycles not of 100 per cent

13

Japanese manufacture and this dictum was intended to raise the level of technology within the domestic industry. Those that went to Asama had a chance of survival: those that didn't were doomed to failure at least in the domestic market.

Japan contains some 26 volcanos that have been active since 1700. One of these is Mount Fuji, another is Mount Asama, an 8340 ft vertebra in Japan's smouldering backbone. Lying about 85 miles North-west of Tokyo, it is easily accessible to the capital's inhabitants.

Suzuki were committed to compete and a 40 day development programme was initiated to provide a competitive racing machine based on the newly introduced 125 cc two stroke Colleda ST. This meant a head-on clash with Yamaha's YA1. Working seven days a week, Mr Maruyama and his team produced a trial design within the 40 days. The machine they wheeled out was a futuristic attempt with swing-arm rear suspension—the normal ST had plunger-type—a long action telescopic fork, and an early form of expansion chamber. Although the single cylinder engine used the production bore and stroke of 52×58 mm, there the similarity ended. The kickstarter was eliminated and a four-speed gearbox was specified against the roadster's three speeds. A special cylinder with innovative porting helped the engine to produce 8 to 9 bhp at the gearbox sprocket. A new crankcase was used repositioning the cylinder rearwards and was heavily finned for improved strength and cooling. A Mikuni M-type carburettor fed fuel through the piston-ported cylinder whilst the exhaust system comprised a long, slowly divergent tube, squeezed at its outlet and fitting snugly under a specially contoured right-hand engine cover. The ST's saddle was replaced by a dual seat but the standard fuel tank was retained, though a hastily daubed 'SJK' symbol had been added. Rear-set footrests were fitted with curious 'stirrups' to prevent dislodgement of the rider's feet on bumpy sections. The wheels and brakes came from the ST but 'knobbly' tyres were fitted, and to aid control of the bucking machine, high-level bars adorned the headstock.

Prior to the event Suzuki established a base camp about half a mile north of Kitakarusawa, a village in the Asama region. Five machines had now been built and were tested by the Team headed by Mr Maruyama and engineer, Masanao Shimizu. The riders, Rysaku Yamashita, Toshio Kamiya, Michio Ichino, Riichi Itoh and Seichi Suzuki were all SJK employees; Ichino, Itoh, and Suzuki later to establish themselves in European grand prix racing.

They investigated the likely routes—NMRA had not yet announced the official course—preparing both men and machines for the event which had attracted entries from Honda, Yamaha, Kawasaki, Bridgestone, Tohatsu, Showa, Lilac, Yamaguchi, and other smaller manufacturers. Eventually, the route was announced; 11.9 miles (19.2 Km) of volcanic ash roads, normally used as a Government test course, with short sections on 'public highways'. Suzuki, meanwhile, had been experiencing problems in practice with broken exhaust mountings and grounding footrests frequently caused the up-ending of machines and riders. Time ran out on Suzuki.

Saturday 5 November broke with near freezing temperatures and a bitter wind but Yamaha were devious; they had secretly practiced on the actual

A prototype Colleda RB. Suzuki's fixation with long intake systems was later dispelled as they boosted power by *minimising* intake lengths
Archives

racecourse before the rest had eaten breakfast! At the start of the 125 cc event, 28 riders sped away as the flag dropped, the YA1s taking an early lead, but Yamashita holding his own. Itoh, meanwhile, had a misfire, his mount finally expiring on a steep gradient. Breaking all the rules, he turned the machine around and bump-started it before sliding around to re-join the race. After an accident caused by the long footrests, when his foot became caught in the 'stirrup' Itoh was forced to retire. Ichino met a similar fate.

With two of the four laps completed, many riders were fatigued due to the arduous conditions, but the plucky Yamaha riders swamped the field scoring 1st to 4th places. Yamashita, Suzuki and Kamiya were 5th, 6th and 7th. Despite these results Suzuki were disappointed since Yamaha had continued their flush of success first achieved at Mount Fuji a few months before. Suzuki learned that in terms of speed their ST could match the YA1 but the result confirmed the importance of good preparation and fortune. Yamaha had both at Asama.

Despondent, Team Suzuki returned to Hamamatsu vowing never to race again after such humiliation. For this reason Suzuki did not contest the next Asama Plains Races in 1957. Publicly, the reason was lack of finance and the Japanese were astounded that the 1955 Asama effort had cost Suzuki 50 to 60 million Yen—about £50,000—a colossal amount to spend on a single event.

Shimizu became the first member of the racing department which was formed in 1956 and continued to develop a 125 cc engine hoping that one day the non-racing policy would be rescinded. In April 1958 he was replaced by a new recruit to Suzuki's development department, Takeharu Okano. An ex-aircraft engineer, and a more recent university professor in engineering, the 49 year old Okano was to become a key figure in Suzuki's future racing fortunes.

Following Yamaha's sweeping 125 cc victory in the 1957 Asama Plains Races, President Suzuki instructed Mr Okano to enter the 1959 event and to prepare competitive machines. The old 1955 Asama machines were re-appraised: the

transmission was weak, the power was insufficient, the chassis needed re-designing. Mr Okano built a number of prototype machines, each privately tested at Asama, for the track had been made available to the manufacturers supporting the races. On a new 5.8 mile circuit the 1957 Yamaha YA1s had lapped in 6 m 7 s (57 mph), a figure matched by one of Okano's designs. Okano arranged with the President for Shimizu's transfer back to the racing department, an encouraging sign that Suzuki were now committed to the 1959 Asama event. Up to this point, Suzuki executives had been split between the costs of racing, and the possible sales boost should their efforts be successful. It's a specious argument heard many times in boardrooms worldwide.

During the early part of 1959, Mr Okano scrapped all ideas of racing modified motorcycles, and aided by Mr Shimizu, began to design a purpose-built engine. When completed, it was mounted in a Colleda chassis, and taken to a mountain road near the village of Shiomizaka for testing. The road had long stretches of three and four degree slopes, an ideal test site because it resulted in the engine pulling hard for long periods. During these sessions Mr Okano was surprised to note that the Colleda had a maximum speed of 77 mph (124 Km/h).

Strangely, all this testing took place at night! Okano had explained his mission to the local police, who agreed to turn a blind eye, provided the local inhabitants were asleep. As the machines weren't provided with lights, and ran on open exhausts, it was surprising that complaints weren't received.

To simulate racing conditions, the new machines were ridden at Asama, but it proved difficult to break the six minute lap barrier. It wasn't only a question of power: a lack of durability was often indicated. Crankshafts seized even before the first bend—one mile from the start—had been negotiated! Later examination by Shimizu showed that the big-end bearings had been subjected to temperatures approaching 1000 degrees Centigrade; as a result the metal had scorched, and was melted in places. Further development realised sub-six minute Asama laps, the machines proving capable of regularly lapping at such speeds. The best lap achieved was 5 m 39 s (62 mph).

As the third Asama Plains Races approached, the machine design began to gel. The Colleda RB—for *Racing Bike*—featured a new twin down-tube chassis with swing-arm rear suspension. Telescopic forks with exposed springs and increased movement were more pliant. Aluminium rims were shod with 'knobbly' tyres whilst the brakes were much larger in diameter than anything before. A huge aluminium fuel tank with deep knee recesses and a sorbo rubber chest pad adorned the diminutive engine whilst the rider sat in a single seat with classic hump-back. The rolling chassis came off the drawing board of Masanao Shimizu: the engine from Takeharu Okano. Testing of many bore-stroke combinations had proved that a short-stroke motor was superior, and the engine was consequently of 56 mm bore and 50.6 mm stroke. The slightly-inclined cylinder was mounted on a heavily finned crankcase incorporating a new four-speed gearbox. Mixture was fed via a Mikuni carburettor, which, with a long intake trumpet and massive air cleaner resulted in an intake length in excess of 12 inches. The carburettor float-chamber was frame-mounted behind the mixing chamber—an attempt to prevent fuel frothing—although fuel lag during acceleration became a problem. Piston-porting was used, with exhaust extraction by the under-slung 'expansion' chamber. Suzuki claimed a power output of 10 bhp at 9500 rpm for the 176 lb RB.

The Asama opposition! The powerful Honda RC142 first seen at the 1959 IoM TT races was successfully converted for their Japanese racing debut. Note the heavy duty steering damper and the strange clip-on handle bars *Archives*

The 1959 Asama Plains Race programme had changed since Suzuki's 1955 attempt: now it was a three day 'endurance' event, for each race was considerably lengthened. Shell Petroleum became the major sponsor thanks to the foresight and perseverence of their Hamamatsu territorial manager, Akira 'Jimmy' Matsumiya, who had persuaded his managers in Japan to promote the sport. At that time, Suzuki production machines were all factory-filled with Shell lubricants and Matsumiya decided that Shell would provide fuel and oil to all the 1959 Asama entries. Matsumiya became the 'Gold Judge' for the Races, and the starter was Kenzo Tada, a Velocette rider in the 1930 Isle of Man TT races. Just two months before, Honda had returned from their Isle of Man TT debut with the Team Award, and were the talking point of Japan. Now they were at Asama with the same riders and machines — though fitted with 'knobbly' tyres. Honda became the favourites for the 125 cc race.

The Honda RC142 machines were twin cylinder four strokes featuring four valve cylinder heads and developing 18.5 bhp at 14,000 rpm. The Honda team were perhaps the most experienced at Asama: they knew the problems of carburation when the course height varied and the weather conditions were unstable; psychologically, they were 'winners' before the races began. To add to the excitement, Honda announced that Asama would be the racing debut of their latest creation, the 250 cc four cylinder machine destined for Europe's GP's the following year. The 40,000 spectators who had paid to watch the event were euphoric. 319 riders had entered—45 being professional factory racers—attracted by the seven classes ranging from 50 cc to unlimited capacity.

To provide additional factory motivation in the search for racetrack dominance, the organisers now allowed imported machines to enter, although the majority of these competed in the larger capacity classes. The 125 cc event held on Saturday 22 August, had a total of 21 entries for the gruelling 14 lap race, a distance of about 81 miles (131 Km). Only seven of the entries were four strokes; all were Hondas. Yamaha withdrew their entries before the start and the much-relished Yamaha-Honda battle evaporated.

As the 125 cc riders warmed up their mounts, rain began to fall and the experienced Honda mechanics swiftly re-jetted their carburettors. Suzuki stood by, retaining the settings optimised the previous day. Sulphur from the vulcano hung low over the paddock as the Suzuki riders, Yamashita, Ichino, Itoh and Suzuki, acclimatised themselves to the miserable conditions; the acrid aroma of the volcanic gases mingled with the two stroke exhaust fumes was fanned by the breeze over the entire racecourse.

At last, Tada mounted the rostrum flag in hand, and as it dropped the 21 machines hurtled away from the clutch-start toward the first hairpin bend. The RC142 Hondas quickly established a lead but the Showas snapping at their heels in the early stages couldn't withstand the harsh treatment of the professional riders, and soon retired, their place taken by the Colleda RBs holding 3rd, 4th, 5th and 6th positions. Yamashita and Suzuki fell, leaving Itoh and Ichino fighting the might of Honda. One of the seven Honda entries, a Benry C92SS—known in the West as the Benly—ridden by a 15 year old privateer named Kitano, was rapidly gaining and when the deteriorating weather conditions forced the leaders to slow, Kitano grabbed his chance and took the lead.

Meanwhile, both Itoh and Ichino had suffered fuel tank leakage, and although Itoh had earlier held on to Honda's Taniguchi, he eventually slowed and fell, retiring from the event. The volcanic ash had now been transformed into a sticky mud, clinging to the riders' leathers and goggles and causing many retirements. The course was littered with machines, amongst them, three of the factory Hondas. Undeterred, Kitano on the Honda held his lead to the flag, much to the chagrin of the Honda factory team who retained 2nd, 3rd and 4th places with Ichino's lone Colleda RB in 5th. Only seven machines finished the race, Tohatsus taking the remaining positions. After all their efforts and preparations, Team Suzuki had returned with a 5th place. Shimizu put Suzuki's poor showing down to bad luck: if only it hadn't poured, if only Suzuki had carburation experience, if only Suzuki had grand prix experience, if only . . . .

Although the results of the 1959 Asama Plains Races left Team Suzuki disillusioned, in typical Japanese style, the defeat became a catalyst and galvanised the fledgling team to greater things. Honda had returned from *their* Isle of Man TT debut with the Team Trophy. Now was the time for Suzuki to cast its nets a little wider and capture new markets in Europe. This optimism was not felt by Suzuki's management who looked on Asama as the end of the racing road. Miserable and despondent, the Team awaited the decision on their future.

Towards the end of November that year, Shunzo Suzuki chanced to meet Soichiro Honda, his opposite number, who asked Suzuki why he didn't race such a fast machine as the Colleda RB abroad. Alone, Shunzo Suzuki mulled it over and came to a decision that was to be as final as it was historic.

2   Man Island debut: race against time (1960)

When the president's office announced that Suzuki were to contest the 1960 Isle of Man TT races—just six months hence—Takeharu Okano and Masanao Shimizu were overjoyed, but realised the magnitude of their daunting task. The assistance was gained of Shell's Jimmy Matsumiya, who had been actively involved with Honda at the 1959 TT, and from December 1959, Matsumiya played an important part in Suzuki's European racing ventures.

Initially, Matsumiya's task was to solve the problem of finance which had to be organised within the strict boundaries of Japan's Foreign Exchange Control Act which prevented the export of Japanese Yen. In 1959, Honda had returned from the TT virtually penniless, and Suzuki didn't wish their racing efforts to be restricted through lack of finance.

The chief technician in the motorcycle division of the Ministry of International Trade and Industry, a Mr Kaneke, was a close friend of Matsumiya and became the link-man in an intrigue that was to ensure Suzuki's financial base for their foreign racing exploits.

> MATSUMIYA   'I was able to help because Shell Petroleum possessed a "special account" allowing Shell to spend some Yens abroad. I telexed Shell International in London asking if they would support the Suzuki Team at the Isle of Man by supplying them with petrol and oil on a free-of-charge basis'.

In London, that telex was passed onto the desk of Lew Ellis, Shell-Mex BP's competitions manager who was able to supplement the free fuel and oil.

> ELLIS   'I drew up a contract that at least gave Suzuki *some* money. I was also asked to look after the Suzuki personnel who were due to reconnoitre the Isle of Man in February 1960'.

Team Suzuki were thus funded by Shell-Mex BP *and* by Shell Petroleum (Japan), and in addition, all their running costs would be accepted by Shell-Mex BP! The cash was used to provide transport and accommodation, and in later years, to meet the contract fees of professional riders.

Following Matsumiya's telex, Lew Ellis contacted Angus Herbert, the well-known Island exponent, who agreed to accompany Ellis to the Isle of Man and to explain the hidden pitfalls of the Mountain Course to the Suzuki visitors. On Thursday, 4 February 1960, Matsumiya arrived at Heathrow with Suzuki's old Fuji manager, Yoshichika Maruyama, weary after their 24 hour flight. The four men and their mountain of luggage were squeezed into Ellis's own car, and the hired Morris 1000 that Angus Herbert was to drive. In convoy, they motored up

to Liverpool and on to the Steam Packet bound for Douglas, Isle of Man, or 'Man Island' as it is known to the Japanese.

Suzuki had set three objectives for the visit: to inspect and film the Mountain Circuit, to ask Norman Sharpe of the 'Green Un' – *Motor Cycling* about the MZ 'boost port', and to visit Triumph's Meriden factory. Time permitting, they were to purchase a few sets of British race-wear. In due course, the two cars arrived at the Fort Anne Hotel overlooking Douglas harbour, where the Team were staying. Matsumiya noted that the problems of racing a two stroke in the Island were not yet appreciated by Maruyama, and began to explain the effects the Mountain Circuit's change in altitude had on carburation. Fuji and Asama may well have been 'mountains' but the height of the TT course varied by almost 2000 feet.

The day following their arrival, they commenced their task in earnest.

ELLIS 'We walked around the circuit; we drove around the circuit. Then the Japanese took notes of each and every camber and gradient, the included angle and radius of every corner, and then they took literally miles of cine film photographing every inch of the circuit: all $37\frac{3}{4}$ miles of it. I've never seen anything carried out quite so thoroughly in my whole life!'

MATSUMIYA 'It was bloody cold, I remember; some of the course was covered in snow. Mr Maruyama took the film sitting on the bonnet of the Morris because he had to bank the camera as we drove around the corners. I could only drive slowly so the camera was set to run at half speed so that when it was run at normal speed, something like racing speeds would be seen. I sat in the car with the heater; Maruyama sat outside in the cold!'

Filming was often delayed due to snow on the mountain but even such bitter conditions didn't deter the Team from carrying out their task. Mr Maruyama

Upper left Geoff Duke samples the RT60 at the Yonezu test course in April 1960. L to R: Matsumiya, Maruyama (wearing badge), Sakai and Mitsuo Itoh (behind Duke) *Archives*

Above Wearing their recently-obtained Lewis leathers, Suzuki's first GP riders pose at Yonezu alongside the RT60. L to R: Matsumoto, Itoh and Ichino. Notice the rice fields *Archives*

Upper right Team Suzuki riders used roadsters (like the prototype Colleda SB shown here) to gain extra TT practice during 'roads open' periods *Archives*

Left The Fernleigh Hotel today. The first seeds of defection were secretly sown between Degner and Matsumiya within these walls. The workshop is just visible to the right of the hotel *Author*

never flinched from his duty: no detail was left to chance. Filming generally took place in the early hours before the Island's traffic ventured on to the roads but occasionally, the Team would film around sunset. When there was sunshine in Douglas, often the mountain would be clothed in mist. The course was not filmed in continuity; the crew recording whichever section was available, and it would be up to the Hamamatsu technicians to edit the rolls of film into a cohesive production representing one complete lap of the TT circuit. Soon the Manx people ignored the Morris 1000, crawling slowly over the mountain with the little man sitting cross-legged on the bonnet.

The film would be of limited use without an expert commentary and so Jimmy Matsumiya visited Geoff Duke.

MATSUMIYA   'He showed us where to peel off for the corners, where a tree would be dripping even after rain had stopped, where the road was slippery, where there were bumps and man-holes. He even explained where the rider should go right—but watch the wall—or left, but watch the tree and man-hole. He taught us so many tricks!'

Duke also confirmed his intention to visit the Suzuki factory in April.

The Team were often beseiged by Manx journalists who regularly reported their progress, but on 12 February, their task was completed and they left the Island bound for London, calling at Meriden en route. There they met Edward Turner, Triumph's managing director and the designer of many successful motorcycles.

MATSUMIYA   'He told us that he'd just returned from Japan saying, "We have nothing special to learn from Japan; I was not impressed at all! However, I hope that one day, a Japanese motorcycle will manage just *one* lap of the TT Mountain course!" I remember thinking at the time, "One day you'll see!"'

Turner was referring to Honda's efforts the previous year on a shorter, less demanding Clypse circuit. The Team then called on Norman Sharpe, who had no knowledge of MZ's much acclaimed, though elusive, 'boost port'; heralded as the secret of their super-quick two stroke racers.

The Team had more success at Lewis Leathers' London emporium where a Lewis executive explained the technicalities of tailor-made racing leathers. The Japanese had never previously understood why western riders wore such baggy leathers and why, when in the paddock, the rider's chests were often exposed! Japanese leathers were of a more supple cow-hide whereas English gear was made of tougher horse-hide designed to hug the rider whilst in a racing crouch. This misunderstanding illustrates Suzuki's road-racing knowledge at that time, and before leaving Lewis's they bought four sets of leathers, 'crashing helmets' and Mk VIII goggles. During the following week, Maruyama and Matsumiya finalised Shell-Mex BP's sponsorship before returning to Japan.

Suzuki's Hamamatsu headquarters flanks the Pacific Ocean, alongside which Suzuki had recently constructed a two kilometer test course at Yonezu as part of their racing programme. The ten feet wide course had a distinct midway kink, where it widened to provide a maintenance area. The tree-lined course made testing a hazardous occupation in those early days of rapid seizure. To make matters worse, a number of small farm tracks crossed it which had already caused the death of test rider Hiroshi Naito when he hit a farmer's ox-drawn cart. Clearly, signalling points were needed.

Susumu Saito commenced his Suzuki career straight from high school in 1960, and he joined the 20 engineers in the research department which encompassed the racing section.

SAITO   'I was a very young boy—just 18 years old when I joined—and I went many times to check the racing machines at the Yonezu test course. At that time the riders were Matsumoto, Ichino and Mitsuo Itoh. . . . My job—I was only an assistant—was to stand by one of the farm tracks and hold a red flag to warn the riders in case a farmer was coming'.

Testing at Yonezu was restricted, by its nature, to top speed and acceleration testing although some tests were designed to provoke piston seizure. Some of the test riders, such as Riichi Itoh, were also technicians. He broke off the traditional university education to satisfy his ambition to become a professional rider. Like Seichi Suzuki, he joined the Tokyo Jychoku Racing Club and raced in so-called 'speedway' events as a professional. Seichi Suzuki was also responsible for some Suzuki design work whilst Riichi Itoh doubled up as a Suzuki mechanic. Thus, many of the Japanese riders who scored grand prix points one day, would be designing, testing and fettling machines the next. Everyone had to be flexible in their roles; the race department had only about ten full-time employees at that time. Nobody complained: if this was the means of gaining glory for the factory and Japan, then they would surely carry out these duties, however humble they may appear to the outsider.

To a European, the Japanese concept of work may appear tyrannical: a left-over from Japan's recent feudal system. To the Japanese worker, loyalty to their employer is important, and since the employer reciprocates this loyalty, it provides the employee with that feeling of well-being and security such mutual respect alone can generate. Most Suzuki workers join the company direct from

Suzuki's heroes return home from their IoM baptism. L to R (garlanded): Kamiya, Nakano, Itoh, Matsumoto, Ichino and Shimizu. Also, Kenzo Tada (4th from left), and Maruyama (seated in front of Ichino) *Archives*

school or university, remaining faithful employees until their retirement. Many of the Japanese who figure in Suzuki's racing story are still employed by the company.

When Yoshichika Maruyama returned to the factory in late February, he knew that the information he had collected about 'Man Island' would shock his colleagues: not simply the severity of the tortuous circuit with its 200 bends but the fact that unlike Mount Fuji and Mount Asama, the course was totally paved.

Work on the TT machine—the RT60—had commenced late in January 1960 with another 40 day development programme requiring non-stop work throughout the January holidays. The new twin cylinder engine was designed by Masanao Shimizu to be installed in a chassis similar to the Asama Colleda RB, but Maruyama's story resulted in many last-minute changes to the RT60's design, because by then, Geoff Duke's Suzuki visit was imminent.

Meanwhile, Toshio Matsumoto, Michio Ichino, and Mitsuo Itoh, the three chosen TT riders, studied Maruyama's film and the script describing the bends and the recommended racing lines around them. Other engineers pored over gear-ratio charts, deciding on the important compromise of internal ratios for the six-speed gearbox. Somebody was busy completing the TT entry forms and in his haste, mistakenly wrote the word 'Colleda' in the space marked 'Manufacturer', an error repeated in the official TT programme.

The first trial design of the RT60 was tested at the Yonezu course by Michio Ichino and Mitsuo Itoh just prior to Geoff Duke's arrival on 19 April. Duke's tour of the Japanese manufacturers had been arranged and sponsored by the Japanese magazine *Motorcyclist* and Shell Petroleum, and when Duke, Fumito Sakai, the editor of *Motorcyclist*, and interpreter Jimmy Matsumiya arrived at Suzuki's headquarters, they were quickly steered toward the Yonezu test course where a couple of RT60s were standing, already warmed up. Would Duke-San like to try one out? Duke squeezed into the leathers and Cromwell pudding-basin bought by Mr Maruyama in London. He even wore the Mk VIII goggles! Once aboard the machine, Duke seemed to enjoy his brief ride but had some trouble turning at each end. He told Mr Maruyama that he'd never ridden such a quick two stroke before, but was able to pinpoint a number of areas for improvement which were passed on to Mr Okano and Mr Maruyama. At the end of one test run, he drew to a standstill posing for photographers in the milky sunlight. Through Jimmy Matsumiya, Duke projected the message that the dampers were too spongy, demonstrating by pressing sharply down on the saddle leaving the rear-end quivering. Duke also suggested that the RT60 was not as quick as a four stroke and that rotary valves may be the answer. The Suzuki technicians nodded amidst a hail of 'Ah, so desu ka's'. ('Is that so?') Before Duke left the factory, he was persuaded to lecture some of their research personnel in order to maximise the benefits of his visit.

Further testing of the RT60 now showed that a reliable top speed was 86 mph, which didn't compare with that of the Honda 2RC143 — the factory entry for the 1960 TT races which produced 23 bhp and a 110 mph top speed. The Honda developed 10 bhp more than the RT60 even though Suzuki had incorporated a mild form of expansion chamber exhaust system. It would be two years before Suzuki's two stroke mastery was to gain them the edge over the mighty four strokes.

Suzuki had little experience in shipping motorcycles and spare parts to Europe; the crating was familiar, but the carnets and customs declarations required were unknown. Honda came to their aid when Mr Okano asked the advice of one of his old students, Mr Kawashima. Both he, and another Honda man, Mr Nizuma, led Okano through the tangle of European regulations in force at that time. Mr Kawashima later became the president of Honda. This assistance from a rival factory may seem strange but Soichiro Honda, like Suzuki's president, was Hamamatsu born and bred and they thus shared an affinity. Originally, Yamaha was also close, but a rift during the mid-fifties left Yamaha out in the cold. At one stage, it was even agreed that orders for motorcycles that could not be fulfilled by the recipient company, would be passed on to their rival. Furthermore, Suzuki and Honda were billed in Japan as forming the 'Japanese Racing Team' for the 1960 TT races. Suzuki were prudent in developing good relations with Honda, for Honda had taken control of the destitute Motorcycling Federation of Japan — the MFJ — in order to form a Japanese racing association that would be recognised by the FIM and thus allow the staging of a Japanese grand prix. Originally, the MFJ had been competing against another non-affiliated organisation, the MCFAJ, and was rapidly becoming swamped before Honda took control. If Suzuki wished to race abroad and to enter a future Japanese grand prix, friendship with Honda would go a long way to help.

Upper Tom Phillis (Honda) and his mechanic seem confident unlike Ichino (20) and Itoh who nervously await a 1960 TT practice session. Just visible between them is Nakano
Archives

Soon all was ready for Suzuki's first grand prix, and the few remaining members of the research department organised a 'Sayonara' party before the

Lower Toshio Matsumoto gained Suzuki's first GP trophy—a bronze replica—by achieving 15th place over the gruelling 113 mile mountain course
Archives

Team left for Haneda airport on the first leg of their journey to 'Man Island'.

In London, Lew Ellis had made Suzuki's reservations on the Island at the Fernleigh Hotel, which possessed a four-car garage sufficient to house the Team machines during TT fortnight. It was here that Lew Ellis brought the Team at the end of May, whilst the machines and spares were transported to the garage on Shell's low-loader. On the Island representing Suzuki were Mitsuo Itoh, Michio Ichino, Toshio Matsumoto, (riders), Takeharu Okano, Masanao Shimizu and Hiroyuki Nakano, (managers) and a squad of mechanics headed by Yasunori Kamiya. Accompanying them was Jimmy Matsumiya, who was officially representing Shell and would therefore have to aid Honda too. The Fernleigh housed a rival team, the MZ equipe headed by Walter Kaaden, and another TT rider Tommy Robb. All were Fernleigh regulars. Eric Teare, the hotel manager, was sceptical of Mr Okano's hopes for a TT victory, and suggested that the first TT served to let the rider learn the course, the second simply to remind him of what he'd forgotten, whilst the third *could* result in victory. In the event, Eric Teare was correct.

Whilst the riders became accustomed to the TT ritual of early-rising for dawn practice, Matsumiya contacted Renolds and Avon for chains and tyres. Ralph Newman, an Avon tyre fitter for the TT, was working at their Island base, a small garage close to Nobles Hosptial.

NEWMAN 'Jimmy Matsumiya asked if we could help and naturally we were delighted to oblige, especially since there had been a lack of bona fide factory entries since 1957 when most of the European manufacturers pulled out.

'The initial problem was one of supply: had we sufficient stocks of tyres to equip the little Colleda? In fact, we managed to find enough to fit up three pairs of wheels to enable Suzuki to test them during practice. I was amazed, the Japanese riders went straight out onto the full circuit and started their tests in earnest. The tyres proved a success; the riders were happy, and we just changed over the whole team.'

However, during one of the practice sessions, Mitsuo Itoh fell at the Bungalow, badly damaging his right knee and gashing his lip. He was rushed to Nobles Hospital where he joined fellow Fernleigh resident Ernst Degner! The machine was repaired and Castrol-sponsored Tommy Robb immediately asked to replace Itoh but Suzuki were with Shell, and furthermore, Lew Ellis had already contacted a suitable replacement rider for the Colleda, Ray Fay.

ELLIS 'When Itoh was put in hospital, Jimmy Matsumiya asked me if I knew a steady reliable rider. I'd heard that Fay's 125 cc Bianchi hadn't materialised and Matsumiya suggested that I take him on. As a Shell contracted rider of old, I asked Ray Fay if he'd ride and he said he'd give it a go. There was no written contract between Suzuki and Fay, his services were free'.

This fact helps to justify the choice, for Suzuki had very little money in 1960, despite the Shell support, and besides, if Suzuki *had* possessed the finance, the Colleda's performance was unlikely to attract a top class professional. Fay had been TT racing for six years mostly riding large four stroke BSAs and Nortons. His best place was 19th in 1956 on a 350 cc Gold Star BSA so he was hardly a potential TT winner on the Suzuki, but it was to Liverpudlian Ray Fay that the historical honour was granted of becoming the first European rider to race a Japanese factory machine, outside Japan.

Between practice sessions, Geoff Duke tutored the three riders, taking them around the course until they could absorb no more information. It was time well spent, serving Itoh particularly well in his future Island appearances. The performance of the Colleda could not have been remarkable, for Ray Fay barely recalls the race or practice sessions. He does remember one day when he took the Colleda in the back of Geoff Monty's van to Jurby airfield for testing.

> FAY 'After three or four laps, I had learnt to use a new technique for riding the Colleda, and with the help of Suzuki's methodical mechanics, I soon became accustomed to riding fast, a comparatively slow machine.'

The qualifying time for the 125 cc class was around 34 minutes, a poor performance by Mr Okano's standards. The Colleda, he figured, was underpowered, lacked development and the riders were inexperienced. Additionally, the riders were unaccustomed to European food and were still adjusting to the new environment.

Despite the 'Japan Racing Team' title, Honda paid little attention to Suzuki's difficulties in the Island: Honda had their own problems to solve. Suzuki could have done without Edward Turner's acerbic comments though.

> MATSUMIYA 'He came to me one day and said, "Your machine looks beautiful, but, will it run?" at which point a mechanic started up a Colleda.
> Turner went on, "What an extraordinary sound! Will it last the race?"
> Turner was in an extremely sarcastic mood that year, but I thought, "I met many people like you in university, so I'm accustomed. You'll see!"
> I told him that we were very careful with money. "We have enough land in Japan to test our motorcycles to see if they're good or not."

After the months of preparation the race was an anti-climax. The factory MVs of Ubbiali, Hocking and Taveri trounced the field and after an undistinguished ride, the three Suzuki teamsters finished 15th (Matsumoto), 16th (Ichino), and 18th (Fay). Matsumoto's average speed for the race was 71.88 mph, whereas Ubbiali's winning average for the three laps was 86.10 mph. However, the Team didn't leave the Island empty-handed; Matsumoto gained a Bronze Replica Trophy, sufficient reward to whet the Team's appetite for battles to come.

The Team re-crated their equipment between visits to Mitsuo Itoh and were soon ready to depart. The problem now became Itoh who had been joined in Nobles by yet another Fernleigh resident, Tommy Robb, who'd broken his neck at Windy Corner. The hospital staff were against discharging Itoh, who was, however, so determined not to be left on the Island that he furtively climbed out of a window and cut off his plaster cast with a pair of hedge-trimmers!

The Team arrived back in Hamamatsu, travel-stained and fatigued. To their friends and colleagues, they were heroes, but the Team had a difficult task showing much enthusiasm for the massive welcome home party staged by Suzuki. Even as the party was in full swing, test riding of the new RT61 and RV61 machines had commenced in preparation for the 1961 season.

> MATSUMIYA 'When the Suzuki Team returned to Japan, they really tried hard. We had *smelled* the Isle of Man air! We vowed to return!'

3 In search of perfection: the Degner solution (1961)

Matsumiya appears to instruct Paddy Driver on the correct throttle action required for his 250 cc RV61 *Archives*

Suzuki were envious of Honda's success in 1960 and for 1961 followed their example with new twin cylinder 125 cc and 250 cc machines, and by contracting western riders to supplement the small Japanese contingent.

In Suzuki's London office at Montrose Court in Knightsbridge, Jimmy Matsumiya, who had joined Suzuki in January 1961, acted as linkman between the Hamamatsu race-shop and Europe, and often met Lew Ellis to discuss possible future riders. Paddy Driver, a South African GP campaigner, was signed up for the year, whilst Alastair King agreed to ride for Suzuki at the TT races.

The race Team was strengthened when Masazumi 'Mike' Ishikawa, fresh out of Michigan State University with an engineering degree, joined Suzuki as manager on 1 February. The new Team hierarchy was headed by Mr Okano who was responsible for Research I, II and III groups. Masanao Shimizu, in direct charge of Research III — the racing department — had two managers reporting to him, Hiroyuki Nakano, responsible for engineering, and Mike Ishikawa, the logistics man, organising the race programme, travel schedules, and finance.

Paddy Driver was invited to test ride the new machines and early in 1961 he arrived in Hamamatsu with his fiancé, Janet Smith. There were a few raised eyebrows. Frank Perris, who later joined the Team, knew the ropes.

PERRIS 'Taking your wife or girlfriend there was absolutely taboo, unless invited. Paddy's girlfriend actually asked the president, Mr Suzuki, why he didn't make four strokes. Don't forget that Suzuki were, at that time, the largest two stroke manufacturers in the world.'

Paddy bitterly complained to Suzuki's engineers about the temperamental throttle response of the Suzuki, comparing it to his more usual Norton, and had trouble adjusting his riding techniques. After a miserable test session in Japan, the future looked grim.

Ishikawa's plan for the 1961 season involved Suzuki in their first full GP programme. Commencing with the Spanish, a nightmare of technical problems were to beset the Team: on that occasion Driver withdrew from the competition before the 125 cc race began! The West German round showed the Suzukis to be lacking competitive power; now all hopes rested with Suzuki's return to the Isle of Man, and the strengthening of the Team.

Frank Perris had been unsuccessfully badgering Jimmy Matsumiya for a ride ever since Barcelona, but at Hockenheim he persuaded Paddy Driver to let him have a secret ride on the 250, the RV61.

PERRIS 'I suddenly found that if you closed the throttle slightly it would go very quick. Paddy however, used to slam the throttle wide open, not realising that by feeling the throttle, there was a noticeable power surge.'

MATSUMIYA 'Paddy later told me that Frank had ridden the machine but I wasn't annoyed because I had already spoken with Frank at Barcelona and liked him immensely from then.'

Apart from a power deficit, the machines would often slip out of gear, or the rider would be unable to engage one correctly. Suzuki's pistons were cast aluminium alloy and were not oval-turned or barrelled as is normally required. The material lacked that important element, silicon, and consequently the expansion rate was high, leading to rapid and regular seizure. Occasionally, the carburettor would flood, and the fairing design did not allow sufficient air-flow to the carburettor intakes. This led to unequal performance in the left and right cylinders and accurate jetting became virtually impossible.

Earlier in the year, a young New Zealander, Hugh Anderson, had signed a Shell contract, and Lew Ellis—a powerful force in recommending riders to Shell-sponsored factories—had virtually guaranteed Anderson a factory machine. It was to be either Bianchi, MZ or Suzuki, as Anderson remembers, and it was to be decided at the TT. Whoever contracted Anderson was onto a winner.

Meanwhile, back in Japan, Suzuki were preparing for the TT, and had bought a pair of Hino coaches which Mike Ishikawa converted into race transporters. The front half contained the seating, whilst the rear became a mobile store and workshop. Channels up both sides allowed the machines, mounted on wooden pellets, to be slotted in above other machines strapped to the deck below. The walls were lined with lockers and benches for spare parts storage. These two vehicles were shipped over to Belgium in readiness for the TT. Up to that point, the Team had been able to travel round Europe thanks to Paddy Driver: the machines were carried in his trailer, whilst the personnel travelled by car. With the two large trucks, transport would no longer be a problem, or so it was hoped. Initially, the insurance companies were reluctant to insure such large, and hitherto unknown vehicles, to be driven across Europe by diminutive Japanese, but once resolved, all the equipment was transferred into the Hinos with some newly-arrived machines. The Team took the ferry from Ostend to Dover, and drove on to Liverpool where they were met by Lew Ellis. He couldn't believe his eyes.

ELLIS 'The trucks were massive great things and when they were driven down on to the ferry, they wouldn't fit on the boat!'

All the machines, crates, spares, engines and tools had to be unloaded on the quayside and put on to the ferry as loose items, and the two transporters were left parked in Liverpool for the TT fortnight. By the time the ferry had docked in Douglas, Ellis had decided on a course of action. He contacted Shell's depot at Battery Quay and arranged to borrow their flat-truck on which all the Suzuki gear was ferried to the Fernleigh Hotel over two or three trips.

Alongside the MZ Team—also staying at the Fernleigh—the Suzuki mechanics began preparing the machines and setting up shop. Shunzo Suzuki, the president, arrived shortly after and was accommodated at the Castle Mona, just down the road from the Fernleigh. The recruitment of Hugh Anderson was

Above For the 1961 Classics, Suzuki made the seven RT61s seen here at Yonezu. L to R: Ichino, Toshio Matsumoto, Okano, Masuda (later to be known as Matsumoto) and Itoh *Archives*

Above right Testing at Yonezu was often hazardous as shown by the schoolgirl strolling alongside the track. Here, Itoh looks pleased with his RT61 whilst Nakano watches Shimizu and another rider change the carburettor jetting *Archives*

initiated when Lew Ellis called to see him on his way to the Fernleigh.

ANDERSON 'He took me to the Suzuki garage in his car and introduced me all round, and that was it. Nobody else was involved with my recruitment because it was simply that Suzuki were supported by Shell, and a Shell rider was going to ride Suzuki. That meant myself, Paddy Driver and Alastair King.'

In Anderson Lew Ellis had found for Suzuki their brightest racing prospect, as his results later proved. Anderson's Japanese team-mates were Toshio Matsumoto, Michio Ichino, Shunkichi Masuda and Mitsuo Itoh, a formidable team, mingling a wealth of GP talent with Japanese ability to ride well on strange circuits. Backing them up was strong team management: Takeharu Okano, Mike Ishikawa, Jimmy Matsumiya, Masanao Shimizu and TT veteran Kenzo Tada, who'd flown over specially for the event. There were dozens of mechanics.

Problem followed problem as the Team attempted to master the troublesome machines. The Team took every opportunity to practice and would fine-tune the bikes at Jurby airfield. Lew Ellis was on hand for one such session.

ELLIS 'I remember this day particularly well; the weather wasn't brilliant, but was good testing weather. When we arrived, who should be practising but Bob McIntyre. Anyway, "Mac" and Alastair did a few runs but Bob put up much quicker times than Alastair. He so enjoyed the bike, a 250 cc machine, that he stayed on it for about an hour.'

Bob McIntyre later turned down a Suzuki ride for the TT, saying that he had very little two stroke experience, and preferred not to make such a major change in the Island.

Suzuki had brought along two 250 cc Colleda TBs for roads-open practice. One day, Shimizu was out riding when he was thrown off, spinning in the air and landing badly. It was a narrow escape from death: *his* TT was spent in Nobles

Hospital and he wasn't discharged until after the Dutch TT when he returned to Japan.

Meanwhile Suzuki were facing another problem with both 125 cc and 250 cc models: magneto drive gears. If meshed tight, ignition timing was accurate, but the teeth frequently broke. If too loose, the inaccurate timing caused piston seizure. Reluctantly, it was decided to withdraw some of Suzuki's entries from the 125 cc race, in order that the mechanics could concentrate on preparing fewer machines. The original seven entries were thus reduced to the four Japanese riders.

As practice wore on, there was much press theorizing as to the 250 cc results. Yamaha were on the Island for the first time with their RD48, reputedly producing 35 bhp, apparently no match for the 45 bhp Honda RC162s. The unreliable 28 bhp of Suzuki's RV61 appeared totally uncompetitive.

Of the six Suzukis that started the 250 cc TT—Matsumoto's didn't make the start—three retired on the first lap (Masuda, King and Driver), leaving Anderson, Ichino and Itoh carrying the flag. Itoh stopped on the fourth lap whilst Anderson and Ichino finished 10th and 12th gaining a Bronze Replica for Anderson. Both machines had lapped 20 mph slower than Hailwood's winning Honda . . . .

By comparison, the 125 cc race became a nightmare; Suzuki's entry had already been reduced to four machines and then, at the last minute, Matsumoto's entry was withdrawn. On lap 1 Itoh retired followed by Masuda and Ichino on laps 2 and 3! Not one of the initial seven man team had finished, and Suzuki personnel, from president Suzuki downwards, were mortified, but this only served to deepen their resolve to conquer the Island.

Their TT hopes of victory dashed, Suzuki were desperate to raise their technical know-how literally overnight, and Matsumiya realised that the stakes would be high. He began to nurture a friendship with MZ's rider and development engineer, Ernst Degner.

MATSUMIYA 'Degner constantly listened to jazz music in his room at the Fernleigh. Nobody with Suzuki liked jazz except myself and Degner and myself became close. His English wasn't good but we were able to communicate. Degner said, "I'd like to stay in the UK, what can you do to help?" Being a trained lawyer, I didn't offer my help immediately, but said, "You need some money, don't you?" '

Other conversations took place, often on the bleak Manx hillside around Snaefell.

DEGNER 'We had to talk on this subject very secretly because we had two or three people from the Communist Party with us at the TT, so we had to move out of their way and talk for only ten or fifteen minutes before splitting. Matsumiya asked me if there was any possibility of me moving over to the Western side, and said Suzuki were prepared to offer me a contract.'

Who first broached the subject of defection is immaterial, but Matsumiya and Degner provisionally agreed terms. Matsumiya realised that he must obtain top-level approval, and that its timing was critical. What better opportunity than when the whole Suzuki racing effort seemed to be in tatters after the

Dateline Haneda airport, Tokyo. Ready for departure are L to R: Toshio Matsumoto, Fumiyaki Kawahara, Shimizu, Morishita and engine designer Seichi Suzuki *Archives*

disappointing race results? Matsumiya says that a meeting was called at the Castle Mona between himself, Mr Okano and Shunzo Suzuki. Mr Okano could not offer the president any guarantee of success within the following year.

MATSUMIYA 'I told the president that research and development was a risky way of spending money; you could spend a lot of money with no guaranteed return. The easiest way is to obtain that which is already established.'

The president agreed and left it to Jimmy Matsumiya to organise directly with Degner. The Team withdrew from the Island, and having reloaded their Hino trucks, headed south towards Assen and the Dutch TT. After even more transport problems at Dover, where HM Customs were reluctant to allow them on to the ferry for lack of British documentation, the Team, still in company with Shunzo Suzuki, checked into the Norge Hotel at Assen.

The MZ team were also in Assen, and a further meeting between Degner, Shunzo Suzuki and Takeharu Okano was secretly convened close to the Norge.

DEGNER 'I had already written down my terms, in English, for joining Suzuki, and when Mr Okano saw how much I wanted, he thought it was too much. Mr Suzuki said to him, "Well, are *you* able to bring that much horsepower by the start of next year?" and he said that he couldn't. Mr Suzuki then continued, "In that case, we must sign the contract".

'I had a *working* contract with Suzuki, which said that I must develop the 125. 22 bhp was the target written into my contract, but I got more, 24 bhp! It was not difficult for me to achieve this increase because I had made all these improvements at the MZ factory. It was easy for me!'

Meanwhile, Frank Perris, well-placed in the 500 cc World Championship on his private Norton, had been asking Jimmy Matsumiya for a factory ride. The latter was so impressed by Perris' determination, that he asked Mr Suzuki if Perris could be given a contract. The president agreed and Perris was delighted that he would make his Suzuki debut at Spa-Francorchamps the following weekend. The contract was worth £1100, a fortune in 1961.

PERRIS 'I can remember Matsumiya making my contract in his flat, and I had the money when I returned to my flat in Penge. I'd been paid in cash, and we laid the money out on the floor, and Rita and I rolled in it! We'd never seen so much money in all our lives. My previous AJS contract fee was just £200 . . . .'

Joe Ehrlich, the boss of the UK-based EMC concern realised Suzuki's dilemma and approached Mr Okano offering to assist Suzuki in whatever way he could. This proposal was given some serious thought but was eventually turned down. Suzuki figured that although the EMC machines were as fast as the MZs, they were also unreliable. In addition, the EMC was water-cooled which suggested an overheating problem, unlike MZ's air-cooled machines.

The Dutch TT became a further frustrating experience: the RT61s of Ichino, Itoh and Matsumoto finished in 14th, 16th, and 17th places. In the 250 cc race, Driver's 250 broke its rear suspension on the second lap, and the remaining RV61s all retired. Team Suzuki were relieved to leave Assen and move on to Spa and the Stavelot Corner Hotel.

The Belgian GP provided no respite for the Team; Ichino was placed 14th in the 125 cc race and Driver 7th in the disappointing 250 event. Newcomer Perris had made 5th fastest practice time on his 250, but on the grid his RV61 refused to start. In desperation, Okano telexed Hamamatsu, 'It is impossible to continue racing because of the magneto gear trouble.' Ten days later, the factory had agreed and the Team withdrew for the remainder of the season.

For the next few weeks, Ernst Degner organised his defection. *He* would not defect until certain his wife Gerda, and two boys, Olaf and Boris were inside West Germany. 13 August was to be the defection date.

DEGNER   'I had to concentrate, not only on racing, but on bringing my
family over—trying to find the best way. Originally, the plan was for my
family to cross the border in Berlin, but the wall was built. I had flown to
the Ulster GP and I got a newspaper the next day and it said that the
Western side was completely closed and nobody could cross the border in
either direction.'

A new date was fixed coinciding with the Italian GP on 13 September, when Ernst himself would defect having first confirmed his family's safety.

The Matsumiya family drove to Monza disguised as tourists: Jimmy hoped MZ would not be too suspicious if they saw him and Ernst together, after all, any committed racing man would break his holiday to see a GP, wouldn't he? Degner told him that he hadn't yet been able to arrange his family's defection, and a new venue was arranged, the Swedish GP on 17 September. With the new border restrictions, Degner had to reorganise his family's method of escape.

DEGNER   'I remember I obtained the help of West Berlin and West
German friends, and whilst they arranged things in the West, I worked on
the problem in East Germany. I have never talked about how my family
managed to escape even though many people have asked me. But now the
time has passed—20 years now—so why shouldn't I explain?'

One of Degner's helpers was a West German named 'Petri'—a nick-name—and he agreed to drive a car back and forth over the East German border at Helmstadt, ostensibly visiting the Leipzig Fair. Soon, the guards would recognise him on sight and took little interest in him, or his Lincoln Mercury limousine.

DEGNER   'The boot of the Mercury car had a double compartment. If you
opened the boot, you could only see half of the space, the other half was
made for my wife and two boys to lay in. On the day of their escape, I
brought them to a pre-arranged point about 20 kilometers before the East
German border in my car, where they had to move over into the other car.

'I had a good doctor and I told him that my boys weren't sleeping very
well. The eldest was 18 months old, and the youngest just six months old. I
didn't tell him of my real plans. He gave me some very mild drug that
would be sufficient to keep them quiet. On Wednesday September 13, on
the way to the border, the two boys seemed to come more awake, so we
had to give them one more pill—a double portion—and slowly they went
to sleep. When my wife changed cars, she took the small one into the boot
and I passed her the big one. There were a lot of blankets stuffed in, a
light, and also there were a few big holes so that they had enough fresh air.

'I then drove north towards Sassnitz, and stayed at a pre-arranged hotel, where I waited nervously all night for a telephone call. Then I heard that it had been received one and a half hours before my arrival. The message was just a code, meaning that my wife and family were safe in West Germany. I was quite nervous, because if they had been caught, I would have gone to jail. I was able to drive my Wartburg car out of East Germany because the Communists didn't know that my family had left East Germany and they thought that I had to return. So why shouldn't they let me leave?

'I took the ferry from Sassnitz to Trelleborg and then drove north to Kristianstad along the coast. I stopped at the first post office and telephoned my wife because I wasn't happy that we'd had to give the boys a double portion of medicine, and I thought that maybe it was too much and they would be ill. My wife said, "Don't worry about it, they're quite well." '

Reassured Degner drove on to Kristianstad to proceed with his own defection. At that time, Jimmy Matsumiya and a colleague were also driving toward Kristianstad in an Opel hire-car. They booked into the same hotel as Degner and the MZ Team, adopting the role of 'talent-spotters' at the GP.

DEGNER   'The MZ people all stayed in the same hotel and I took a bedroom overlooking the front of the hotel so that I could see all the cars and lorries of the MZ team. On Sunday morning—race day—I waited until everybody had left for the track, and then I went down and packed all my belongings into the boot of my car. I then went to the track. I had no need to return to the hotel because I didn't leave anything there.'

Meanwhile, the two Japanese were waiting for Degner as practice for the grand prix got under way. Bertie Schneider—a future Suzuki rider—competed at the Swedish GP. Wasn't Suzuki's presence there suspicious?

SCHNEIDER   'A lot of meetings were attended by the Japanese, just watching and taking photographs. There was nothing unusual in this at all.'

On Sunday in the 125 cc GP, Degner's MZ broke its crank on the third lap and he retired. Now he put his defection plans into gear.

DEGNER   'The paddock was in the middle of the track, and we could only leave the paddock between races. I left the track just before the 500 cc race and drove south towards the ferry for Denmark, together with Matsumiya and his friend in their hire car.'

Keeping well back, the two Japanese watched as Degner drove through the customs shed.

DEGNER   'The policeman said, "You don't have any visa to get into Denmark!" Then I told him that I was on my way from East Germany to West Germany because of the political situation there. He asked me to wait whilst he made a telephone call. I waited for three-quarters of an hour when a few gentlemen from Copenhagen came to talk to me. I didn't know at that time where they were from—whether they were policemen—but actually they were Americans from NATO. They wanted to know some military details of East Germany but I was unable to help them. After half an hour of talking, they gave me permission to enter Denmark. I then took the next ferry to West Germany.'

According to Jimmy Matsumiya, shortly after the races, he and his colleague returned to the hotel with the MZ team and proceeded to ply them with drink to cover up Degner's non-appearance at the hotel. It appeared to work and eventually the conspirators slipped away into the night in Degner's wake. Driving quickly, they overtook Degner before he had caught the ferry out of Sweden. Matsumiya remembers inspecting MZ engine components to be sure that Degner had stuck to the contract he'd signed at Assen, but Degner emphatically denies having taken anything from MZ when he fled to the West.

DEGNER   'I did not *need* to take anything; I had worked for them for such a long time that I had it all in my mind. It was easy for me to build a new engine.'

However, Tadao Matsui, a Team mechanic at the time, Jimmy Matsumiya and Mike Ishikawa recall things differently.

MATSUI   'Ernst Degner brought with him an MZ piston and cylinder which we thought most important because of the different materials used. The porting was also advanced and by using parts similar to MZ we were able to reduce piston seizures and improve performance.'

MATSUMIYA   'He took a cast-iron cylinder sleeve from an MZ together with a piston and connecting rod, and some drawings which I checked: I wanted to know what I was buying.'

ISHIKAWA   'Degner brought with him some schematic drawings, and some pieces of the 125: a piston, cylinder, crankshaft and a disc valve.'

Suzuki's acquisition of these items was possibly more important than Degner himself. With such items, Suzuki could have made a replica of the MZ RE125 engine. Once details of materials and detail design were known, it would have been a relatively simple matter to optimise carburation and expansion chamber design on the test bench.

Meanwhile, back at Kristianstad, the truth was dawning on MZ team manager Walter Kaaden: whilst it was not unusual for Ernst to be absent from his bed, usually he'd resurface at the hotel for breakfast.

PERRIS   'Rita and I had breakfast with Kaaden that morning and I remember him asking us if we'd seen Ernst. The word was just then beginning to buzz about and Walter repeated, "Where's Ernst?" We both said that we had no idea.'

This was particularly embarrassing for Perris and his wife since Frank had taken over the role of buying the drinks for the MZ team the previous evening once the two Japanese had left. The Avon tyre crew including Ralph Newman were also breakfasting that morning.

NEWMAN   'Walter Kaaden came through the restaurant asking everybody, "Have you seen Ernst?" We just treated this as a normal request and the whole thing was forgotten. Mind you, Kaaden looked a little concerned

A small team contested the 1961 Singapore GP where Seichi Suzuki (the *rider*) finished 2nd to a Honda 2RC143 *Archives*

that morning. It wasn't until later that the paddock grapevine came up with a solution to the mystery and it was only days later, back in England, that we realised the significance of it all.'

Degner's defection became a *cause célébre* overnight and was reported in many German newspapers. Consequently, when he arrived in West Germany, the immigration officials allowed him to enter on his East German passport and to travel to Saarbrucken to join his family. The only condition was that he report to the local police station who would fill out the necessary documentation.

The difficult part over, Ernst Degner began to think of his career and the fact that he was still leading, and could still *win* the 125 cc World Championship, if only he could be ahead of Phillis at the final round in Argentina on October 15. He met Joe Ehrlich at the EMC factory in Hatfield who agreed to provide him with a 125 cc EMC. Degner remained in England for a few days, staying at Ehrlich's home and working on the machine which was later air-freighted to Argentina. But when Degner had arrived in Buenos Aires, eagerly awaiting a chance of riding the machine, he heard that it had been held up at New York airport. He is convinced it was collusion on the part of East German and Argentinian communists that scotched his plans. In the paddock, Degner argued with the organisers who offered him a Bultaco which he declined, convinced it would be too slow for Phillis' Honda. But this was only the storm clouds brewing, for later that day, Degner heard that the FIM had received a telex from the East German Motorcycle Federation saying that his competition licence had been suspended. Degner's previously obtained West German Competition licence was ignored by the officials. In the upshot, Degner had to be content with 2nd place in the 125 cc World Championship, watching Phillis snatch the World Championship so rightly his own.

After returning to Saarbrucken, he had to attend an FIM inquiry in Geneva where the East German Federation alleged that he had 'overdriven' his MZ in Sweden and intentionally broken down, that he had divulged MZ secrets and thus broken his MZ contract, and that he had failed to notify the East German Federation that he no longer required their racing licence. Degner received a reprimand and was fined 250 Swiss francs, about £21.

Meanwhile, rumours of Degner's plans had already commenced in the English motorcycle journals. On 28 September, less than two weeks after his escape, *The Motor Cycle* suggested that Degner was 'heading for Japan.' By the 2 November, the same journal asked, 'Suzuki for Degner?' and mentioned that Jimmy Matsumiya was visiting West Germany at that time. A few days later Degner flew out to Japan, the first of 35 such visits. During his four months stay, he lived at Suzuki's Lake Hamana hostel, 'Kore da so', close to the factory.

Degner was in great demand at that time, and he recalls receiving a telex from Signor Bulto of Bultaco offering him a job. He was also approached by Yamaha in Argentina who asked if he would help them to develop their engines.

Attempting to avoid any bad publicity, Suzuki went to extraordinary lengths to keep Degner's true identity secret.

DEGNER 'That's why they gave me some visiting cards printed with the name "Eugen Muller, of Zurich" which I had to give to Suzuki people who were not to know that I had joined them to work on racing motorcycles. Only a very small amount of people knew who I really was.'

'Eugen-San', or the familiar 'Gen-San', suited Degner since his full name is Ernst Eugen Degner.

Suzuki wanted Degner to concentrate his efforts on the 125 cc models and he commenced the routine work of designing, building and fettling engines, but it

After Degner's defection, MZ recruited British riders such as Alan Shepherd, seen here being congratulated by MZ chief Walter Kaaden and the team after finishing 2nd in the 1964 125 cc East German GP. Shepherd recalls they were constantly accompanied by Communist Party 'minders'
Shepherd

was soon impossible for him to continue with his false identity. A Japanese magazine photographer waited for him to appear outside the Suzuki factory and having taken the picture, the irrefutable evidence of Degner's involvement with Suzuki was circulated world-wide.

Apart from his undoubted abilities as an engine designer, Degner's role was more wide-ranging.

DEGNER 'My objective when I got to Japan was to build new engines, but I was also very interested to have a really good chassis. You can have a good engine but if you are unable to bring that power to the ground it is no good.'

Degner's tuning abilities were first recognised in the early part of 1962.

DEGNER 'Normally, we had a cast-iron liner surrounded by the aluminium cylinder casting and before I joined Suzuki they formed the exhaust port bridge only in the liner. I bridged the aluminium also to conduct the heat from the bridge into the cylinder. Without the aluminium support, the cast iron bridge distorted when it became warm and caused piston seizure. I also showed Suzuki how to drill small holes in the piston skirt that aligned with the bridge, which helped to cool the bridge.'

With resolution, Ernst Degner applied himself to solving Suzuki's technical problems. Never before had he worked for such appreciative masters.

DEGNER 'I remember when I finished the first 125 cc cylinder by hand. I had told Mr Okano and Mr Ishikawa, "Don't come to the workshop today, I'll do the finishing work on the cylinder. I'll phone you when I'm ready but it will take at least six hours." I phoned them, and when Mr Okano saw the cylinder, he grasped it under his arm and rushed to show Mr Suzuki what I had done. Mr Suzuki called a few other directors there, and they looked at it and then, I was no longer only half a god for they had seen what I was able to do. Not only were the ports polished, also between the liner and the cylinder casting material so that there would be good contact and the heat would be easily transferred to the cylinder.'

After that, Suzuki were able to duplicate Degner's hand-fettling principles, but it was all done by sophisticated machinery.

One important contribution made by Degner during this period, concerned the transmission difficulties experienced in 1961. Degner redesigned the selector mechanism to prevent incorrect selection or, worse still, the engagement of a false neutral. Degner was a perfectionist: Susumu Saitoh recalls that he was so fastidious about wheel balance that it became a joke within the research department.

Suzuki gained all these technological strides as a consequence of Jimmy Matsumiya's first chats with Degner in his Douglas hotel room the previous June. It could so easily have been another manufacturer who gained Degner's knowledge.

NEWMAN 'Ernst was such a good rider, having proved himself on the MZ, and still with a lot of racing left in him, that it was obvious that he'd be picked up by another works team, and as things were in 1961, it could only have been the Japanese.'

4 Hostile territory: war of attrition (1962 to 1964)

Degner's race-shop activities produced the RM62, RT62 and RV62 machines for the 1962 season. The Team were confident of success but Degner's Suzuki contract gave him first stab at the 125 cc World Championship which had eluded him in 1961. To improve his chances, he used a special rear exhaust version of the RT62.

DEGNER 'I told them I'd tried both types of exhaust at MZ and that the rear exhaust had better acceleration. But they made both because money made no difference.'

There were two support crews for 1962. Whilst the First group looked after all GPs up to the West German round, the Second group in Japan would pander to their requests. Then, their position would be reversed apart from a few key personnel, and the First group would commence work on the 1963 machines. The First group was headed by Takeharu Okano with Mike Ishikawa and Hiroyuki Nakano in support whilst Matsumiya would often join the Team at the GPs. Yasunori Kamiya was chief mechanic. Seiichi Suzuki and Mitsuo Itoh doubled as mechanics and riders. The Team's European HQ was moved to the warehouse of Suzuki's distributor in Paris, Pierre Bonnet, where the Team built their machines, often testing them in the surrounding streets!

Suzuki's classic season commenced at Barcelona but despite working night and day, the Team could not overcome the many problems—mainly piston seizures—and without scoring, the Team packed up and drove to France. Clermont-Ferrand on 13 May will never be forgotten by one rider.

PERRIS 'I went out in practice and the machine had a seizure which threw me off. The 250 also seized in practice and again I fell. In the 125 race I was just entering a left-hander and it went W-H-A-C-K! I couldn't catch it so down I went again. I picked it up and returned to the pits and I remember Mr Okano asking if the bike was OK. By this time, I was a little browned off and I threw the bike at Jimmy Matsumiya and told him where he could stick his bikes!'

Degner on his 125 couldn't catch the four Honda RC145s and finished 5th, whilst in the 50 cc event, Suzuki, Itoh and Degner finished 5th, 6th and 7th.

After licking their wounds in Paris, the Team arrived at the Fernleigh in Douglas, Isle of Man, where they were joined by Osamu Suzuki, the president's son-in-law. Anxious to avoid a confrontation, MZ now lodged elsewhere.

Tyres for the 50s caused problems for Avon's Ralph Newman.

NEWMAN 'During the off-season, Avon had no technical contact with

Above Before the 1962 GP season commenced, Matsumiya and his wife Noa hosted a dinner at London's Edmundo Ros Club. Seated with them are, L to R: Rita and Frank Perris, Perris' sister-in-law Gitti, and Degner *Eros*

Right Viva Suzuki! Itoh, Degner, Ichino, Morishita and Anderson line up on their RM63s at Barcelona *Archives*

Suzuki and when the 50 came along, it had a different size of tyre compared with previous Suzukis.'

But tyre selection, to a canny rider, could be a useful tuning aid.

DEGNER 'In 1960, when I raced the MZ, the final gear ratio I wanted was just in-between that which was available, so I had a new rear tyre fitted and that was it. I was able to beat Ubbiali's MV easily! If you rolled the new tyre on a length of one kilometre, that might be worth 20 or 30 metres; that's a lot.'

When Degner won the 50 cc TT there was jubilation in the Suzuki pit. Itoh and Ichino were placed 5th and 6th too! Suzuki's win was the first TT victory by a two stroke since 1938. It sounded a death knell throughout the four stroke world. But for Suzuki, they'd conquered the mountain at their third attempt, as predicted by Eric Teare—their hotel manager—in 1960. Moreover, this was Suzuki's *first* World Championship victory.

Ironically, Degner only managed 8th in the 125 cc TT; Perris and Anderson retired, but Suzuki's 50 cc win hit the headlines world-wide and Osamu Suzuki threw a party at the Castle Mona. The crowds, too, were delighted.

MATSUMIYA 'I remember driving the van back from the Sulby Straight; so many people were shouting, "Suzuki won!" And even driving back from Liverpool, motorcyclists would recognise us and our TT victory. This was the time I thought that Suzuki business could now begin.'

Perris had already raced the 250 to victory at Cadwell Park, setting a new lap record, but during TT practice the 250s proved embarrassing and were withdrawn. At the Dutch TT Anderson was injured, but Degner was 4th on the 125 and won the 50 cc GP with Suzuki and Itoh in 4th and 5th places, sandwiching the Kreidler team. In the 250 cc GP Perris finished 5th but Degner hit Tommy Robb's Honda—lying on the track after Robb fell—bending the Suzuki's wheel, and putting him out of the hunt.

Earlier in the year, Mike Ishikawa had found a new Team HQ in Holland, the Hotel d'Orange at Badhoevedorp, which had a number of lock-up garages and was close to Schippol airport. The Hotel d'Orange became the Team's HQ until 1967.

Anderson's injuries prevented him contesting the Belgian GP, and in the 250 race, Degner had a seizure whilst Perris—4th for four laps—retired with a broken plug terminal. Perris made his 50 cc debut in Belgium.

> PERRIS 'Mr Okano insisted that I rode it, but for me at Spa, the only place you shut off and braked was at the 'La Source' hairpin. I had five laps to ride where I had to hold it open—no riding was involved—because every corner was flat out. I just sat there trying to get myself wrapped around the 50.'

Perris finished 14th with Degner and Suzuki in 1st and 4th places.

During the West German GP practice, Perris had lapped on the 250, 25 seconds slower than Redman's Honda, and in the race retired after one lap, whilst Anderson also withdrew from the race. In the 50 cc GP, Degner repeated his flush of 50 cc victories, with Itoh, Suzuki and Ichino in 3rd, 5th and 6th places. Anderson finished 6th in the 125 cc GP—the highest-placed Suzuki rider. The 125s hadn't proved particularly reliable.

> ANDERSON 'In 1962, we all kept seizing up and breaking down. Solitude was the first time that I finished on the 125.'

Transport was becoming a headache and Mike Ishikawa purchased five Commer 1500 vans to replace the troublesome Hinos which were shipped back to Japan. The First group now returned to Japan, whilst Shimizu's Second group flew out to the Ulster GP, where they fitted new rear exhaust engines to the Perris-Anderson 125s. Shortly after the start of the 125 event, Degner fell at Cochranstown.

> DEGNER 'It wasn't raining, but on some parts it was wet. Where I crashed it was my fault because I went around there on the limit. The road was dry but the rear wheel slipped and I couldn't catch it and I went with both knees into a wall. My left knee was split into eight or ten pieces and I also severed a tendon. Then they operated but I still had to do a lot of exercise before I was able to use it again.'

Meanwhile, Hugh Anderson maintained contact and finished 5th. In the 250 cc GP, Anderson was in 2nd place when his RV62 seized—like Perris.—three miles from the start, due to a jetting error. Injured Degner was a non-starter.

En route to Sachsenring and the East German GP, the Team collected the 50s from Badhoevedorp but Degner was unable to defend his 50 cc Championship because of injury. Furthermore, his team-mates weren't keen on contesting in a communist state; East Germany still smarted over Degner's defection. Eventually, Itoh and Anderson agreed to ride and Itoh—using Degner's machine—finished 2nd with Anderson 3rd. At the Italian GP, new teamster Isao Morishita substituted for Degner, finishing 5th in the 50 cc GP with Itoh and Anderson in 2nd and 4th places, stealing Championship points that would otherwise have been gained by Kreidlers. Perris attained 5th place in the 250 cc

DANIEL HUSTINGS R
THE FINAL LINK BETWEEN
LADBROKE HALL TO AMSTERD

Upper Five new Commer vans were delivered to Team Suzuki's HQ at Badhoevedorp during 1964. Commers succeeded the earlier Japanese Hino transporter *Muller*

Lower Anderson (RV62) holds a short-lived 2nd place behind Jim Redman (Honda) in the 1962 250 cc Ulster GP. The unreliable RV62 scored only two championship points that year *Nicholls*

GP but retired along with all his team-mates, whilst on their RT 62s, Perris and Anderson finished 7th and 8th in the 125 GP.

Whilst Degner was fit for Tampere, he was reluctant to ride.

MATSUMIYA 'Before Ernst and I flew out to Helsinki, we bought a couple of small tear-gas pistols because . . . Degner was worried by MZ's presence.'

DEGNER 'I was afraid that the communists would take me back and so I had bodyguards. They were two friends who had pistols and took care of me. Finland is half and half politically, and everywhere I went, they were there.'

The moment Degner came into the pits after finishing 4th in the 50 cc race, his bodyguards surrounded him and Matsumiya drove the three men back to the hotel. For Perris, the 1962 Finnish GP was an event he'd sooner forget.

PERRIS 'They wanted to make up the numbers at the Finnish GP, and I had to ride a 50 again. Tampere is very hilly and you came down this very steep hill, around a 90 degree corner and up another steep hill, and I actually had to paddle it up! I was rather glad when it seized on me because I was making a fool of myself.'

Perris later made amends in the 125 cc GP by finishing in 5th place.

At Badhoevedorp, spares and machines were crated up, to be flown to Japan and the Argentine where Degner needed to finish 2nd to clinch the 50 cc World Championship. Anderson and Itoh also contested this final round.

ISHIKAWA 'The 50 cc Championship was decided at the Argentine GP and Degner was determined to win the title, but his knee still caused us some anxiety. Anderson was asked to support Degner as much as possible during the race. Degner gained the Championship as a result, although Anderson himself won the final round. Without Anderson's help, Degner could not have won the title.'

Degner rode Anderson's number one machine, but proving his *riding* ability, Anderson led the race almost throughout. Initially, Degner was 4th with two Kreidlers ahead but by intentionally slowing, Anderson caused the two Kreidlers to lose concentration—one crashed—thus assisting Degner to achieve 2nd place, and Suzuki their *first* World Championship. In the 125 cc event, Anderson took the chequered flag—Suzuki's first 125 cc GP victory—his job made easier by Honda's absence.

By then, Honda had already clinched the 125 cc and 250 cc World Championships, and their new test circuit, Suzuka, became the venue for Japan's first International Road Race and which would see the launch of many new racing models in future years.

The First group had been designing a new twin-cylinder machine, the RT63X—the 'X' denoting front exhaust—to be assessed against the rear exhaust single during the Suzuka practice periods.

DEGNER 'The outcome of the test was the same as with the single cylinder tests; the rear exhaust RT62 had more acceleration than the RT63X, so I chose to ride the single cylinder model in the race.'

PERRIS   'This was the first time Suzuki realised that they had something
with the 125 that year. In practice, I'd ridden the RT63X but preferred the
single.'

Perris' choice was wise; he finished 2nd, proving the benefits of the rear exhaust
concept, whilst new teamster Haruo Koshino was 6th. Anderson chose to test
ride the new RT63X in this non-Championship event, and finished 10th. In the
50 cc race, Anderson, Morishita and Suzuki finished in 2nd, 3rd and 4th places
(Degner crashed due to strong cross-winds whilst holding 4th place) but Perris'
125 cc result vindicated the rear-exhaust design.

Suzuki didn't provide a 250 cc machine for 1963, preferring to concentrate on
the smaller classes. Austrian Bertie Schneider was added to the Team's strength.

PERRIS   'Schneider joined the Team in 1963 after Suzuki had said they
wanted somebody who would be compatible with us. Unanimously, we
agreed on Bertie because he was one of the top private owners.'

At the Daytona season-opener—a non-Championship event—the Team used old
RM62s and RT63Xs, swamping the field in both classes. During practice, TV
crews filmed as the RT63Xs lapped as quick as the best 500 cc Manx Nortons
and G50 Matchlesses. Suzuki gained profitable publicity.

Following Honda's temporary withdrawal from 50 cc racing, the Kreidlers of
Anscheidt and Pagani became Suzuki's challenge, but the new 125s appeared
superior to the Hondas. At Barcelona Schneider made his Suzuki debut, but
achieved no higher than 7th in the 125 cc race in which Anderson had retired
with ignition trouble whilst holding 2nd. Perris retired on the first lap whilst
Degner, after an early fall, later retired. In the 50 cc GP, Anderson was pipped at
the post by Anscheidt, with Morishita finishing 4th, but at the West German
GP, Anscheidt was thoroughly beaten—finishing 4th-with Anderson, Morishita
and Degner ahead. Itoh and Ichino were 5th and 6th too! Degner had his first
Suzuki 125 classic victory at Hockenheim with Anderson 2nd. Things were
looking good. At the French GP, Anderson won the 125 cc GP with Perris and
Degner in 4th and 6th places, but Anscheidt beat Degner and Ichino's 50s;
Suzukis taking 2nd and 3rd places. In the Island, Anderson won the 125 cc event
with Perris, Degner and Schneider in 2nd, 3rd and 5th places; a Suzuki 1–2–3!
Suzuki also won the 50 cc race when Itoh became the first Japanese rider to claim
Mountain victory. Anderson held off Anscheidt's Kreidler, relegating the
German to 3rd place with Morishita and Ichino in 4th and 5th!

The Hondas were again beaten at Assen when Anderson and Perris kept
Taveri at bay with Schneider in 4th. Degner retired with a broken crankshaft. In
the 50 cc Dutch GP, Suzuki took the first five places; Degner, Anderson, Ichino,
Morishita and Itoh finishing almost within sight of each other!

Schneider was becoming more familiar with the little Suzukis, but the Belgian
125 cc GP was handed to him when Degner and Perris retired, and Anderson,
who finished 2nd, was off form.

SCHNEIDER   'On the 125 we had a power band of only 500 rpm, and at
Spa, changing from 5th to 6th meant slipping the clutch because it was
slightly uphill. It would slip below the power band unless you did that.'

In the 50 cc event, Morishita took the chequered flag ahead of Degner, with
Anderson and Itoh 4th and 5th.

One of the originators of the
modern aggresive riding styles,
Anderson riding his RM64 at
Hockenheim *Rauch*

Mitsuo Itoh (right), finished 3rd behind local rider Kissling (DKW) and victor Anderson in the 1962 125 cc Argentine GP
Archives

At the Ulster GP, Anderson characteristically set a new lap record in winning the 125 event from Schneider with Perris finishing 6th. A win in East Germany would clinch Anderson's 125 World Championship, and this he accomplished in fine style, with a 2 minute lead over Alan Shepherd's MZ, and setting yet another lap record in the process. Anderson again humiliated the Honda 125s in Finland, raising the lap record and leading Luigi Taveri over the line by $1\frac{1}{2}$ minutes! In the 50 cc GP, Anderson took the lead from Anscheidt in the early stages, but lost the ultra-light machine on the damp and difficult pit corner. After a long uphill push, Anderson remounted and in attempting to catch Anscheidt, raised the lap record. There wasn't enough time and Anscheidt won with Itoh, Anderson and Morishita finishing 2nd, 3rd and 4th. Anscheidt now led the 50 cc World Championship with 32 points to Anderson's 30. It would have to be decided in Argentina, an unpopular—and expensive—round. With the 125 cc World Championship already won, Suzuki didn't contest the Italian GP—which didn't include a 50 cc round—and the Team enjoyed a five week break before consolidating their 50 cc position in South America. Were Team orders issued here to help Suzuki's chances?

ANDERSON   'One year before, I had supported Degner in his quest for the World Championship and now Ernst was doing the same for me.'

Their plan succeeded, and Anderson won the race with Degner 2 seconds behind, thus retaining Suzuki's 50 cc title. The 125 cc GP was not contested.

The riders flew to Japan for the crucial pre-Japanese GP testing where they started as holders of the individual *and* Manufacturer's World Championships in both the 50 cc and 125 cc classes. The Japanese GP, held at Honda's test track Suzuka, enjoyed full World Championship status and saw the debut of the new RZ63 250 cc square-four. This had had to be announced prematurely after Yori Kanda—a Japanese photographer—had taken a sneak shot of it being tested by Haruo Koshino at Yonezu. This blurred photograph was published worldwide in October.

In the 50 cc event, Anderson, Masuda and Ichino finished 2nd, 3rd and 4th behind Taveri's flying Honda—Honda's first 50 cc GP in 1963. Then came the 125 cc event which Perris won whilst Degner and Anderson picked up 3rd and 5th with Mitsuo Itoh in 6th place. Perris' win created some amusement for the Japanese.

PERRIS   'Jim Redman was the same size as me, five feet eleven inches, and when I won the 125 cc race it had been him and I that were dicing for the lead. The Japanese thought it highly hilarious that these two big guys had led the 125 cc race with all the little fellows behind them!'

The 250 cc event followed, and Degner, Anderson and Perris were down to ride the new RZ63s. Schneider had a broken collar-bone, and could only spectate.

DEGNER   'I made a very bad start, and I had to risk a lot on that first lap to get the connection to the top. On the second corner, the front wheel tried to slip away, I caught it again and I went off the racing line, because at the edge of the track there was no grass, only sand, and if you touched that it is dangerous. And then I laid the motorcycle down myself because I didn't want to touch the sand, and my head hit the ground so hard that I was immediately unconscious. When I awoke, I saw the motorcycle about ten yards away and I ran up to it—I wanted to pick it up—but inside the streamlining it was burning. I didn't see that because I was dazed. When I started to pick up the motorcycle, I became unconscious again and a big flame spread to the tank which exploded and that was the end. I was told later that I was burning for 25 seconds before a fire extinguisher was used.'

PERRIS   'I couldn't get my 250 to start and when I came around the corner, there was Ernst lying in a pool of petrol and I pulled him out of it, waited until other help arrived and then zoomed around to the pits. There, I was asked why I had stopped. I explained that Ernst had been terribly burnt, but I was told to carry on racing. They couldn't understand my feelings—I'd just seen Degner's flesh burning. Ernst and I were good friends . . .'

DEGNER   'Sometimes the Japanese are so soft in their hearts, and at other times they are so hard. I was unconscious for about two minutes and I awoke inside the paddock. I was shouting because they hadn't given me an injection and I felt the pain, and it was horrible. The doctor wasn't sure of my injuries so he wouldn't give me drugs until I had been x-rayed.'

Degner spent one month in a Japanese hospital, then returned to Germany for the first of 56 skin-graft operations.

Meanwhile, in the 250 cc race, Anderson was leading the Morini of Tarquinio Provini—a contender for the 250 title—but towards race-end, he struck trouble, finishing 9th.

ANDERSON   'I was riding in 4th or 5th position and dicing with a Yamaha rider who fell off right in front of me on the last lap, and I had to get off the Suzuki. But for that I would have been either 4th or 5th on the RZ's first outing.'

At the 1962 Japanese GP, the riders assessed the new RT63X twin. Anderson (10) samples the twin (notice the fairing bulges for the disc-valve

Despite Degner's cruel luck, Suzuki were delighted with the RZ's performance and with Perris' 125 cc victory. The future seemed promising: they had successfully defended their 50 cc World Championship, and picked up the 125 cc title and they were determined to build from this firm foundation during 1964.

Anderson admits that Team orders were in force at the Daytona event—the US GP—in 1964. Orders were based on the likely success of each Team rider throughout the year, in order that they could contest the European rounds from a good position. At the Daytona 50 cc event, Anderson, Morishita and Itoh scored a 1—3—2 victory. The 125 cc GP was a further Suzuki demonstration; Anderson, Itoh, Schneider and Morishita taking the first four places! Practice showed the 250 cc RZ64 to be competitive on the fast, banked circuit, where power counted far more than handling.

PERRIS   'Bertie and I were on the 250s and we were trailing each other along and we came up to this big red machine. It was Hailwood on his 500 MV. We caught him up and suddenly I got caught up in his wake and was quite easily able to pass him.'

SCHNEIDER   'The MV did 246 to 247 km/hour [about 152 mph] but we didn't actually *race* against Mike because he was in a different class, it happened during practice. We joked that we were as fast yet only half the size! We did have some seizures though . . .'

Adrenalin was flowing freely in the riders' veins, and an off-track incident amused an FIM official who thought he'd seen the dwarf-like Schneider punch a burly US policeman!

SCHNEIDER   'We had problems with the bike and I came into the pits. I wanted to use the toilet urgently and there was a toilet outside the gate which was guarded by a Sheriff armed with pistols around his belt. I had no trouble getting out, but when I returned he asked me for my pass. He could see my leathers and my helmet so I said to him did he think I was dressed like that for a masquerade? I was already nervous, and late for qualifying, but he grabbed me from behind and said I had to stay there. I was shaking with rage. I didn't hit him . . . but maybe he stumbled a bit!'

Soon after, things turned a little sour when Perris stepped off his 250 at high speed.

PERRIS   'I was zooming around in practice taking a right-hander and the front-end let go. My ankle was trapped under the fairing dragging me with the machine. In trying to rid myself of the machine, I kicked large dents in the tank. We both went over the banking and landed on the grass. This snapped my leg back below the knee. I had to pay £1300 to have nine screws put into my leg—almost half my contract fee—because we were never insured against such things by Suzuki.'

induction) whilst Perris straddles the RT62 single which he later raced to 2nd place *Perris*

After Daytona, Anderson and Schneider raced at the unrecognised Singapore GP that Suzuki had contested in 1961. But why should Suzuki enter such a low-key event?

SCHNEIDER   'The Singapore GP had a very good write-up in the Far

Eastern countries, and Suzuki had a very strong importer there, so they went there for this publicity. Mike Ishikawa, Mitsuo Itoh and Hugh Anderson were also there with a few Japanese mechanics. I rode only the 125 there and I retired when my engine seized.'

ANDERSON   'I remember Bertie, he loved the sun and the swimming pool, and I remember that I was faster on the 50 than he was on the 125! In the race we had ignition bother, and this time it really was ignition—Suzuki would often claim ignition problems when the true problem was a broken crank or con-rod—and otherwise, I would possibly have won the open class. I was fluctuating with a Yamaha rider that I would pass on the twisty sections, and he would pass me on the straights because of his more powerful 250 cc machine. Finally, I had condenser trouble and I was out.'

The Spanish GP saw the Honda–Suzuki battle renewed, and in practice Anderson had achieved the fastest lap. In the 125 cc race he was forced to slow whilst lying in 2nd place, eventually finishing 5th, directly behind Schneider. Anderson had the same position in the 250 cc GP, with Schneider in 8th place, whilst Anderson took 2nd in the 50 cc GP with Itoh and Morishita in 3rd and 4th places.

At the French GP, Anderson and Taveri were disputing the lead on their 125s, when Anderson's RT64 expired, leaving Schneider and Perris to take 2nd and 3rd places. He made amends in the 50 cc GP, claiming victory with a record-breaking lap in the bag. The 250 cc GP was Anderson's last ride on a Suzuki 250. He retired in the race, with Schneider taking 3rd place.

ANDERSON   'The 250 hadn't really been developed since the Japanese GP,

Left L to R: Ichino, Anderson, Degner and Itoh during the 1963 West German GP at Hockenheim where Team Suzuki scored their first GP hat-trick *Schwab*

Centre Perris gesticulates to his mechanic Shunkichi Matsumoto whilst Teruo Sasaki struggles to understand having just ridden the RT63 from the Fernleigh Hotel to the IoM TT paddock *Perris*

46

Above Another hat-trick for
Team Suzuki! A 1963 IoM TT
shot showing Degner (3rd),
Anderson (1st) and Perris (2nd)
with their 125 cc RT63s.
Behind them looking relieved,
L to R: Ishikawa, Kamiya (just
visible), Okano, Shimizu and
Shigeno *Perris*

and I was drawing up a list of things that had to be changed. Frank and
Bertie would often disagree with me, and so I decided not to ride it. It was
pointless carrying on and I wasn't contracted to ride it anyway. The 50 had
nine speeds, the 125 had eight and the 250 had six, and when you're trying to
organize what gear to use round which corner, and what gear ratios to choose
for each machine, it became virtually impossible. In addition, when you had
to get off a 250, hop onto a 125 or a 50, the colossal difference in weight for
each machine made things very difficult. As events proved, my assessment
was perfectly correct.'

At the TT, Suzuki were beginning to miss Degner and so at the
suggestion of Perris and Schneider they contracted Australian Jack Ahearn
on a race-by-race basis. In practice, the 250 was plagued with problems:
the long wheelbase and the front-end heaviness made the machine difficult
to handle around the bends, although once in a straight line, it could be
squirted without much trouble. Like all two strokes, carburation was critical.

SCHNEIDER 'Jack Ahearn didn't have much success because he did not
have any feeling as far as carburettor setting was concerned. That is most
important, because you have to feel in the first half mile if the carburettor
setting is too rich or too lean and adjust the lever. If you don't do this, then
definitely the engine will seize up. This was Jack's trouble; he only had four
strokes before and they're not so critical.'

Perris retired at the Highlander, Ahearn seized on the third lap, and Schneider's
chain broke on the second lap . . . In the 125 cc race, neither Anderson, Perris
nor Schneider finished.

ANDERSON 'At Union Mills, I passed Luigi Taveri and in the process, over-revved the engine a fraction. As soon as I took it to peak revs—14,000 rpm—I knew I was in trouble, and sure enough, within a mile, it locked solid.'

Anderson claimed 1st place in the 50 cc race, with Morishita and Itoh in 3rd and 5th positions. Ahearn was offered further rides on the 250 cc, and manfully accepted although disaster haunted him whenever he rode it.

At the Dutch TT, in the 50 cc event, only five riders finished, but Morishita and Itoh took 2nd and 3rd spots whilst Schneider, Anderson and Perris secured 4th, 5th and 6th in the 125 cc race. At this point, Nakano's 1st group returned to Japan to be replaced by the 2nd group with Shimizu in charge. With him he brought a recent Suzuki recruit, Takashi Nakamura, an excellent English-speaker, acting as assistant to Mike Ishikawa. As usual almost the full complement of mechanics were exchanged.

At the very fast Spa circuit, the 50s lapped at 92 mph, and Anderson finished 3rd, only half a second behind the winning Honda! By contrast, the 250 cc event was a disaster; the Suzukis having engine trouble, a sore point with Schneider, the easy-going Austrian.

SCHNEIDER 'We had trouble with big-ends and they sometimes had to be changed during a single race meeting: Suzuki said that they were working together with a German university to develop something, but in those days, I was more interested in making money—and racing—to be interested in how they solved their technical problems.'

With no 125 cc grand prix at Spa, the Suzuki vans were driven to the West German GP, where Degner was well enough to spectate. Anderson led the 125 race and raised the lap record, but regrettably fell. Schneider finished 4th. True to form, the 250s were troublesome once again. In the 50 cc GP, Morishita and Itoh finished in 2nd and 3rd places.

SCHNEIDER 'At a lot of the races, I had fastest or second fastest qualifying times, but the 250 always seized on the first lap, and nobody knew what was the cause. At Solitude the same thing happened, and afterwards, Degner discovered the mistake that had been made. He suggested that because of the better cooling obtained by using water, the actual piston clearances were less when the engine was warm, than those on an air-cooled engine. So, when I went out for practice, I was able to idle along for one or two laps gradually going faster and faster—warming it up slowly. In the race, I would go on to the starting grid and be waiting for 5 or 7 minutes, allowing the water temperature to drop down to 50 or 40 degrees, and then the engine would suddenly be flat out. Outside, the engine stayed cool, but inside, the pistons became suddenly hot and caused the seizures. Soon this problem had been solved.'

Two weeks after the East German, where Anderson finished 16 seconds ahead of Taveri's Honda in the 125 cc race, the Team had arrived in Ulster with their convoy of blue Commer vans. The 50 cc category was not catered for, and in practice for the 125 cc GP, Anderson had engine problems and used Frank Perris' 'spare' engine for the race. After crashing at the hairpin on the first lap Anderson remounted, but a lap later his engine stalled as a result of poor

Above The horrifying fire that engulfed both Degner and his RZ63 during the 1963 250 cc Japanese GP and which kept Degner out of the saddle for most of 1964, (see p 44) *Archives*

Right One for the road! Daytona-bound in 1964, the GP stars enjoy a pre-flight drink at Gatwick. L to R: Perris, Taveri, Vittorio Carrano (Hailwood's MV mechanic), Shepherd, Read, Schneider, Driver and Hailwood *Perris*

carburation. With sheer guts, determination and brilliant riding, Anderson raised the lap record by 15 seconds, as he strove to make up his lost time. Meanwhile, Perris and Schneider were contesting the lead with the Honda fours of Taveri and Ralph Bryans, but on the penultimate lap—Anderson's fastest— he passed Perris, taking the lead. On the last lap, Perris slowed with ignition trouble and the two Hondas swept past, but Schneider, who caught Perris about one mile from the flag, intentionally fell in behind his team-mate finishing 5th. Without doubt, the 1964 125 cc Ulster GP was Anderson's finest ride of his racing career, but Perris too had been equally determined to win, and had earlier broken the lap record himself by about 11 seconds!

In the 250 cc GP, Jack Ahearn rode the RZ64, but the man who christened the square-four 'Whispering Death' fell.

SCHNEIDER   'Ahearn always said you must ride a bike thinking that around the next corner, there may be oil on the ground, it may be damp, and there may even be a tree-trunk lying in the road. You must ride so carefully so that you don't hit the tree, or slide off on the oil patch. He said this at the Ulster GP, but two laps later, he was lying in the ditch because he fell off on some oil!'

In that same race, bedevilled by pouring rain, Schneider coaxed his 250 into 6th place.

Practice for the Finnish GP at Imatra was held under wet conditions, and Anderson caused some amusement when, after out-braking his rivals on the slippery track, he was asked to name the glue that enabled him to stay aboard the machine! It was theoretically possible for Anderson to win the overall 125 cc title, and for the race he tuned his 125 as lean as possible to extract a little more power. Whilst leading the race, a piston melted and Anderson was forced to retire, with the World title clinched by Taveri, whereas Schneider finished 4th. In the 50 cc race, Anderson and Anscheidt fought a close battle, but Anderson emerged the victor, finishing just 0.7 seconds ahead of his Kriedler rival. Anderson's win gave him the World title for the second year, and Suzuki Japan the World Manufacturer's Championship.

The Italian GP ended Schneider's Suzuki career after just a couple of seasons.

PERRIS 'Bertie was a marvellous bloke; but he really was the Team joker. At Monza, Bertie was playing around outside the hotel chasing Gerda—Ernst's wife—over the flower beds, when he fell and broke a bone in his ankle. It didn't put him out of the race, but he wasn't as fit as he should have been. Shimizu had seen it all and realised that Bertie wasn't taking it seriously enough..'

SCHNEIDER 'During the 125 cc race my foot was hurting a lot and on the last lap, something broke in the engine and I had to push it all the way back to the pits. The mechanics said that they couldn't repair it and I said that I would concentrate on the 250 instead, but this broke down in the race too and again I pushed it back to the pits. Again the Japanese said that they couldn't repair it since they'd returned all the spare parts to Japan ready for the Japanese GP. Then I thought; after a whole year of risking my neck always knowing that on the first lap something would happen, and nobody would know why, was it worth it? I suspected that the Japanese may have wanted to cancel my contract, so I said "Bugger it!"'

Monza marked the return of Degner to Team Suzuki, but he was doubtful of his riding ability.

DEGNER 'After such a long stay away—it was nearly a year—I thought that I would never find my racing form like I had before. At Monza, just after I left hospital, I had fifth fastest practice time in front of Ralph Bryans, but in the race I had a lousy start and tried very hard and finished 3rd.'

In that same race, Anderson finished 2nd, with Perris in 5th. Monza concluded Suzuki's European season and they returned to the Hotel d'Orange to finish packing their equipment.

Since Anderson was himself based in Holland, the Suzuki HQ was handy.

ANDERSON 'I used to go up to Badhoevedorp quite a lot; I did a lot more testing than the others. I'd go to Zandvoort testing because after Ernst crashed in Japan, I became the number one rider. The Team carried a log of everything that occurred at all the meetings, and all the settings of the machinery; they took my settings as the standard.'

Badhoevedorp also had a number of other less-welcome visitors.

DEGNER 'Security was very bad and there were often pieces missing; sometimes items such as cylinders and crankshafts. They couldn't use these parts because they didn't have all the other pieces but some people in Germany who produced their own engines, needed some information – maybe how the crankshaft was balanced.'

TADDY MATSUI (mechanic) 'I remember in 1964, we had some thefts, and we lost a complete 50 cc cylinder engine which was never recovered.'

ANSCHEIDT 'The garages were always being broken into and spares stolen, such as engines, wheels, and frames. At this time, I saw many private bikes being raced with Suzuki parts on them. One Dutch machine was seen with a Suzuki clutch and brake but the Japanese couldn't say anything because they didn't know exactly where they had come from. They may have come from crashed machines which had been kicked out.'

Schneider inspects an RT64 cylinder whilst his RZ64 awaits final race preparation. The numbers on the silencer cover remind the mechanics of the sprocket sizes for the race. Compare the detail design with that of the earlier RZ63 (see p 218) *Gruber*

Prospective teamsters also visited the Hotel d'Orange.

SCHNEIDER 'In those days, everybody was trying to get a ride, and were friendly towards the Japanese. There was a Dutch man, Jan Huberts, who tried to join the Team. He tried several times at Badhoevedorp but was not successful.'

Another, more illustrious rider, was seriously considered.

PERRIS 'I tried to get Hailwood to ride for us when he left MV. I spoke to Suzuki at the end of the season and Mike came down to Hamamatsu. Suzuki offered him a ride on the 250.'

HAILWOOD 'I was a bit fed up with MV, and Honda weren't very interested, and Frank Perris said I ought to have a chat with Suzuki. I was a little concerned about Suzuki's bad reputation for seizing up and also that they only made the smaller machines, so we didn't get very far in our talks.'

Hailwood's possible inclusion in the 1965 Team raised a few other problems too.

NAKAMURA 'Suzuki were only half interested: Hailwood would be too expensive and that would spoil the balance of the existing Team members' payments. I never actually spoke directly with Mike, but with Frank Perris, and I remember that I telexed the information to head office from

Monza in 1964. They didn't trust me—maybe I was too young—and told me not to worry about it. "We'll manage this from Japan, you just carry on with the racing. It's not your job."'

Hailwood wanted a bigger Suzuki, but the 250 represented the limit of Suzuki's engineering at that time. Hailwood visited Hamamatsu and Takashi Nakamura met Mike in the president's office just after the 1964 Japanese GP. In the upshot, nothing came of this meeting and the matter was dropped.

The Japanese GP saw a new teamster, Yoshimi Katayama, who rode well in the 125 cc GP, finishing 3rd, whilst Degner took the flag just one second ahead of Taveri's Honda. Earlier, Anderson had stormed into the lead, demolishing the lap record, but regrettably, an ignition wire came loose, side-lining him. This race was Degner's first GP victory since his terrible accident—at the same circuit—the previous year.

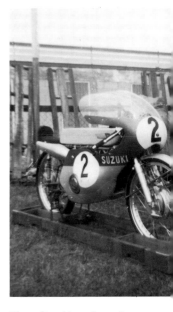

> DEGNER 'I had ridden with Taveri the whole race, and I watched him— where to overtake—and on the last lap at the last corner, was able to pass him.'

Suzuki didn't contest the 50 cc race, and only four Hondas came to the line, so the FIM withdrew its classic status.

Suzuki's relations with MZ after Degner's defection had never been sound at management level, although Perris was quite friendly with MZ race-chief Walter Kaaden, but at Suzuka in 1964, MZ and Suzuki came a little closer.

> ANDERSON 'The East Germans were never friendly, but Walter Kaaden would nod his head to me and to other people who he recognised; Kaaden was a good man. When MZ raced in Japan in 1964, they lost all their tools and a lot of gear in transit, and Suzuki provided transport for them from the airport and out to Suzuka. Suzuki really did quite a lot for them.'

During these hectic years, Degner's expertise at developing two strokes had been noticed by other manufacturers, keen to follow in Suzuki's footsteps to victory.

Team Suzuki used wooden pallets to simplify handling of their fragile machines *Archives*

> DEGNER 'After the first two years, Yamaha tried to get in contact with me—just as they had done when I first left East Germany—but I was under contract with Suzuki and I told them that I was not interested. Shortly before I gave up racing in 1965, Kawasaki spoke with me on two stroke technology. Then a Japanese engineer came over to Germany and had talks with me about a contract. In 1966 they flew me over to Kawasaki for more talks, but they didn't give me a contract, even though I spent two weeks in Japan; they wanted to know specifications and details before I signed a contract!'

During 1964, Suzuki had taken the 50 cc World Championship for the third time running. Race pundits wondered when Honda would mount a real challenge to Suzuki in this class, as they had done with the 125s that year. They hadn't long to wait, for 1965 marked the commencement of a three-cornered battle in the 125 cc class; Yamaha entered the racing arena and Honda made a more determined effort to steal Suzuki's 50 cc title. The 'phoney' war was over: now it was battle stations.

5 No surrender:
racing truce (1965 to 1967)

For 1965, Hugh Anderson, Frank Perris, Ernst Degner and Jack Ahearn were joined by Yoshimi Katayama who'd proved himself at the 1964 Japanese GP.

> PERRIS 'The Japanese are a very proud race and didn't like having to ask Europeans to ride their bikes; they'd sooner have Japanese riders.
> Katayama was my team-mate on the 250 in 1965 and on the 125 in 1966.'

Mitsuo Itoh, Haruo Koshino and Michio Ichino were to support the main team on the track, riding the same new water-cooled machines. Mike Ishikawa and Hiroyuki Nakano managed the Team, and again were assisted by Takashi Nakamura.

As in 1964, the Daytona result was predetermined by the Team, and all went according to plan when Degner won the 50 cc race, followed by Anderson, Ichino and Koshino. In fact, they crossed the line almost abreast—just 0.4 seconds covering them. In the 125 cc event, the finish was a little less exciting; 0.6 seconds separating the first three, Anderson, Degner and Perris. With Yamahas present, ridden by Phil Read and Mike Duff, the 250 cc race couldn't be a foregone conclusion, and the Yamaha pair lapped the entire field, including Frank Perris, who finished 4th.

The factory Hondas did not appear for the 125 cc West German GP, leaving Anderson, Perris and Degner to finish 1st, 2nd and 4th, but in the 50 cc GP, the Hondas of Bryans and Taveri led Anderson home by 20 seconds with Itoh a further 16 seconds adrift in 4th place. Honda were taking Suzuki's 50 cc mastery *very* seriously.

Hugh Anderson was beginning to worry about the task that lay ahead upon his arrival in Barcelona for the Spanish GP.

> ANDERSON 'I couldn't sleep the night before first practice, and lay awake until 3 am when I made a cup of tea and thought things out. I was lumping all the GPs together, and so was looking at a mountain; individually, they weren't so hard to conquer. I was also worried about whether I was doing the right thing. It didn't take long to realise that contracts were signed and I was fully committed; I decided that if I was going to race, I shouldn't worry about it, and hopped into bed and slept. A couple of days later I won both classes.'

Despite relegating Bryans' 50 cc Honda to 2nd place in the GP, Anderson's victory became his last in this class. In the 125 cc GP, Perris secured 2nd place behind Anderson.

At Rouen for the French GP, the factory 50 cc Hondas outpaced the Suzuki

By 1965, Team Suzuki outgrew their Fernleigh TT workshop and rented another garage at the Falcon Cliff hotel. Here, chaos seems to reign as Shigeno prepares Perris' RZ65 *Perris*

RK65s, with Degner, Itoh and Anderson taking 3rd, 4th and 6th. Anderson started the 125 cc GP leading the classic series with three successive wins, but Degner was looking for glory too, and led the race until the last lap when Anderson, after a succession of record-breaking laps, eventually overtook his team-mate whose machine was suffering from a throttle cable problem which caused it to misfire. Perris finished 3rd behind his two team-mates. Anderson's record-breaking ride resulted in Bruce Beale—finishing 5th—being lapped twice by the winner! In the 250 cc race, neither Perris nor Ahearn finished; Ahearn had a mid-race fall whilst Perris' RZ65 seized on one cylinder. But in the Isle of Man, Perris had his most successful 250 cc GP race.

> PERRIS   'I finished 3rd, but I got a fouled plug at Ballacraine and did the first lap on three cylinders, came in for a plug change, and from then on it was beautiful. I got with Provini and we did the remaining five laps together. We refuelled together on the third lap but because I'd caught him, it meant I was actually ahead of him on corrected time.'

In the 50 cc race, Luigi Taveri cleared off leaving Anderson and Degner in his wake. At Ballaugh Bridge on the first lap of the 125 cc race, Anderson led the Yamahas of Read and Duff by ten seconds, but on the Mountain, Anderson's RT65 struck plug fouling, and he stopped to change them. (Most GP Suzukis had a small pouch mounted on the fairing containing a plug spanner and fresh spark plugs.) Having lost his lead, he broke the lap record in chasing the Yamahas, raising it to 96.02 mph! But his gallant attempt was in vain; he finished 5th with Degner in 8th place. Both Perris and Katayama retired.

Takashi Nakamura recalls the 1965 TT for a different reason.

> NAKAMURA   'We had about 20 mechanics to support the 17 machines in the Island, and when we arrived, Lew Ellis arranged for a lorry to transport our equipment to the Fernleigh Hotel. Ishikawa asked me to tip the driver £2, and I mistakenly gave him £20! The next day Lew Ellis suggested that perhaps I had made a mistake but I was embarrassed, and

Veteran GP campaigner
Frantisek Stasny (Jawa) leads
Perris off the 1965 250 cc TT
start-line. The small cover in
the Suzuki fairing enabled
jetting to be rapidly changed
during practice *Perris*

when I told him that it was arranged in that way, he was surprised. I
thought I hadn't fully convinced him, and I later told Ishikawa of the
error, but I don't know how he claimed it on the Team expenses.'

By the Dutch TT, Suzuki were leading the 50 cc World Championship and
the 125 classic series by virtue of Anderson's four successive wins, but Yamaha's
new 125 cc water-cooled twin was a certain threat. In the race, Anderson made a
poor start, losing about half a mile on the leader — Phil Read. As usual, a handful
of record breaking laps brought him within striking distance of the leaders by
mid-stage, and when Read retired, Anderson inherited 3rd place behind
Katayama and Duff, the Yamaha rider taking the flag, with Katayama and
Anderson 2nd and 3rd. Both Perris and Degner retired in the early stages. Ralph
Bryans won the 50 cc GP race from Anderson — who set *another* lap record —
whilst Itoh and Degner finished 4th and 5th. Katayama had his first 250 cc ride at
Spa, partnered by Perris and Ahearn. All three machines suffered problems in
the race — Ahearn retired on lap 2 as did Perris in the later stages. Katayama
initially battled with the Hondas and Yamahas, but a misfire slowed him and he
finished 4th.

In the 50 cc classics, Honda and Suzuki went to the Belgian GP level-pegging,
but on the fast Spa circuit the super-quick Suzukis came into their own with
Degner first home, ahead of Hugh Anderson, despite the fact that Anderson
needed to score maximum points to consolidate his overall position. Behind
them, Bryans and Itoh crossed the line together with identical times, but the
verdict for 4th place went to Itoh. The Belgian GP was the last race for the
problematic 250 cc square-fours; Katayama and Perris ended its career in fine
style, finishing 4th and 5th. But this result did not mask its overall unreliability
and Suzuki chose to withdraw from this class.

PERRIS 'The handling of the 250 was getting better all the time and
towards the end of 1965 it wasn't bad at all. We started to go fairly quick
even though we had a lot of problems with fouling plugs. This put me out

of many races but once the motor got hot it was good. You'd start off, and then after one lap you'd have to come in for a plug change. It was just beginning to come into its own when they took it away from us . . .'

Anderson also rode in motocross events, and just prior to the East German GP his leg was damaged in an accident, but whilst he missed the Sachsenring event, he was fit to ride in Czechoslovakia. At this time, Ishikawa, Shimizu and Nakano, together with some mechanics, returned to Japan leaving Takashi Nakamura and three mechanics, Kamiya, Nagata and Shunkichi Matsumoto. Atsuto Daiza—from Suzuki's European sales office—took charge of the Team's affairs. His first event was at the East German GP where Ahearn was to be substituted for Anderson. However, the organisers wouldn't allow this and only Perris went to the line on his Suzuki 125. The factory MZs gave Perris a hard race, but eventually Perris drew ahead of the leading MZ and cruised home with one minute in hand. It was Perris' first Suzuki victory since the 1963 Japanese GP.

Ten days after his motocross accident, Hugh Anderson was practicing at Brno with his leg in a special splint. The press were never informed of Anderson's disability and they would never have guessed, as Anderson and Perris diced in the early stages. But Anderson was having none of this, and decimating the lap record, he began to pull out a lead over Perris of about five seconds each lap. Anderson's race ended when he crashed, leaving team-mate Perris to take the flag almost two minutes ahead of his nearest rival, Derek Woodman on an MZ. Anderson's uncharacteristic spill was caused by a broken spark plug electrode! Hugh thought the plug lead had become detached.

The highest 250 cc GP placing attained by Suzuki was Schneider's 3rd in the 1964 French GP. Perris, seen here rounding Ramsey hairpin, equalled this in the 1965 250 cc TT *Nicholls*

ANDERSON 'They were in place, but I continued to fiddle, and for far too long. I looked up and was at the end of a short straight. I got into the corner as far as possible and layed the bike down, bursting three straw bales and coming to a painful stop. X-rays showed that my leg hadn't re-broken, but it was painful enough.'

Ulster was Degner's final Suzuki victory. In the 125 cc GP, Frank Perris retired with a broken crankshaft, and Anderson's RT65 also hit mechanical trouble, but Degner's win was popular, and no doubt pleasurable for him as he convincingly thrashed the factory MZs. Because Anderson had failed to score in East Germany and Czechoslovakia, whilst Perris scored maximum points at both events, the pair contested the Finnish GP with only 2 points between them. If Perris and Anderson finished 1st and 2nd at Imatra, the two would be level-pegging on 44 points each. Imatra put great pressures on the Suzuki teamsters. From the start, Perris and Anderson shot into the lead, with Perris marginally ahead. The lap record was shattered by both riders during their dice, as Perris attempted to leave Anderson behind. But Anderson's race was going to plan.

ANDERSON 'I stalked Perris in a planned move until the beginning of the last lap, when we caught a bunch of slower riders. I dived past Perris through a gap and into the lead, winning the race.'

Perris later claimed that he was under Team orders to ensure an Anderson victory, and whilst there is some merit in this claim, it is reasonable to ask why it was necessary for the two Suzuki teamsters to open up a gap of almost three minutes on the 3rd place rider. Furthermore, the results indicate that in gaining

Perris looks dumb-founded at Takashi Nakamura (holding stop-watch) during practice for the 1965 Czechoslovakian GP. Anderson looks on impassively, awaiting a new front wheel for his RT65 (just visible)
Anderson

the lead, Anderson raised the lap record by seven seconds which would have been totally unnecessary if Perris had slowed to allow Anderson to pass. Conversely, it was not Anderson's normal race tactic to stalk Perris, and as in the past, it would seem that Anderson was often capable of outriding Perris. Certainly, the 1965 125 cc Finnish GP leaves many questions unanswered, but the results should be considered in context. If Anderson was never informed of Perris' orders, it is possible that both riders recollect the event accurately.

The Italian GP at Monza adds strength to Anderson's case, for Degner would surely have been involved in any plan to support Anderson's title bid.

DEGNER   'At the time we had no race orders, and after two laps I was very far into the lead—in front of Hugh Anderson and Frank Perris. Then it started to rain and I crashed on the third lap. The upper part of my leg was broken into eight pieces and I had to spend another nine months in hospital.'

On the rain-soaked track, many riders came to grief, but after four laps, Anderson led his team-mate Frank Perris by over half a lap, and at three-quarters distance, Anderson actually lapped Perris! It was a brilliant display of frictional judgement between Dunlop rubber and Italian asphalt on the part of Anderson, who continued to extend his lead to the finish thus regaining the 125 cc World Championship from Honda's Luigi Taveri.

The Team returned to the Hotel d'Orange to sort the spares and crate the machines for despatch to Japan; for the Japanese GP, new machines would be available. But Perris was talking of retirement, and Degner was lying in hospital recovering from his Monza accident, and with Hugh Anderson showing interest in motocross, it was clear to Suzuki that fresh blood should be brought into the Team. Hans-Georg Anscheidt had been told by Kreidler of their competition withdrawal at the end of 1965. Suzuki heard and were tempted. . . .

ANSCHEIDT 'Suzuki contacted me first by telexing their European office and then someone from there asked me to race in Japan. There, I was recruited by Suzuki, at Suzuka race circuit, even though I was still under contract to Kreidler. They paid me to ride at the Japanese GP and then signed me up for the 1966 season.'

The Perris-Anderson rivalry came to a head in a Japanese night-club when a major row developed, and many things were said by both riders which otherwise would never have been vented. It certainly cleared the air and didn't appear to destroy their mutual respect. Both were re-contracted for 1966 following the Japanese GP.

Anscheidt's up-grading from the 12 bhp Kreidler single cylinder to a 16.5 bhp Suzuki twin cylinder 50 cc, required familiarisation.

ANSCHEIDT 'The bikes were very different to ride compared with the Kreidler: they were twin cylinder and had much more power but the power band was much narrower.'

In spite of his inexperience, Anscheidt finished 4th in the Suzuka 50 cc classic race, with Mitsuo Itoh 3rd behind the victorious Hondas of Taveri and Bryans. Anderson crashed whilst holding 2nd place, but remounted and finished 8th, establishing a new lap record. In the 125 cc GP, Honda's 125 five cylinder made its debut, and Taveri led the race until he had engine problems, when Anderson snatched the lead giving him a maximum of 56 points over the 125 cc classic series! Suzuki were happy at having regained this championship but were equally disappointed at losing the 50 cc title, which they were determined to win back in 1966.

Anscheidt's contract was only for the 50 cc class in the classic series although Suzuki loaned him a 125 cc machine for use in the German National Championships. Yoshimi Katayama was also signed for both 50 and 125 cc classes. Anscheidt and the new RK66 became formidable opposition, not only to Honda, but to Anderson, who never finished higher than 3rd in the 1966 50 cc classics. The same applied with the totally out-classed RT66, although Katayama finished 2nd on two occasions. Anderson scored a solitary 3rd at the TT with three 4th places and a 5th in Ulster. Perris finished no higher than 4th in a 125 cc GP in 1966, but in the 50 cc class, Anscheidt was able to chalk up wins at Hockenheim and Monza, with 2nds at Spain and Fisco (Japan) and a 4th in Holland. This was sufficient to clinch his first world title.

The seamen's strike delayed the TT until the end of August, and Team Suzuki were weary and raw-nerved.

PERRIS 'I'd already told Suzuki that when I was 35, in 1966, I would be retiring, but after the TT that year, Suzuki told me they were going home with the 125s, probably because they'd had a bad season. I wanted to go to Monza—one of my favourite circuits—and I remember saying to Mr Shimizu at Jurby one day, "Come on, you *must* give me a bike for Monza," and Shimizu said no. I said, "Well you can stuff your bikes."'

Perris left the Island that afternoon amidst a hail of rumours. Frank was still determined to race at Monza.

PERRIS 'I rang Benelli's and flew out to Modena for practice on the 350

Upper Perris waits calmly as Shunkichi Matsumoto warms up his RT65 at Brno. Astride his MZ, Heinz Rosner is unperturbed by the opposition. Rosner finished 3rd whilst Perris claimed victory *Perris*

Lower A rider relaxes behind his RK65 at Assen, whilst Suzuki's expansion chamber expert, Yoshihiko Murai, (wearing sunglasses) and Taddy Matsui (foreground) re-jet the carburettors *Gruber*

but they didn't have enough time to prepare a machine for Monza and offered me a ride for the Japanese GP. Then I received a telegram from Suzuki: "Holding you to your contract until 31 December 1966." I had to cancel the Benelli deal.'

Motor Cycle News carried a banner headline, 'Perris on Benelli' but during that week Gilera offered Frank a ride on their 500-4 at the 'Race of the Century', and the headline changed the following week to 'Perris on Gilera'.

The TT marked Ernst Degner's return to GP racing, and he finished 4th in the 50 cc race behind Anderson. But Degner, too, was becoming disenchanted with his racing career.

DEGNER   'I didn't feel like risking things as much as I did before, and so in a few races, I hadn't been very successful. Suzuki watched it of course, and we talked about it and I told them that I was tired of racing because of so many accidents and then it was nearly the end of the season and I gave up. After that, I didn't race on motorcycles anymore.'

Only Hugh Anderson remained from the 'old school' and he wasn't too pleased with the way things were progressing.

ANDERSON   'In the Isle of Man practices, I seized up, locked up or broke down 15 times; I only managed two laps on the 125 without breaking down and just one lap on the 50, and after some pretty good years it's just a bit hard to accept that kind of thing. I'd been used to being on the front row of the grid for four years, and here I was, dumped on the second, third or fourth row. The machines weren't going well—too many disappointments—and Team orders to finish behind Anscheidt in the 50 cc class at Fisco were too much. At Monza I was current world champion, and I was way down on time, possibly a minute behind, and it was rather hard to accept.'

Above The start of the 1966 50 cc Dutch TT. On the front row, Anscheidt is sandwiched between Bryans (Honda, 1) and Taveri (Honda) whilst Katayama (7), Anderson (3) and Degner (5) were relegated to lower grid positions. Lack of 50 cc interest is reflected by the depleted grid *Rauch*

At the Japanese GP, Honda handed Suzuki the 50 cc title, for prior to Fisco, Bryans led Anscheidt by 4 points, but Honda withdrew their entries from the event claiming that Fisco was too dangerous. Cynics said Honda were annoyed that their own circuit, Suzuka, was not being used. To gain the title, Anscheidt had to finish no lower than 2nd and thus Katayama was allowed to win his first GP in front of an ecstatic home crowd, with Anscheidt 2nd and Anderson— under orders—in 3rd place. In the 125 cc GP Katayama and Itoh finished 2nd and 3rd, a result that reflected Suzuki's overall 125 cc performances that year; they hadn't won a single race in 1966.

Meanwhile, Honda withdrew its 50 and 125 cc machines for 1967, resulting in Taveri's retirement and the sacking of Stuart Graham. Anderson now announced his intention to retire from road-racing and take up motocross—with Suzuki of course. He was commissioned by Suzuki to find someone suitable to replace him. He chose Stuart Graham.

GRAHAM   'About three days after Christmas Hughie Anderson telephoned me, asking if I would be interested in a Suzuki contract for 1967. Suzuki had a short-list including Ginger Molloy, Peter Williams and myself. It seemed my name was at the top of the list. Hughie told me that if I agreed,

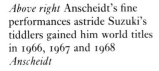

Above right Anscheidt's fine performances astride Suzuki's tiddlers gained him world titles in 1966, 1967 and 1968 *Anscheidt*

we'd both go out to Japan where I could test the machines, and if I liked them, sign a contract.'

The 1967 line-up was to be Anscheidt, Katayama and Graham on the 50s, with Graham and Katayama on the 125s. The Team was managed by Mike Ishikawa with some assistance from Akira Yoshimoto whilst Yasunori Kamiya again led the mechanics including Shunkichi Matsumoto (formerly Masuda), Tadao (Taddy) Matsui, and Toshio Matsumoto, with Mitsuo Itoh helping in the paddock or on the track.

The Spanish GP resulted in a decisive 50 cc one-two for Anscheidt and 'Kat', but in the 125 event, the Suzukis were no match for the Yamahas of Read and Ivy, with Katayama and Graham finishing in 3rd and 4th places.

Hockenheim, Anscheidt's 'home' GP round, saw Graham getting to grips with the 50. In practice, he found he could beat Anscheidt, the German national hero.

> GRAHAM 'I had instructions that I wasn't to win and this is the worst thing when you suddenly find yourself out in front. Then Georg's bike went sick enough to enable me to pull out a two second lead within one lap. Then *my* engine went "pop" just as Georg's chimed in again and he eventually won.'

Anscheidt, having a rare 125 cc ride finished 2nd to Katayama with Stuart out of contention.

At Clermont-Ferrand, Graham's 125 suffered clutch slip just after passing Read and gaining on Ivy. This allowed Read and 'Kat' to overtake Graham who finished 4th. In the 50 cc GP, Suzukis swept the field with Katayama, Anscheidt and Graham finishing in that order.

By now, Stuart Graham—traditionally a big-bike rider—was getting used to riding the 50.

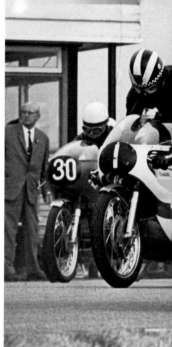

GRAHAM 'Once I'd learnt the technique for keeping the motor within the power band—16,500 to 17,000 rpm—it didn't bother me at all. Below the band, it just stopped—there was no flywheel effect. You never ever stopped changing gear, even around corners where you had to change gear all the way round making sure you didn't wipe your foot off. I never used the clutch or "kill-button" either. Why stop the spark? I was always terrified of oiling up a spark plug anyway because they were so temperamental.'

Above left Count the Suzukis! At Hockenheim in 1967, Anscheidt relaxes during practice, and later finished 1st in the 50 cc and 2nd in the 125 cc GPs *Anscheidt*

The riders were being regularly told that a new four cylinder 125 would be available at 'the next grand prix' but they never arrived.

GRAHAM 'When I signed up, Suzuki showed me a 125 cc *square*-four on the test bed and they said we'd be racing them for the TT. The TT came and the fours didn't arrive but then we learned there'd been a change of plan: the square-four was being redesigned as a V_4, just like Yamaha. The intention was to design, manufacture and develop the V4 by September which was absolutely incredible.'

The 125 cc Suzuki-Yamaha battle continued at the TT where regretfully, Graham made a poor start. First man on the road, he relied totally on signals regarding his race position.

GRAHAM 'Suzuki's signalling point was on the Sulby straight—just about the worst place because the bumps would make your goggles float up and down on your face—and I hadn't seen a signal until on the last lap. I read, "PLUS 3 SECONDS Y", which I thought meant I was in 1st place, 3 seconds up on Yoshi Katayama. I guessed that Katayama would not be allowed to pass me so I slowed a little since I thought I'd nipped a piston earlier. Down the Mountain, I richened up the mixture too, using the hand lever, but by the time I'd finished, I'd lost the race to Read. The "Y" on the signal board referred to Yamaha. That's what made me so determined to win the 50 cc race.'

Taking advantage of the Yamaha 125 cc V4's poor starting record, Graham is first off the 1967 Dutch TT start-line. Read (1) is just mounting his Yamaha RA31 but his team-mate Bill Ivy (2), is still pushing. Graham finished 3rd behind the V4s *Carling*

For maximum publicity, it was decided that Katayama should win the tiddler event, but Anscheidt and Graham were told that if Katayama retired, they could win but that Anscheidt had first priority.

GRAHAM 'Katayama made a mess of the start and Georg and I hung around for a lap—we'd started together—and eventually, Katayama caught us up and turned around to look at Georg and put his wheels down a ditch! Katayama was *quick* around the Island but he was wild, riding all over the place like an accident waiting to happen. Anyway, Georg and I decided to race but when we got up to the Black Hut, Georg sat up and I thought his engine had stopped. I kept going and when I looked behind me at Creg-ny-Baa, he was just coming around Kate's Cottage. So I thought, "To hell with this!", and got stuck in and won the race.'

Anscheidt finished 2nd, about one minute behind Graham.

GRAHAM 'Georg was a little upset, and said "Why did you go so fast?" I told him that I had wanted to win it and I don't think he ever forgave me for that.'

The Yamaha struggle continued, and Graham soon adopted his own way of holding the fort until the Suzuki V4s arrived. One method was to jet the twins so lean that the rider could stay with the Yamahas, at least until the Suzukis overheated and seized. This was Katayama's method. Graham decided that a good race position and reliability were important, and jetted accordingly, taking advantage of the Yamahas' sluggardly starts, and when the two Yamahas came screaming past, tried to hang on in 3rd place. Sometimes he'd manage to split the Yamaha pair.

At the Dutch and East German rounds, Graham finished 3rd behind Read and Ivy but at Czechoslovakia he was 2nd to Bill Ivy and he won the Finnish GP.

On the 50s, Katayama won the Dutch with Anscheidt 4th, the Suzuki duo split by the Derbis, but at Spa-Francorchamps Suzuki scored a 1–2–3 with

Anscheidt, Katayama and Graham. The Belgian marked the end of the 50 cc World Championship rounds in Europe. Suzuki decided to virtually withdraw the 125s after the Finnish GP and the machines, spares, and most of the personnel, were flown back to Japan to prepare for the Fisco round.

Ulster was a continuation of Graham's battle with the V4 Yamahas.

GRAHAM   'In practice, I hadn't been able to gear it correctly because of clutch slip. In the race I was able to pass Bill and Phil within the first two laps, but the machine soon lost its edge.'

Stuart stopped twice to change plugs and *still* finished 3rd, two minutes behind Read and Ivy who crossed the line wheel to wheel, the verdict being given to Ivy.

Graham turned down the Italian GP — where Anscheidt was 2nd — because of poor start money and before he entered the Canadian GP at Mosport, he was called to Japan for testing.

The 125 V4 Suzuki, the RS67, proved beyond doubt that at last, Suzuki had a Yamaha-beater. During practice for the final round of the 125 cc World Championship at Fisco in Japan, Katayama, Graham, Morishita and Itoh tried out the new model but Katayama fell, breaking his collarbone. In the race itself, Graham had to scratch to catch up with Ivy and as Stuart's diary states; '2nd all the way in the 125 race to Little Bill. Bike went well. Nearly crashed on last lap (exhaust loose).'

In actual fact, Graham made a poor start and Ivy built up a good lead. Graham was within three seconds of Ivy when the exhaust grounded on the penultimate lap. This cost him half a minute but he retained 2nd place.

GRAHAM   'The 125-4 was great. If I'd been 110 per cent fit at the time — I was suffering from 'flu — and had had a bit more sorting-out time, I think we could've had Little Bill away. Because at last, we had a bike that was as good as the Yamaha.'

The 50 cc race was dominated by Suzukis, only a lone Derbi breaking up the first six places. Graham's diary: 'Finished close second to Itoh under orders. Could have won.' Anscheidt finished 4th, having already retained the 50 cc World Championship.

Stuart Graham finished 3rd in the World Championships for both the 50 and 125 cc classes and Katayama was 2nd in the 50 cc, and 4th in the 125 cc World Championship.

After the Japanese GP Stuart Graham and Anscheidt visited the Suzuki factory to discuss 1968 contracts.

GRAHAM   'Everything was agreed; new 125-4s and 50-3s for Georg and myself, and then we came home. We didn't sign our contracts then.'

Meanwhile, rumoured changes in the FIM rules would outlaw both the twin and the new three cylinder 50 cc model. It was obvious to Suzuki that to continue 50 cc racing would be foolish.

Then, early in 1968, Honda announced plans to withdraw from grand prix competition. It shocked a world familiar with the sight and sound of the silver and red multis and it drove Suzuki to decide about its own racing future.

GRAHAM   'Ralph Bryans had been testing the new Hondas in Japan, and on 13 February, he broke his journey to call at my home. His first words were, "Have you signed your Suzuki contract yet? If you haven't I'd sign it quick and get it off because Honda have quit and I think Suzuki are going to do the same!" It was a bombshell. Panic stations! I rushed upstairs, signed my contract and rushed off to the post. Then I sent a telegram to Suzuki accepting their terms. It wasn't too late, Suzuki agreed to pay about three quarters of my fee and to send me a 125 cc twin with a spare engine and parts so that I could race in International races. I was told that I couldn't enter the World Championship rounds.'

Accordingly, Stuart's machine arrived on 14 March, and it turned out to be his 1967 machine. Two days later, he left England for his first race in Italy.
    Anscheidt struck a similar deal.

Business as usual; Read, Ivy (Yamaha RA31s), Katayama and Graham (Suzuki RT67s) prepare to renew the battle at the 1967 125 cc East German GP *Graham*

ANSCHEIDT 'Even though I hadn't signed a contract, I asked Suzuki if they would supply me with some machines for the 1968 season. They agreed to this and also to give me some money and a Commer van. They said that I could try for the World Championship again on the 50 cc but not on the 125 cc. Maybe this was because the 125 cc was not quick enough.'

And so Suzuki withdrew from the World Championships. The path to success had not been easy but during their eight years in Europe, they had won 53 motorcycle grand prix races, 27 in the 50 cc class, the remainder in the 125 cc category. They had gained seven individual World Championships; five in the 50 cc and two in the 125 cc class. Suzuki accumulated six World Manufacturer's Championships, four in the 50 cc class and two for the 125 category. They had raced 21 different models in the hands of 20 contracted riders.

Without doubt, their most successful rider was the brilliant and consistent Hugh Anderson. His determination matched theirs and his riding courage made their efforts worthwhile. During his six year tour of duty, Anderson had won 25 GPs, was 2nd 12 times and 3rd on ten occasions, he also set 21 GP lap records on 15 different GP circuits. Without his two 50 cc and two 125 cc World Championships Suzuki's results would have been mediocre.

But this was not the last the world would see of Suzuki World Championships; Anscheidt retained the 1968 50 cc title with ease, and Dieter Braun won the 1970 125 cc World Championship on his ex-Anscheidt machine. Suzuki would not forget their experiences during these years of competition and in the future, would return with a vengeance.

Above Graham's perseverance won through at Imatra in 1967; aboard his RT67, he vanquished the Yamaha V4s and claimed victory *Graham*

Left On the eve of the 1967 Czechoslovakian GP, Seichi Suzuki the rider works on Graham's RT67 watched by manager Akira Yoshimoto *Anscheidt*

6 Power struggle: grand prix weaponry (1960 to 1967)

Suzuki's first serious road-racer—the RT60—was directly descended from the 1959 Colleda RB; but whilst the new twin cylinder engine—piston-ported—spun to 11,000 rpm, the RB's longer stroke limited rpm to 9500. The chassis were almost identical, sharing suspension systems and general concepts. To fool the press, Suzuki disguised the crude expansion chambers by clothing them in 'silencers'. Suzuki optimistically claimed 30 bhp for the 13 bhp engine, and to protect the RT60's delicate crankshaft bearings, a rich 8:1 fuel-oil ratio was used! A new air-cooled clutch transmitted the power via Suzuki's first six-speed gearbox. The RT60 was also Suzuki's lightest-ever 125 cc machine; 180 lb (82 Kg).

In 1960, Suzuki noted the successful MZs and their rotary valves. After much testing, Suzuki incorporated similar valves in their RT61 which retained the same basic dimensions as the RT60. The RT61 cylinders were more inclined, with Mikuni M22 carburettors—sporting huge bell-mouths—delivering the mixture. Rotary valves forced the magneto to be repositioned atop the six-speed gearbox. A twin leading shoe front brake was introduced on the RT61, and a fibreglass fairing superseded the RT60's hand-beaten aluminium type.

The engine produced a disappointing 15 bhp at 10,000 rpm with a 1000 rpm power band; to compete with the 23 bhp Honda 2RC143s, RT61 riders had to over-rev the engine, resulting in total unreliability. Other problems appeared during the heat of the races.

> ISHIKAWA 'We had many problems with ignition because the drive-line used three spur gears, and to reduce backlash, the meshing was very tight. The teeth were overstressed together with the magneto bearings and we suffered many failures of these components. Piston seizures were also experienced when the ignition timing varied.'

Similar problems were encountered with Suzuki's first 250 cc machine, the RV61. With a power band of only 500 rpm, its six gears were insufficient and riders found they were below the power band despite having changed gear at the maximum allowable rpm. Whilst Honda's dominating RC162s developed 45 bhp, the RV61s produced only 28 bhp and were prone to piston seizures, handling problems and slipping clutches. The 1961 250 cc Suzuki was a total failure.

Suzuki, however, were determined; they had an unlimited racing budget and with the defection of Degner came the missing link—two-stroke expertise. Degner's formula for success—the humble single cylinder—completely reversed previous design philosophies. During a four month stay in Japan, Degner was given a free hand and produced a virtual replica of MZ's RE125

racer, the Suzuki RT62. Knowing the advantages of a rear exhaust—enhanced power because of the easier flow of exhaust gases and resultant cooler-running pistons—he made such a version of the RT62 for himself—others had to use front exhaust types.

DEGNER 'It is normally very easy to do; you reverse the sand core forming the crankcase-inside so that the transfer ports align, and then simply reverse the cylinder.'

But Suzuki's engineers had previously been sceptical about rear exhausts.

ISHIKAWA 'Everybody thought that the exhaust was the hottest spot so it had to face toward the wind—at the front. So when we reversed it we expected there to be not enough cooling and we soon expected there would be piston scuffing or seizure. But Degner tried his own way and we observed that the cooling of the rear exhaust is sufficient for a race. Also we had run many tests.'

The Suzuki RT62 that Degner designed was a mirror-image of the MZ RE125; where MZ had components on the left, Degner positioned them on the right, but this had little effect on power output and the RT62 finally produced 23 bhp, a 3 bhp improvement over the first model. The rear exhaust model had a revised magneto mounting positioned behind the disc valve housing; on the front exhaust model, it was gear-driven and mounted above the gearbox.

DEGNER 'It took only three months from being on the drawing board to testing on the bed and on the track. Unbelievable!'

For the first time, Suzuki used aluminium cylinders with cast-iron sleeves, and the piston material became a high silicon aluminium alloy which reduced its expansion rate and helped prevent seizure. Earlier exhaust port bridges had been

Above A prototype RT61 125 cc twin. Note the huge carburettor bell-mouth and the unusual cylinder finning designed to reduce weight *Archives*

Above left MZ technology (via Ernst Degner) was instrumental in Suzuki's racing fortunes. By 1964, whilst Suzuki's 250 became a complex square four, MZ's relatively simple 48 bhp RE250 proved more successful *Shepherd*

Above In spite of its compact design, the 250 cc RV61 was totally unreliable. Magneto drive gears and crankshaft bearings became both its, and the RT61s, achilles heel *Archives*

Above right Although the rear engine mounts of the RM62 appear over-engineered, this diminutive racer weighed just 132 lb (60 Kg), the legal FIM-imposed limit *MCW*

weak, but now it was found that the additional cylinder bridge withstood the distortion which previously forced the bridge into the cylinder to seize on the piston. Degner also drilled a small hole in the piston skirt to align with the bridge so that cooling oil could lubricate the heat-stressed bridge.

It was this technology that elevated Suzuki to a position of leadership in the forthcoming grand prix battles. Ironically, it was not the RT62 that drew Suzuki's first GP blood, but the 50 cc single, a miniature replica of the RT62, the design of which had commenced before Degner's defection. Although too busy designing the 125s to become involved with the RM62, Degner's influence can still be seen. Like the 125, the RM62 cylinder incorporated a boost port.

One of the problems of high-speed two strokes had been inadequate cylinder scavanging; if some unburnt gases remain in the cylinder, the new mixture is contaminated, severely reducing power. The boost port had been developed at MZ and the Hatfield base of EMC, where Joe Ehrlich had determined that a small groove in the cylinder wall opposite the exhaust port, and a corresponding window cut into the piston skirt, allowed some mixture to pass through into the port. As the piston approached bottom-dead-centre the puff of new mixture cleared any residual exhaust gases. Furthermore, cold gas passing through the piston skirt improved its cooling. The boost-ported RM62 initially developed 8 bhp at 10,500 rpm, but a change in carburettor size—20 to 22 mm bore—increased power to 10 bhp at 12,000 rpm, and maximum speed to 90 mph (145 Km/h) by season-end.

Suzuki's new 250, the RV62, was virtually a pair of the RT62 cylinders mounted on a common crankcase. This 130 mph air-cooled front exhaust twin produced 42 bhp at 10,500 rpm, but suffered from gearbox and piston seizures, *and* doubtful handling. After the Ulster GP, the RV62s were returned to Japan.

Apart from Degner, the riders recruited by Suzuki had little or no two stroke experience. Setting up the carburation was crucial.

DEGNER 'Everybody had to learn how to set up the carburettors taking into account the weather conditions *and* the final drive gearing. For example, if you drive on a circuit like Monza where the lowest speed is about 80 mph, and then on a circuit with many corners like Barcelona, then you have to change the secondary gear. This should also include the carburettor setting; you rev much quicker from say 10 to 12,000 rpm than when you have gearing set for say 110 mph. I think Hugh Anderson picked it up from me very quickly, this relationship between gearing and carburation, and also the mechanics because they have watched me for a long time and they know exactly what to do.'

ANDERSON 'Ernst did pass on information to me—no more than he really had to—but quite sufficient to allow me to get the basic idea of how these engines operated and what they would respond to. I *learned* from Ernst; he had an uncanny ability to fine-tune his machine to gain speed and reliability; perhaps this is where the idea of me having faster machines than anyone else came from.

'I used to sit in the garage with Ernst for two hours just to decide on what sprockets to use on *one* machine, so that I could get my gearing to suit 90 per cent of the corners, and I'd just have to do my best on the remaining corners. This was the art of getting the best from these machines; hours in the workshop.'

Two stroke technology and Europe were synonymous and it was in Europe that Suzuki searched for reliability. First regarding piston design, where the German Mahle was predominant.

DEGNER 'We asked Mahle to send over to Japan some pistons, and when they arrived, the piston makers in Japan sent over to Suzuki some engineers. I told them the whole story; how Mahle used a forging method and not a casting and other details. Within a few days, they had sent us the first few pistons and when we tried them, they were a lot better than the Mahle pistons. The problem with the original Japanese pistons was that we had to give them a big clearance because if the piston gets warm, it grows like a cake, and we have a lot of seizures. With the new Japanese pistons, we could have less tolerance than with the Mahle without seizing, therefore more power.'

Big-end bearings too were troublesome, and again Europe provided the solution.

DEGNER 'A friend of mine who worked for INA in Germany sent me some INA bearings to Japan. Those bearings were taken over to INA in Japan and then we got new cages for the needle rollers. Before this, the cage would break and then the needles would become square.'

Suzuki was rapidly gaining useful experience with expansion chambers but progress was too slow. Europe supplied the ground-rules.

DEGNER 'We had to make experiments with lengths and then with a little more volume in the middle and a smaller volume at the end. In that way we got a number of different power curves and we saw which way we had to go. And so we learnt the effect of different shapes on the power curves.

Following his defection, Degner created the rear-exhaust RT62, re-siting the magneto to accommodate the expansion chamber, but the then-unused magneto drive-gear case was retained, (see p 68) *MCW*

Aachen Technical High School in Germany made a formula for a low-speed engine which was available in a technical book. Nobody from Japan made contact with them; I brought a lot of those formulae in my brain with me to Japan. If the engine runs at 2 or 2500 rpm it can be worked out exactly, but if the engine runs at 12,000 rpm we have to find a better volume to make the power band as wide as possible. You could take the formulae as a basis to find the optimum. This is not only the method at Suzuki, but also in the MZ company we did the same.'

For such concentrated development work, Mike Ishikawa installed four Meidensha dynamometers in the test house where a large cooling fan on rails could be aligned with whichever dyno was in use. These dynos were in constant use as engines were developed and new exhaust systems evaluated. Yoshihiko Murai carried out this work whenever he wasn't fettling Anderson's machines in Europe. During 1962 he tested 112 designs for the RT62 before selecting the optimum type. How many were made altogether?

ISHIKAWA 'Uncountable. For the dynamometer we made only a simple shape; a cone and cylinder. Because of this, most of the mechanics were capable of welding them, so quite arbitarily, they would cut and weld, cut and weld. I think maybe over a thousand types were tested between 1961 and 1967.'

Most of the developments concerned improvements to disc valves or expansion chambers and each new design was numbered for later reference.

During the 1962 racing season, Degner made many suggestions to Suzuki's engineers who checked out the theories on the dynamometer, but towards

season-end a 125 twin cylinder front exhaust engine, the RT63X, became the top priority. It was raced only twice; at Suzuka and Daytona.

Searching for power and reliability, Suzuki's engineers scoured the racing world looking for that decisive racing edge.

SCHNEIDER 'When we asked, "What are Yamaha doing or what's Honda doing on this part?" Shimizu would open his drawer and already had the part there; he had somebody in all these factories which made it easy for him to get all the parts. As far as I remember, he even had some needle bearings from Kreidler and a Yamaha con-rod in his desk; he was very well informed.'

The 1963 machines comprised an uprated rear exhaust 50 cc—the RM63—which produced 11 bhp at 13,000 rpm, requiring nine speeds instead of eight. Likewise, the RT63 engine had rear exhausts and was provided with a pump that forced oil directly to the crankshaft bearings, improving crankshaft life and boosting power. An oil pump too was added to the RM63 during the season. But in spite of these extra features, and the special attention paid to weight, the RM63s were below the 60 Kg FIM-imposed limit, and strips of lead were lashed to the lower frame tubes to make them 'legal!'

The RT63 produced 26 bhp at 12,000 rpm—2 bhp more than the RT63X—and weighed 207 lb. The air-cooled twin cylinder engine housed an eight-speed transmission of non 'cross-over' type; the clutch and final drive were both on the left hand side, with the gear-driven Kokusan-Denki magneto nestling in the

Above left Suzuki's engine test department of the sixties. An RT63 engine is on the dynamometer. Murai developed 112 expansion chambers—some can be seen hanging on the walls—in order to gain just 2 bhp *Perris*

Above Degner works on his RM63 at the 1963 IoM TT. Kappei Itoh assists while Ichino can be seen behind *Willoughby*

Right At the 1962 Japanese GP, Anderson rode the RT63X front-exhaust 125 cc twin *Archives*

Far right The 50 cc RM63 was characterized by its rear exhaust (see p 69). Further weight reduction forced Suzuki to *add* lead ballast to the RN63 in order to meet the FIM limits *MCW*

recess behind the cylinder on the right. The 24 mm Mikuni M-type carburettors were mounted slightly up-draught in order to direct the mixture over the flywheels. As on the RT62, the front brake was a double-sided single leading-shoe design.

Despite improvements in reliability, major parts were frequently replaced as part of a preventative maintenance strategy.

ANDERSON 'Bikes are so much more reliable today: if we could get past 80 miles then we thought the crank was good for 200 miles. Today, racers think nothing of getting 1000 miles out of a racing crankshaft.'

The 250 cc class was not forgotten and the race-shop was engaged in the design of a new 250-4, the RZ63. Basically a doubled-up version of the RT63, sharing its bore and stroke dimensions, it was a square-four concept, and was Suzuki's first water-cooled engine. To allow unrestricted water flow around the hotter rear cylinders they were cast in longitudinal pairs. Thus water was fed via long hoses to the rear cylinders and allowed to percolate forward and upward before entering the radiator via short hoses. Each cylinder had three transfer ports, and whilst the rear pair had rear-facing exhausts, the front pair faced forward. With an idler gear between the two crankshafts, they both ran in the same direction. The idler-shaft compromised the total machine; the power unit was over-weight and excessively long, requiring a wheelbase approaching 56 inches—even longer than the later 500s! Cooling water circulation was left to thermo syphon—an oversight that was never corrected. Ignition was by gear-driven Kokusan-Denki magneto mounted behind the rear left-hand crankshaft, whilst carburation was handled by 24 mm bore Mikunis mounted slightly up-draught on the disc valve

covers. The clutch was positioned on the right-hand side and the power was transmitted via a six-speed cross-over gearbox. Lubrication was by pre-mix—an oil-pump was added later.

In preparation for the 1963 Japanese GP, Perris, Schneider, Degner and Anderson were invited out to Hamamatsu.

SCHNEIDER 'During the 250 testing I asked Frank Perris to ride behind me to see if he could see any reason why it didn't handle. It seized on the second lap and he came off too.'

PERRIS 'Bertie just lost the lot in front of me and I clobbered him and he broke his collarbone. We were lying in the side of the field at Suzuka, Bertie was unconcious and I didn't know what was happening. I woke up and tried to help Bertie by waving to other Suzuki riders who were batting round the track. They wouldn't stop. The only one to stop was Hughie.'

With Schneider side-lined, Perris—an ex-AJS chassis designer—continued 250 testing alone.

PERRIS 'The RZ63 had an incredibly weak frame with thin frame tubes. The bloody things were absolutely lethal. I said to Mr Okano, "Please give me a drawing board, I'll design a new frame. We're here for two months." He said to me, "Fak-San, *we* don't design a bike, a computer designs it!" and I said, "OK, then you'd better get a bloody computer to ride it!"'

The message got through; within two weeks, the RZ63 had an improved chassis, with larger diameter tubes. Although the overweight RZ63 suffered from other problems, the handling situation—aggravated by the 1400 mm wheelbase—was serious.

ISHIKAWA 'Due to the square-four construction, the wheelbase was long and the steering was consequently affected adversley. At that time, power was not a great problem, but the riders didn't like the way the machine

Above left Suzuki's RT63 took Anderson to six successive 125 cc GP victories in 1963. The carburettors were up-draught to guide the mixture over the flywheels *MCN*

Below Team joker Bertie Schneider in the race shop office in 1963 following a spill

whilst testing the new RZ63. The chart shows the 1963 results *Perris*

Above The functional cockpit of the RT63. The choke lever and kill-button can be seen on the left handlebar. The central knob is the steering damper *MCW*

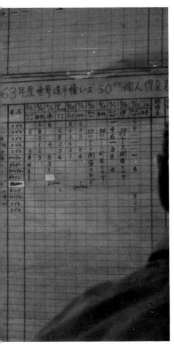

steered around the corners and had to take corners at a much slower speed than their rivals.'

The engine overheated during testing and a radiator header-tank was temporarily installed. This made the machine front heavy and attempts were made to overcome this before its debut.

DEGNER 'Unsuccessfully, we tried to reduce the weight, but we couldn't do it because the engine was heavy—water cooling—and the frame had to be made of thicker tubing. Altogether, it was very difficult.'

Other problems showed up during the season.

SCHNEIDER 'The 250 was hard to start because it was a heavy bike and it did not fire so easily. The main problems were the handling, the gearbox and then the seizing in the race, and I think that was enough, especially from the rider's point of view. The long wheelbase was not too bad on fast corners but on slow ones it was not very good.'

PERRIS 'It had too long a chassis and had slow steering. It was also terribly front heavy. That's how I bust my leg at Daytona in 1964. You'd crank it over and the front would keep going away from you all the time. You'd take your life in your hands if you took a handful. I'd never ever take my four fingers off that clutch!'

The RZ63 had a power-surfeit; 52 bhp at 12,500 rpm, topping Honda by some 4 bhp. The riders prepared their own engines in Japan, and Schneider apparently came across a 'rogue' engine during 1964 when power had increased to about 57 bhp.

SCHNEIDER 'I was working on my 250 four, trying to make it better; stripping it down, building it up, testing it on the dynamometer, and the other engines always had about 57 bhp but mine had only 54 bhp. So again, I stripped it down to pieces, put it together again. They said that I must work more carefully and that was why this engine was not as good as the others. Then I saw that one of the engineers was standing with his foot on the dynamometer and that was why I was getting different results!'

PERRIS 'When the 250s came off the brake, I used to get the best one, but actually, when you got on the thing, I can never remember one of the bikes being any better than another. It was then up to you to get the thing carburated right so it would zip out of the corner better than the others. If it didn't, it was your fault for being lazy and not doing anything about.'

The best 250-four that ever came off the brake gave 58 bhp at the rear wheel, sufficient to blow off larger machines on the straight, but an embarrassment in such a poor chassis package.

To save time and expense of testing at Suzuka, the Yonezu test course was used, but its primitive facilities were less than adequate for the powerful 250 cc models.

ANDERSON 'I rode the 250 there when we were having gear selector problems—the gears were seizing on the forks—and it was raining this day and very cold. There was little control over the people working in the gardens and they'd be walking across the track which was slippery and we were testing gearboxes and doing a good 150 mph! I did as few trips as possible and complained that I was bitterly cold, and opted out of the system.'

To improve the riders' morale, Suzuki showed them the plans for Ryuyo Test Course, due for completion in 1964. Nobody liked testing at Honda-owned Suzuka because of the travelling and the risks that Honda engineers were timing the Suzukis.

SCHNEIDER 'Suzuka was five or six hours drive and Suzuki's drivers were very slow. Instead of looking ahead 100 metres they would be looking just 10 metres!'

PERRIS 'The road that went there was jam-packed with lorries the whole way and so we'd go down there for two or three days.'

Suzuki engineers took detailed notes after testing, and then the riders would relax, either at the factory watching development activities or at Suzuki's hostel overlooking Lake Hamana. For acceleration testing, a small area outside the race shop was provided where it was possible to optimise low-end carburation and to perfect starting techniques.

Two other machines made their debut at the 1963 Japanese GP; the RT64 — little changed from the RT63 — now produced 30 bhp at 13,000 rpm. A shorter stroke for the RM64 allowed increased rpm whilst improved porting produced 12.5 bhp at 14,000 rpm, but in most respects it was similar to its predeccessor.

1964 was perhaps the busiest year yet for Suzuki's racing department. By year-end they had produced new water-cooled twin cylinder 50 and 125 cc models, and already redesigned the RZ model by shortening the power unit. The new 50 cc 'RK' series incorporated all Suzuki's technology. Water-cooling reduced the cylinder temperature-gradients and appeared to be the final step towards completely reliable, seizure-free two strokes. However, water circulation was by thermo-syphon which later proved inadequate. The RK65 had a twelve-speed gearbox in deference to the small power band, the tiny 32.5 mm pistons hammering out 14.5 bhp at a maximum rpm of 16,500! Off-setting the additional weight of water-cooling, Suzuki used duralumin for frame construction — which was of 'open' design — titanium for nuts, bolts and axles, and magnesium for the main castings; the RK65 weighed in at just over the 60 Kg FIM limit! Engine design was similar to that of the RT63 and RT64 models, with twin rotary disc valves, but the clutch was mounted on the right and the gearbox was of the 'cross-over' design with the drive sprocket on the left. The Kokusan-Denki magneto was driven from the left-hand end of the crankshaft and was mounted behind and out-board of the left-hand cylinder.

The new RT65 was similar to the RT64, sharing the same basic dimensions and layout and retaining the non cross-over gearbox but with nine speeds — an additional gear. This model, too, used exotic materials although still using a steel frame. Despite water-cooling, the extra gear, steel frame and twin leading-shoe front brake, the RT65 was lighter than the RT64. With this machine Suzuki were determined to recapture the 125 cc World Championship from Honda and with the RK65, retain the 50 cc title for the fourth successive year.

The RZ65 250 cc square-four had a lubrication pump for the crankshaft

Above right Suzuki's early riders rarely suffered handling problems — apart from 250-4s — and the 125 cc frame changed little in design. This RT64 employs steel tubing *Grüber*

Above far right A mechanic checks the ignition timing of the water-cooled 125 cc twin, the RT65 (note the dial gauge in the plug hole). A hydraulic steering damper — just visible behind the forks — was specified *MCW*

Lower right A familiar sight to Suzuki's 250 cc riders! A dismembered RZ65 awaits new pistons following seizure. The massive turbo-cooled rear brake featured twin leading-shoes to retard the overweight machine *MCW*

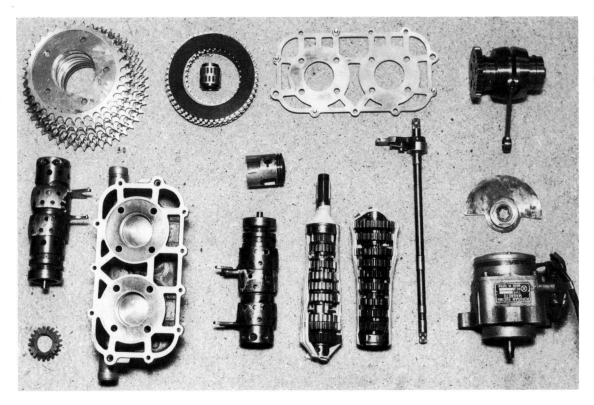

bearings, but the top-end was still lubricated by a lean pre-mix. The redesigned cylinders had integral water-manifolds along each bank to improve water circulation and the engine was shortened by eliminating the idler-shaft between the crankshafts. A newly developed Kokusan ignition system was incorporated and an eight-speed gear cluster helped the rider keep the motor within the power band. Braking had already been improved by using twin leading-shoes on the RZ64, and now the chassis was also strengthened by material and design changes. It was a futile effort to tame the beast, for Suzuki withdrew the RZ65s mid-season, and apart from Katayama's lone ride at the 1965 Japanese GP, they were never again seen by the racing public. . . .

For 1966, minor changes improved both maximum rpm and peak power on the RT66 and the RK66, which now had 14 gears. But whilst Suzuki regained the 50 cc World Championship, the RT66 was outclassed.

Suzuki made many improvements with chassis components and Anderson was particularly active, often testing at circuits such as Zandvoort, which was close to Suzuki's Badhoevedorp HQ.

ANDERSON 'The front forks used to be too hard and you had to hit a brick to get them to move. That sort of energy created at the front of the machine would be transferred to the rear. Later on, I used to relieve the seals and get the fork action softer that way. The rear suspension units were always under a bit of doubt, but they were much better than they felt because I tried to improve on them and didn't have a whole lot of joy; I did a lot of experimenting, but at that time, the springs were quite short and the spring rate suffered. I tried Girlings at the 1964 TT and on the

The RT66 featured two *separate* crankshafts geared together and a 9-speed gearbox with lightened selector drums. Note the gear-shift shaft allowing left or right side gear lever mounting *MCW*

50 cc I won and it went around there perfectly; it sat on the road beautifully and was spot-on. I continued to experiment with Girlings until the end of 1964 at the Japanese GP where I found they didn't have enough damping on the 125 and the rear was letting go in a hell of a big way.'

Like the RK66, the RT66 had an 'open' duralumin frame with a stressed power unit, first used for the 1965 Japanese 125 cc GP. Anderson won.

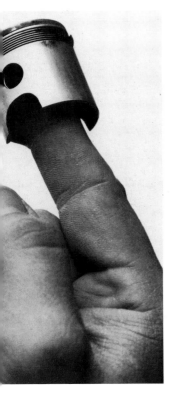

The 32.5 mm diameter single ring piston of the RK67 Suzuki's smallest was just 28 mm! *Anscheidt*

ANDERSON 'There was quite a difference in characteristic between the aluminium and the steel frames; on the fast corners the aluminium frame was quite good, but on the slower ones it was too rigid. The steel frame was sometimes a little bit too flexible at high speed, like going down through Barregarrow in the Isle of Man—or down Bray Hill, whereas the aluminium frame got rid of that. It was rather a hard, rigid type of frame and the feeling was quite different. You felt more bumps, especially on slower corners. On fast circuits, it was good.'

Riders were given a choice of mechanical or electronic tachometers, but most riders opted for a mechanical type. Suzuki were constantly searching for stable ignition timing, and in 1965, Kokusan-Denki perfected their first condenser-discharge ignition (CDI) system for the RK65. CDI was an immediate success and was later used on the 125 cc machines. Because the new system looked outwardly similar to the old types, the riders never realised that their machines were running on a point-less ignition system.

With ignition problems solved, carburation became top priority motivating Mikuni to produce an integral-float instrument, first used late in 1967. Previous Mikunis were notoriously difficult to tune.

ANDERSON 'Whatever was right in the morning, was wrong in the afternoon and there became quite a mystique about it. I used to wait until an hour before the race before deciding what jets to use. I used to allow for a lean period that would occur after about 15 or 20 miles by running mine a bit richer, but you had to know when it was happening, and what was happening.'

DEGNER 'I normally had a few marks on the choke lever and the clamp. If you opened it just one mark that makes such a lot of difference to the power, but only for a short time, maybe 20 or 30 seconds maximum. You make carburettor settings while the mixture lever is in the middle position, so if you feel it is too lean, you close it a bit and then you richen the engine. Later on, we had such a lot of experiments, that we had a standard carburettor setting. All the others—needle jet, jet needle was fixed. Only the main jet then needed changing to suit weather conditions.'

Anderson never trusted his crankshafts to withstand maximum rpm and kept his motors about 200 rpm short. By fine carburation adjustment, he obtained almost the same power output but with more reliability.

Hugh Anderson raced his 125 in New Zealand in the winter of 1965–66 and there, a braking problem already experienced at Brno and Monza, became more apparent. When Anderson visited the factory before the 1966 season, he insisted on a twin leading-shoe front brake for his machine. Katayama used one too.

The small Suzukis required a riding technique which the riders developed in unison with the narrowing power band. Were they difficult to ride?

ANDERSON 'You had to be pretty considerate of the motors and it was very hard to ride in a group because you couldn't hear your engine so well. Otherwise you'd tend to oil plugs or seize up. The power band was extremely narrow and up the Mountain Mile in the TT, you'd be slipping the clutch constantly and when you change gear, you don't shut the bike off, you just keep it wound on, and because you're slipping the clutch and pushing the gear pedal you've virtually got automatic drive.

'You had to be really conversant with the motor in order to get the best out of them and after practice, I used to write everything down: I'd modify the notes after each practice session until I'd built up quite a lot of notes. Before the race, I'd read these things and then I'd remember just how many gears to come down for each corner. When you're riding in two classes, one bike you'd come down eight gears, and another bike it'd be six gears for the same corner, and you had to know—or I wanted to know— how many gears to come down. Not what gear you were in. In this way, when I was on the start-line, I knew exactly what I needed to do and eliminated all start-line nerves. They were definitely difficult to ride, there's no doubt about that.'

The 1967 machines closely resembled their 1966 counterparts. Skew gear-driven water-pumps were added to their cooling systems which allowed yet higher power and engine speeds—17.5 bhp at 17,300 rpm on the RK67 and 35 bhp at 14,000 rpm on the RT67. Ten gears were specified for the 125 to deal with the narrowing power band. Despite that, the engine weighed only 70 lb.

During 1967 Suzuki were secretly developing a new 125 cc machine to combat

Above Built like a watch! The 14-speed transmission of the RK67 exposed. The 'accessory' drives were from the gearbox and primary shafts and the extra shaft for the output sprocket facilitated a more central chain-line. The gearbox is less than 8 in. (203 mm) wide *Anscheidt*

Above left The RK67 developed 17.5 bhp at 17,300 rpm, yet despite its complexity, weighed just 128 lb (58 kg). Note the water and oil pumps mounted behind the clutch. The carburettor settings have been noted on the exhaust heatshield *MCN*

Right The Makoto Hase-designed V4 125 cc Suzuki. The engine used twin Kokusan-Denki magnetos and was the first to feature Mikuni's new integral-float carburettors, the 'VM' series. The RS68 model illustrated has a rectangular aluminium swing-arm *Crosby*

the Yamaha V4 threat, and new personnel were drafted into the research section where two separate design teams worked on totally independent concepts; a square-four, and a V4 designed by Kiyoshi Kushiya.

ISHIKAWA 'Both project teams were competing with each other, and by chance, the V4 project became the leader.'

The two teams amalgamated, finalising the design of the RS67. Just four months after work had commenced, the RS67s had been tested at Ryuyo by Mitsuo Itoh. Now it was time to invite the grand prix riders over to try their hand.

GRAHAM 'I remember walking into the race-shop and seeing about four V4s lined up all ready to go. I just couldn't believe it. They'd started after the TT in June and here they were. They stuck three of them on the back of a pick-up truck and drove down to Ryuyo. I got on one and straight away, I thought, "This is it!" Just what I wanted, because it fitted me better than the little lightweight things.'

The three machines were all set up quite differently, but Graham immediately clipped a second off his previous best lap time at Ryuyo.

GRAHAM 'The only trouble we had was that it was low on ground clearance and I kept grounding the bottom of the lower expansion chambers.'

The RS67 resembled the Yamaha RA31; its cylinders, set at 90 degrees, had the lower bank angled down by 5 degrees and each cylinder had independent cylinder and head castings, and crankshafts which were geared to an idler gear. The engine was water-cooled and incorporated a water-pump. The lubrication system was new, with two trochoid-type pumps and one plunger-type that fed each cylinder via separate pipes. The twelve-speed transmission lubrication operated on a dry-sump principle with oil pumped around the gearbox by a trochoid pump, reducing losses due to oil swirl and heat generation. The V4 produced a tremendous 42 bhp at 16,500 rpm with 1500 rpm power band. The

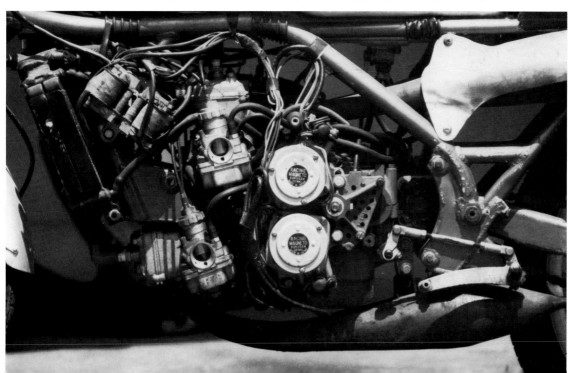

lightweight unit, using titanium and elektron for many parts, was housed in a duralumin chassis. The front down-tubes terminated between the cylinders where a substantial engine mounting was provided; the engine was a stressed member of the chassis. The machine weighed 209 lb, only 13 lb more than the twin cylinder model it superseded!

Initial testing of the RS67 lasted one week, and Stuart Graham's diary tells all:

'October 9 (Monday)—Factory. Went testing all day. Tried new 4 cylinder machines. Seized one. Light bike!

October 11 (Wednesday)—Went to Fisco. Took all day to get there, (typical Japanese)! Caught the 'flu. Machine not bad. Testing all day.

October 12 (Thursday)—More practice. Used 50 and 125s. Still same on 125; 1m 42.5 secs. 50 down to 1m 57.5 secs. in five laps. Then broke.

October 13 (Friday)—Wedding Anniversary. Official practice. 125 down to 1m 41.5 secs. Down to 1m 55 secs on 50. Very warm. Fever coming on.

October 14 (Saturday)—More practice. Pouring with rain all day. 50s in morning, 125s in afternoon. Quick practice with 'flu!'

On 15 October the RS67 made its first public appearance. It represented Suzuki's last titanic effort in the sixties. They'd started with a 13 bhp twin and ended with a 42 bhp four!

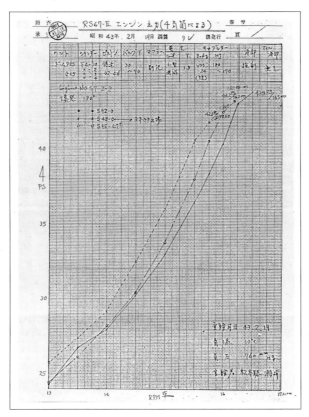

Suzuki were still developing the RS67 in February 1968 when these power curves were taken by Shunkichi Matsumoto (43.8 bhp at 16,500 rpm). The three curves represent different exhausts, proving that mid-range torque sacrifices top-end power *Archives*

7   Second front:
let battle commence (1966 to 1971)

In 1965, Haruo Koshino went to America with an RK65 and a couple of RT65s which he raced in small west coast events. Now the American public could see the blue and silver rockets in action.

Koshino's activities were part of Suzuki's plan to bolster their US sales, using a race-version of the recently announced 'Super 6' — or X6 in the USA — as a spring-board towards that objective. To race these 250 twins, US Suzuki hired three top-line US riders, Dick Mann, Dick Hammer and UK ex-patriot Ron Grant, with a unique contract allowing them to ride other larger capacity marques alongside the X6s in top-money events. Mann riding BSA and Hammer Triumph. Suzuki paid them only travel and accommodation costs, but the riders retained their prize money which produced racing fast and furious. US pro-racing wasn't for the faint-hearted, breeding tough gritty characters; men who could fall at high speed and still have the guts to re-mount and finish. The AMA Grand National Championships favoured dirt-track racing so with only three road-racing events scheduled for 1966, an exclusive pavement rider stood no chance. The best riders were good all-rounders; like Mann and Hammer. US Suzuki service manager Fred Moxley, became Team manager, with Bob Ellison and Chris Young as tuners. During the winter they built a squad of X6 racers which made their debut at Daytona in March. Hammer qualified, but in the heats his engine blew.

Koshino demonstrating his RT65 at Riverside Raceway, California *Cycle World*

HAMMER   'Bob and Chris took it completely apart and put it back together again. In the race I came from dead last off the grid, caught Gary Nixon on the Yamaha and passed him. Then my rear brake lever broke two laps from the end and I had to slow. Nixon won and I finished 2nd.'

In May, at a non-Championship Carlsbad event, Mann's front wheel locked and he broke a collar bone, whilst Hammer led until his engine expired. In practice, Koshino made his X6 debut but he also fell, returning to Japan with a broken wrist.

Now it became clear that the biggest problem was handling.

HAMMER   'We did a lot of work on them; beefing up the swing arms by welding $\frac{1}{4}$ inch steel stiffeners down each arm and under the pivot. When you were going fast in a turn they used to flex too much. Strengthening the headstocks with gussets and so forth improved them; they were just too weak for road racing.'

Initially, a twin disc front brake was fitted but was soon replaced.

HAMMER   'Fred Moxley went to a Fontana double leading-shoe racing
unit and on the back fitted special metallic linings. The brakes were great.'

At a later Carlsbad AMA National Race, Cal Rayborn on the 250 Harley cleared
off with Hammer, Mann and Grant in pursuit. After Hammer fell, Rayborn
lapped the entire field including 2nd and 3rd finishers, Mann and Grant. In a
second 250 cc race, Grant and Mann diced for the lead—there were no Team
orders—but Grant fell, wiping off a footrest and brake pedal. He re-mounted
and finished 3rd behind Mann with Rayborn again victorious. Hammer, too, fell
on lap 9 but still finished 8th.

Because of disappointing results the 1967 race budget was reduced. Mann,
who'd been flown to each meeting from his Hawaiian home at Suzuki's expense,
was dropped. Hammer and Grant were retained.

On much-modified machinery, Daytona success again eluded the Team, but
at Loudon, despite the wet conditions, the X6 duo blasted off to an early lead.
One report described the machines as 'spectacularly swift' and they appeared
uncatchable, Hammer having gained a half lap lead over Yvon duHamel in five
laps! But Hammer soon retired to the pits and Grant later expired on the course.

At Indianapolis, Grant lost 30 seconds at the start, but forged ahead
overtaking Hammer, whose X6 was misfiring due to mal-adjustment of the
mixture lever. Realising this error Hammer gained on Grant, finishing one
second astern in 3rd place, with Gary Nixon 1st aboard his Yamaha.

1968 became the turning point in Suzuki's US racing fortunes; with GP
constraints removed, Hamamatsu produced new machines—TR250 and
TR500 (XR05)—and dictated overall racing philosophy. 1968 was the first year
the riders received a fee in addition to expenses.

HAMMER   'The value of our contracts was $6000 to ride six races. That
was the biggest contract a US motorcycle racer had with anybody at that time.
Yamaha wasn't signing contracts like that then.'

Hammer and Grant were retained, and Cal Rayborn was signed for 250 cc races.
The big wallet had opened!

Mitsuo Itoh, fresh from the grands prix, joined the Team at Daytona as rider-
development man. The new TR250s were out-paced, despite Rayborn's 3rd
place in his qualifying heat.

The XR05, based on the newly-launched T500—500/5 in the USA—had
problems too.

HAMMER   'They had a very narrow power-band—maybe about 900 rpm
and every time you changed up a gear, you had to slip the clutch, and they
wouldn't hold up to that. They didn't really handle that bad going slow
into the infield, but going fast up on that big turn at Daytona, you just
couldn't hold it wide open round the corner because it'd start wobbling
and carry you clear to the outside of the track! It was fast once you got it
going—I qualified at about 133 mph, which was faster than the Triumph—
but as far as lap times were concerned, you could go 5 seconds faster on the
Triumph because of the power band.

Itoh was the fastest Suzuki qualifier at 134.288 mph, and although Grant's
XR05 engine blew in front of the grandstands he still managed to qualify.

Cycle World's then editor and
publisher, Joe Parkhurst (left)
with his technical editor
Gordon Jennings (right) are
definitely enjoying themselves
with Koshino and Riichi Itoh
on Suzuki's sub-miniature
racers at Riverside *Cycle World*

Hammer considered his position; he was a pro-racer dependent on the purse, and he needed a good finish.

HAMMER   'I wouldn't ride the Suzuki in the race, it was too dangerous. I rode Rod Gould's Triumph as he'd had an accident in the 250 cc race. Triumph offered me his 500 and I finished 7th in the race but was disqualified because I'd qualified on the Suzuki.'

Rayborn, aboard a Harley, lapped the entire field in winning the race in which Grant and Itoh finished 5th and 9th. Hammer's desertion severed his contract but he wasn't asked to return the first $1000 installment. Hammer retired from racing in 1970 and is now a construction engineer. Meanwhile, Fred Moxley was becoming a little frustrated and resigned, being replaced by Paul 'Grommet' Garnant.

At Loudon, Grant achieved 7th place in the 500 cc event, and 4th in the 250 cc race, a position originally held by Rayborn who'd ridden his TR250 so hard that it eventually broke. The race was won by Art 'The Dart' Baumann who'd so impressed Suzuki that he was signed for 1969.

Renewed hopes also came with news from the factory of improved XR05 performance, and they became optimistic for Daytona. On the new slimmer XR05 Grant qualified at 146 mph and finished 2nd in the 200 mile event. Baumann finished 13th having suffered gearbox problems and a slow pit-stop.

At the wet Loudon Championship race, Baumann was placed 15th; the XR05 had no front mudguard and the rain obscured his vision, but at Indianapolis Grant was 2nd—again to Harley-mounted Rayborn—with Baumann in 3rd.

Ron Grant gained three National Land Speed Records at Bonneville on his XR05 just one week before the Sears Point National Championship event in September, but had no time to rebuild his tired motor. Baumann was suffering from hepatitis at Sears Point but still rode the gruelling 125 mile race, run with a track temperature of 105 degrees! By lap 4 Baumann had gained the lead from Rayborn and by lap 15 Grant was lying 2nd to Art. On lap 23 Jess Thomas fell, causing Art to take to the grass (temporarily) and four laps later, Grant's

Above 'Hammer Dick' doing his stuff on the X6 racer and wearing his Triumph leathers! The machine bore close resemblance to the stock roadster *Cycle World*

Upper left The X6 racer at Carlsbad during 1966. Team manager Fred Moxley (top left) stands next to Dick Hammer, awaiting his chance to ride. Beneath Hammer, Riichi Itoh squats alongside an RT65 whilst Bob Ellison (foreground) re-jets the X6 *Cycle World*

overworked engine blew and he retired. By lap 37 of the 50 lap race, all but Baumann of the top ten had refuelled and Paul Garnant was signalling madly. Two laps later, Baumann was refuelled in nine seconds without losing his lead and history was made as he crossed the finishing line, claiming his $3450 winner's cheque. It was the first AMA National Championship race to be won by a two stroke, and the first to be won by a Japanese machine. . . .

Suzuki now realised that, as with grands prix, top riders combined with fast reliable machines were the key and for 1970, the Team was strengthened by recruiting Jody Nicholas, an ex-Vietnam US Navy fighter pilot—and violin virtuoso—and no mean rider to boot. For Daytona, Grant, Baumann and Nicholas were joined by US rider Jimmy Odom and New Zealander Geoff Perry, a rider groomed by Rod Coleman in Southern hemisphere events. It was Suzuki's strongest team to date.

Daytona week is renowned for rider frolics—usually in 'rent-a-racer' cars—but Daytona car-hire agencies had a blacklist of riders' names.

NICHOLAS   'Ron and Art bought an old '61 Buick and started selling shares in it. There weren't any takers, but they all certainly wanted to drive it fast, and on a quiet jungle road, Aldana almost totalled it. He was staying with us at the Holiday Inn, and the last night it was alleged that he was going to drive it into the swimming pool . . . After the bar closed we were sitting out there waiting for Aldana; he was just crazy enough to do it!'

Often the idea was to see who could drive a car the furthest into the Atlantic, and still be able to drive back out. Chas Mortimer held the record at one time, his car radio aerial just visible above the ocean!

In the Daytona 250 event, Grant and Nicholas rode the overweight TR250s.

NICHOLAS   'Ron and I had one of the best races we'd ever ridden. We fought like it was a Trophy dash at Ascot—for 100 miles—then finished 8th and 9th. They were genuine factory bikes made out of what, I'm not sure—except lead. . . .'

During qualifying for the main event, it was clear that the XR05s didn't carry enough fuel even to get them to the halfway 100 mile fuel-stop, despite the unintentionally oversize fuel tanks. (Suzuki had fitted six *Imperial* gallon instead of six *US* gallon tanks).

Grant had been racing 'down under' during the winter and had also tested the new XR05 at Ryuyo before returning to the States. At Daytona, Grant was ahead of Hailwood's BSA!

NICHOLAS   'He was really, really quick and was leading when he ran out of fuel just a couple of laps before they were going to call him in anyway. Geoff Perry was doing quite well towards the end but he too had an enormous fuel tank and had he won, he may have been disqualified.'

Nicholas' XR05 seized and for one reason or another, not a single teamster finished the race.

Three weeks later the Team raced at the Kent 125 mile Championship race. Nicholas crashed.

NICHOLAS   'It rained during the first half of the race, but later it dried up and there was a dry line. On the last corner I got off, slid along the racetrack and go up, pushing the bike until I collapsed. But the high humidity had steamed up my face-shield and Suzuki helper John Butcher came over and knocked on the helmet. 'Is anyone in?'. . . .'

Nicholas was holding 3rd place on lap 35 when he crashed, behind leader Grant and 2nd man Baumann. But Baumann too crashed, on the 40th *and* 46th laps, remounting and finishing 5th. But even crashing was used by US Suzuki to good effect. In a press release they quoted Baumann.

BAUMANN   'The fact that I was able to finish the race in 5th place after two crashes, shows the tough reliability engineered into Suzuki machines.'

At Talladega, a 200 mile race run on the Daytona-styled banked circuit, it was reported that the factory Suzukis had 'speed, reliability, and handling.' But a 250 start-line incident upset the form-book. Jody and Art had by then quit racing the TR250s and were watching as Grant stood on the grid.

NICHOLAS   'He started in the first wave but the bike loaded up on the line and whilst it was eight and twelve stroking—barely pottering along—the second wave came through the smoke-screen. Dave Bloom accidentally hit Grant and left Ron on the line, his left foot literally hanging. Art and I tried to look away because it made our hearts sink. They kept him at the track for about 15 minutes before they moved him.'

Grant had a compound fracture of his left leg.

In training for the 200 miler, Grant had been 5th fastest at 150.258 mph whereas Nicholas had had gearbox problems and barely qualified. But Team Suzuki feared disqualification if they won, because of the illegal fuel tanks.

NICHOLAS   'We had to find some way to take up space inside the tanks so we found some plastic bottles that held outboard motor oil and we figured it would take three bottles in each tank to get them down to the proper capacity. We were in rural Alabama but we went out and found some Texaco station and this big black fellow came out and brought twelve quarts of oil. He was kinda bewildered about what we were going to do with it and his eyes must've been two feet in diameter seeing these crazy Gringos pouring this perfectly good oil down into the waste-barrel!'

Starting from the back row, Nicholas overtook *40* riders in five laps and lay 3rd behind the the Tridents of Nixon and Dave Aldana! After a lap 20 fuel-stop he was relegated to 7th place but was soon in 2nd behind Aldana after Nixon fell. Nicholas still needed another fuel-stop but lost only 35 seconds and maintained 2nd place to the flag. Baumann had a steady ride and finished 4th.

The final 1970 event for US Suzuki was at Loudon for the 100 mile championship race where again Nicholas crashed.

NICHOLAS   'That was where I figured out that I had either an overflowing carburettor or a broken fuel-line because as I was coming down off the big bend, I hit the ground and the bike burst into flames. We figured that the little cavity under the carburettors had filled with gasoline and the acceleration caused it to swish back on to the rear tyre when I was still

History in the making! The 1969 Sears Point event where Art Baumann raced his XR05 to its first US victory. Despite its crudity, *this* refuelling rig worked. L to R: Garnant, Grant (just visible) and Bud Parker *Cycle World*

banked over and I went down. I remember trying to drag it off the track and having people drag *me* off to get me away from it.'

Nicholas had been lying 2nd to Mark Brelsford at the time of his accident but Baumann continued for a few more laps before his engine expired. Injured Grant was a non-starter.

Ron Pierce, another US rider, joined the Team for 1971 but Odom was dropped from the Daytona Team, where all five teamsters, Nicholas, Grant, Baumann, Pierce and Perry, retired with seizures caused by the fitting of an electronic ignition system. It was a disastrous start to the AMA road-race season, now increased to seven events. Six weeks later, the Team raced at Atlanta, where catastrophe reigned supreme. It all revolved around the fuel-stop.

NICHOLAS 'We reckoned it kinda hard to get in and out of the pits; you'd come down the long straightaway and on an off-chamber downhill *right*-hander, you'd have to go off to the *left* into the pits. 'Grommet' decided it would be better if we stopped on the back someplace — out of the traffic — and fuelled up there.

'The rules about refuelling weren't that specific about *where* you refuelled, it was just taken for granted it would happen in the pits. We set up the fuel-stop about a mile from the pits — just at the start of the long back straight. All the fuel was stashed up behind the fence there and they signalled Ron Pierce to stop on the track-side. I was circulating and had seen some activity over there — I was having a real go with Dick Mann on his three cylinder BSA and had just reached 3rd place — and was waiting my turn when I ran out of fuel.

'After someone saw how Ron Pierce was refuelled, they made the crew get out. I'd been watching a while and the crew couldn't make it back to the pits — they were trapped in the in-field section with the race in progress. Ron Grant stopped at the K & N pit — the air-filter people had a fuel-dump in the pits — and he kept going along with Pierce. Art and the rest of us just ran out of gas!'

Bud Wilson, US Suzuki's service manager, was helping the Team at Atlanta.

WILSON 'It was embarrassing, I stayed in the pits. It did create a lot of press coverage though!'

Pierce was disqualified and Grant didn't figure in the results.

When Team manager Paul Garnant returned to Santa Fe Springs, he found in his office a beautifully-made gold petrol can with the inscription in black: 'The 1971 Golden G-*ASS* Award'. At the time, nobody admitted responsibility, but US Suzuki's current service manager, Geoff Mazon, now confesses the can was all his own work!

Loudon — where Nicholas retired with mechanical problems — Kent and Pocono events followed that year, but after Pocono, the machines needed an engine-tune.

NICHOLAS 'Grommet and Chris Young drove across the States to US Suzuki's east coast parts warehouse to freshen up the bikes, and then drove on to Talladega. When we got there, the bikes hadn't been touched, there

Above Grant leads Baumann at the 1970 Kent races. Between them they led the field for 52 of the 56 laps. Including the last . . . *Archives*

Above right Jody Nicholas exploring the limits of his tyres whilst riding his XR05 at a 1970 Orange County race *Archives*

were no standard-size piston rings in the spares and the Suzuki dealer in down-town Talladega had just one set of rings for the four machines. It was incredible; here was this huge lorry with room for half the parts supply from Santa Fe Springs and there was nothing in it!'

Nicholas couldn't complain; he finished 2nd at Talladega, and would have probably won but for *two* fuel-stops.

NICHOLAS 'Aldana and Don Castro on BSA and Triumph 3s were batting around together—we were almost dead-even going down the back stretch because we were going into a head-wind—and by riding side by side they were creating quite a pocket and I watched my rev-counter go up to 8200, 8300 rpm whilst staying right between them. Coming off the banking on to the straightaway, there was a tail-wind, and I could slip up and pip the both of them going into the first turn and lead through the in-field. Then, about half-way down the back straight, here they'd come again. Doug Hele couldn't understand why I was so fast, but I wasn't *into* the wind, but with a "tow" from these two big beasts in front of me, I could slip right by them. I couldn't hear for a week afterwards—I've never heard a noise like that in all my life. Two of them without silencers. Just big open pipes!'

The Ontario meeting in October—where Grant was 3rd and Baumann 4th—ended Suzuki's sixth US racing season and, with only two wins to their name, it was obvious that better machines were needed. What they got in exchange for their veteran XR05s, was a device so fearsome, that it took the Team riders by surprise, and shook the very foundations of the American road-racing scene.

Left Loading a Team XR05 at Daytona 1971 are L to R: Riichi Itoh, Michio Ichino and Mitsuo Itoh *MCW*

Below 1971 teamster Ron Pierce riding his factory 500 XR05 at Pocono *Cycle World*

8   American dreams:
Daytona disasters (1972 to 1975)

Towards the end of 1971, Ryuyo residents heard the characteristic scream of an open-piped three; Mitsuo Itoh putting through its paces an early version of what became known as the TR750 to the racing buffs, and the 'flexi-flier' to its riders, a nickname coined by Ron Grant (—and the XR11 to the factory).

The debut of the new XR11s was Daytona 1972, where they were ridden by Grant, Baumann, Nicholas and Perry—Pierce was dropped for 1972. Yet again, the refuelling bogey haunted the Team.

NICHOLAS   'The dump-tank was all set up for practice and they pushed the bike up with the Japanese standing around with their stop-watches. Grommet, with the hose in his hand, couldn't get it in the tank and he almost pushed me over a couple of times. Someone suggested they glue some fur around the tank orifice so that he could find it! I remember if it hadn't been for Shoji Tanaka and Bill Buchka on my right side, I'd have been pushed over for sure.'

Bill Buchka joined US Suzuki as a race mechanic in the autumn of 1971 and he recalls other difficulties with the XR11s.

BUCHKA   'There was a series of problems we experienced then; shredding tyres in four or five laps—chunks of the tyre coming out. Daytona was our initiation with that motorcycle. I'll tell you that period of two weeks at Daytona was like two *months*. So much work; so many problems. If it wasn't tyres it was the chains that weren't up-to-date at that time. Man, it was unbelievable!'

Development of 'bolt-ons' such as tyres and chains just hadn't kept pace with the new, super powerful XR11. Prior to Daytona, the fastest machines in the US were the 79 bhp BSA-Triumph factory triples, but they were less powerful *and* less peaky than the 100 bhp Suzukis. The XR11 represented a quantum leap in technology—suppliers of 'bolt-ons' would have to follow, but soon.

Nicholas qualified at 169.81 mph for Daytona with Art Baumann ahead at 171.75 mph—a new record and the first 170 mph-plus officially timed racing motorcycle. The tyre manufacturers were distinctly worried, hoping that race day would be cool, minimising tyre temperatures. Grant and Nicholas used Dunlop tyres for training but Baumann was faithful to Goodyear.

NICHOLAS   'After four laps of practice, Dave Buck of Dunlop knelt down by the rear tyre and stuck his pyrometer into it. I can remember seeing his mouth come open as the needle went up. He said to me that Dunlop would

like us to use their tyres, but they couldn't guarantee them. Then, Tony Mills of Dunlop said that much as they wanted Suzuki to use Dunlops, they'd just as soon we didn't.'

Goodyear then arranged for some tyres to be specially made from a stock-car rubber compound which was more temperature-resistant, but even Goodyear were not too optimistic and their new tyres weren't available until Thursday of practice week. It was frustrating.

> NICHOLAS   'We were desperate; we had the fastest things on the track, and no tyres?'

During the race, Mike Babbich, Goodyear's tyre technician, planned to check rear tyre temperature and wear at each fuel-stop, and if required, new tyres would be fitted then, but when Jody stopped after about 80 miles only about two-thirds of the tyre circumference was visible to Mike Babbich—the remainder hidden by the rear fender. The tyre wasn't changed.

> NICHOLAS   'By then, I'd got an enormous lead so I backed it off and started cruisin' around. Going through the in-field—about 110 mph left—I just started to pitch it down and it went sideways, just like Ascot on the cinders.'

Nicholas straightened it out going on to the grass, and just stopped it before he re-crossed the track *against* the traffic-flow! The rear tyre was flat, its cords visible for about 12 inches of its circumference. . . .

Grant, meanwhile, had lost time at his fuel-stop.

> BUD WILSON   'They messed it. Paul Garnant just couldn't get the nozzle

Factory mechanics worked long hours at Daytona 1972, enabling the new XR11s to raise the qualifying speed record to 172 mph (279 km/h). Here, an engine is about to be removed *MCN*

For the late-season Ontario
meeting, the XR11s had been
fitted with 'standard' cylinders.
US Suzuki mechanics John
Alnut (left) and Brian Lunnis
warm up Geoff Perry's
machine *Dixon*

into the tank. He was standing there by the tank and twisting it. It took
over ten minutes and there was gasoline all over the place.'

Leaving the pits, Grant overcooked the clutch which soon caused his retirement.

BUCHKA   'I recall that we were having a lot of trouble with the clutches
overheating and cooking themselves, so we tried several different things to
get more air through them.'

And Baumann? Whilst dicing for the lead on the 12th lap he too retired with
magneto trouble.

At Road Atlanta, Nicholas and Grant gave the XR11s their head, finishing
1st and 4th. But the race had been run under protest with rumours that Team
Hansen—the factory Kawasaki team—weren't too happy with the cylinder and
head specifications of the XR11s. The AMA, whose rules had only recently
been amended to allow the faster 750s into the National Championships, were
closely monitoring the situation; only certain engine parts were allowed to be
modified from the roadster versions. Merv Wright, like Ron Grant, was an
English ex-patriot and originally became involved as Grant's mechanic in 1971.
Later, after joining Suzuki's service department, he became Garnant's
successor.

WRIGHT   'We had to submit items such as crankcases and cylinders to the
AMA which they brought to each of the races in case of protest. In
fairness, there really was no intention to cheat; it was actually a mix-up
between verbage in the AMA rulebook and the FIM F750 rules.
'I have a distinct feeling that the Atlanta protest had something to do with
the fact that two Kawasaki's were in 2nd and 3rd places. Jody won the

race, went into the winner's enclosure, but then a protest was put in anonymously and suddenly, the Suzuki got thrown out and Kawasakis became 1st and 2nd.'

But what was it all about? Wright considers the cause was a typographical error in the FIM rulebook where acceptable engine modifications were not to change the 'Cylinder barrel *casting material* . . .' Wright contends that Suzuki Japan made their XR11 cylinder and head to comply with this rule which appears to control only the casting *material*. But the AMA rulebook, based on the FIM F750 rules, inserted the word '*and*' between 'casting' and 'material' thus limiting the cylinder barrel to the same material *and* casting as the GT750. Team Hansen succeeded in their Atlanta protest because the XR11 cylinders were obviously dissimilar to those of the GT750, being sand-cast and without the GT750's vestigal finning.

This severe blow caused Suzuki to withdraw from further US competition until they could extract similar horsepower from the GT750 cylinder casting. The new parts were ready for Talladega.

Above Dunlop tyre boffin Dave Buck and Team Suzuki manager Paul Garnant quietly consider the tyre-shredding capabilities of the 100 bhp XR11s at Talladega *Cycle World*

NICHOLAS   'Boy, was it hot in Talladega that year! I pulled off with heat-exhaustion. I grew up in that sort of heat, but *I* couldn't take it. The water temperature was 95 degrees, and at the racetrack, humidity was close to 100 per cent. I'd unzipped my leathers almost down to my navel but the wind caught them and they spread out and almost blew me off the back of the bike! Without a tail-piece, I'd have been blown right off it.

'I was in 2nd place behind duHamel—maybe four or five seconds down—and going down the back stretch, I remember one of the lane-divider stripes, painted on the road, going back and forth either side of the front wheel. I thought it was kinda strange and decided to check it out on the next lap but I came around again, and the lane was still *moving*! I thought, "Jeez, I'd better stop." I came in, and Shoji Tanaka got down on his knees with his hand on the throttle and kinda looking up like "Ugh?" There was nothing wrong with the bike, it was just fine. I remember getting off the bike, sitting down on the wall and then I went, tilt! And I was out!'

In a pre-Talladega tyre testing session Baumann had crashed at 150 mph, but in the race, riding in great pain with a lashed-up broken collar bone, he finished 3rd, epitomising the tough US riders.

The final National Championship race in 1972 was at Ontario in California. Here Perry finished 2nd but Nicholas crashed. He was not to ride in a major event again, medical reasons forcing his retirement. He was one of the best US road racers in the early 1970s, but to Bill Buchka, who prepared his machines in his last year, he was more than that.

BUCHKA   'I always had a lot of respect for Jody; I felt that as far as intelligence levels go, there were few guys like him who race motorcycles. To find a guy with such a high intellectual capacity was refreshing for me because I like to think that I'm not your average mechanic either; I like to read, I appreciate culture and music, and you don't get too many opportunities to discuss that sort of thing, so I enjoyed his company for that.'

Above right Baumann, (wearing 'modified' leathers to accommodate the splint supporting his collarbone) leading Nixon at Talladega *Waaser*

When Jody retired from racing, Bill Buchka left US Suzuki. Recently he tuned Graham Noyce's World Championship winning Honda moto cross machines.

With improved XR11s promised for 1973, US Suzuki contracted Don Emde and Englishman Paul Smart, and with Grant and Perry, they were a formidable team for Daytona. (Art Baumann had switched camps to Kawasaki.) Smart was rammed at the start of the 200 mile event, but eventually got under way. Grant achieved 4th place before his chain broke, whilst both Smart and Perry retired with ignition troubles. Only Don Emde, riding a tactical race, finished for Suzuki, in 7th place.

For 1973, the AMA increased the number of Championship rounds to nine—two more than in 1972—and eliminated re-fuelling problems by running two-leg races. When Team Suzuki raced at Dallas International Raceway in April, Paul Smart led the entire field and earned the $10,000 winner's cheque, but the American public weren't really interested in road-racing; only 8000 spectators attended Dallas.

At Atlanta, it was Perry's turn. Riding a magnificent race he took the lead on lap 10 of the 30 lap race, and remained there until race-end. With two successive victories, it was time to celebrate.

> WRIGHT 'It was traditional that there would be a party and the race winner usually got bunged into the swimming pool, clothes and all, and if the Team manager was around he went in too! At Atlanta, Geoff thought he'd avoided it—everyone was well-lubricated and forgot about it. He quietly crept off to bed and shortly afterwards, Yvon duHamel remembered and Geoff woke up in the pool—still in bed! They'd carried Geoff and bed down to the pool and had a ceremonial launching!'

Suzuki's celebrations were premature; Kawasaki's teamsters were offered special victory bonuses by their factory; Nixon taking advantage on his semi-works Kawasaki by winning the Loudon, Laguna Seca and Pocono 75 mile events in a clean sweep.

Geoff Perry was only a semi-professional racer and often returned to New

Zealand between races, where he worked for Air New Zealand as a technician. He was returning to Laguna Seca on 23 July when the plane crashed into the Pacific near Tahiti. There were no survivors.

Geoff's tragic end cast a gloomy shadow over Laguna Seca, where Smart was the best placed Suzuki rider in 4th place. Meanwhile, even Kawasaki's domination was coming under threat from the 350 cc factory Yamahas, and at Talladega, the little Yamahas took the first four places, (Grant was 6th) whilst at Charlotte, Roberts' Yamaha was 2nd, splitting the factory Kawasakis with Grant lying 4th. During these events Suzuki had little luck, and at the final round at Ontario, Smart managed 5th, Kawasakis taking the first three places with Roberts' Yamaha in 4th.

Bad luck had dogged the Team during 1973, and it was no surprise that after an eight year association with Suzuki, Ron Grant left. Only Smart was re-contracted for 1974, to be joined by his brother-in-law Barry Sheene, and ex-Team Hansen riders Nixon and Cliff Carr, following Kawasaki's withdrawal from AMA competition. Cal Rayborn had just signed a US Suzuki contract when he went to New Zealand in December 1973. There, racing a private TR500, he fell to his death when it seized. It was his first ride aboard a 500 cc Suzuki. . . .

At Daytona in 1974, over 30 of the new F750 rule-bending Yamaha TZ700s had entered: the pressure on Suzuki was enormous. During practice Smart qualified with an average speed of 107.949 mph, Sheene with 107.013 mph. But Sheene was determined to improve the handling of his XR11 for his Daytona debut.

> WRIGHT 'We were messing around with different combinations of swing-arms and shocks and I was keeping track of the lap times and I could see which combination was working the best. But Barry disagreed with my figures and suggested we refit the other swing-arm. We tucked the bike away while Barry watched Gary Nixon, and did nothing whatever to the bike. Half an hour later, Barry leapt back on it, did a few more laps, came back in and said, "Perfect! Don't touch it!"'

Conditions were hot and humid for the 200 mile race as Smart took pole with Sheene also on the front row. From the start Agostini's factory Yamaha took the lead with his team-mate Hideo Kanaya in 2nd. Sheene was the first Suzuki casualty, with ignition trouble. Soon it was time for refuelling and Smart was the first to pit.

> WRIGHT 'There was a bit of a debacle on the refuelling. We were trying to refuel Paul but the fuel just wouldn't flow and we ended up with a queue of riders waiting for gas. I'll never know what prompted me to take a second refuelling system along, but somebody was watching after us, I guess.'

During a later post-mortem on the fuel hose, a flap of loose rubber was revealed which had completely blocked fuel flow.

With the Team refuelled, Suzuki's Daytona chances were never better as Nixon led the field with Agostini 12 seconds in arrears and yet to make *his* second fuel-stop. By an error of judgement, Nixon used too much power and crashed as he left the in-field section. Smart was now Suzuki's best hope in spite of the

Above Art Baumann (right), 3rd at Talladega 1972 despite a broken collarbone, sweats it out in the winner's circle with duHamel (1st) and Gary Nixon on their Team Hansen Kawasakis *Waaser*

delayed fuel-stop, but *his* XR11 was suffering and he finished 9th with Carr two places behind. Nixon had brought Suzuki the closest they had ever been to that elusive Daytona victory.

For Atlanta, the Team received three brand-new XR11s accompanied by the evergreen Mitsuo Itoh. Wright had impressed upon the factory that Daytona machines were unique and unsuitable for other US racetracks. During practice the new machines were tested.

WRIGHT   'We put Smart, Carr and Nixon on to their respective machines and sent them out. After one lap, Paul Smart pulled in with a deathly white face saying that he couldn't ride the thing. Cliff came in and shrugged and said it was OK but could be better, and Nixon thought his was pretty good. To try and solve the problem, everyone exchanged bikes but the result was exactly the same and was a classic illustration of my theory.'

This test proved the importance of the rider's physical size; Itoh and Nixon were similarly built, suiting the new machine. Moreover, US tracks were quite different to Ryuyo.

WRIGHT   'Ryuyo's like a billiard table and you've got a little Japanese test rider weighing 98 lb dripping wet in his leathers, and you get the bikes over here, where you've got an undulating track *and* rough surfaces . . . You've got Smarty going around corners with only his toe-nails left on the bike, Cliff Carr bending off the bike in a most peculiar manner and Nixon just sitting bolt upright. No wonder it's different.'

Predictably, in the race Nixon finished 3rd whilst Carr and Smart struggled with their ill-handling Suzukis out of contention.

Nixon's mechanic, Erv Kanemoto—US-born despite the name—decided to improve the chassis himself, and with a Santa Anna company, C & J Frames, built his own frame with adjustable rake and trail. Wright knew the factory frowned on private development and heavily disguised the new chassis. Nixon's new machine raced at the next National, Loudon.

Geoff Perry claimed victory at the 1973 Road Atlanta meeting. Kel Carruthers (2nd) and a youthful Kenny Roberts (3rd) rode 350 cc Yamahas *Cycle World*

The factory mechanics immediately recognised the bogus frame but Nixon persisted and rode to victory in the 75 mile race, leaving Smart struggling in 13th place on his standard-framed XR11. Both Carr and Smart persuaded Kanemoto to modify their frames with steering geometry identical to Nixon's in time for the next race at Laguna Seca.

Meanwhile, Nixon agreed to test ride Suzuki's new 500 cc GP racer—the XR14, or RG500—at Ryuyo, but two days after his Loudon victory, he crashed at Ryuyo, returning to the States with both arms severely broken.

Only Smart and Carr contested Laguna Seca with their modified XR11s, but during practice, Smart had the fright of his life.

WRIGHT   'Smarty was honking up the straight already dangling off the side of the bike in preparation for the crest of the hill and the left-hander that followed it, and just as he was shifting into top, the crankshaft broke. All hell was let loose in the engine and I have never in my life seen anybody move so fast; from hanging off the side and "blip!" he was up on top of it in just a split second. He coasted off to the side and undoubtedly needed a change of shorts, but it was funny to watch!'

In the heats Smart was 3rd whilst Carr's engine blew and a new one was hastily fitted for the main race but then Carr suffered front brake trouble and having reached 7th place was forced to retire. Smart gained 4th in the early stages and held on to this position to the flag.

Sheene's GP commitments completed, he was able to fill in for the injured Nixon at Talladega, but both he and Carr slowed towards the end of the race due to imminent lack of fuel, finishing 4th and 5th respectively. Smart had already retired with a suspect front tyre. The final National Championship round at Ontario became the subject of a Hollywood motorcyling documentary, *On the limit*, but unfortunately the race was a Yamaha walk-over. Ironically, having qualified the fastest, in the race Sheene suffered from a failing rear brake and finished 4th—the highest-placed Suzuki rider.

Suzuki's race development had centred on brute horsepower, and aerodynamics had been simply a matter of wrapping the fairing around the machine. At Ontario, Wright was accompanied by a McDonnel-Douglas aircraft engineer, Dr. Bob Leibeck, who had a PhD in aeronautical engineering. He'd already designed the 'wings' on Dan Gurney's Indianapolis cars and when he saw the XR11 fairings he wasn't too impressed.

WRIGHT 'Bob shook his head and was horrified, saying, "That is *so* wrong!" I asked him to build me a new one, and in conjunction with Camber Fairings of Costa Mesa, they developed a new fairing.

Wright planned to use the new fairings at Daytona in 1975, but the factory disapproved and they eventually arrived in England 12 months later.

Daytona preparations commenced in December when Merv Wright organised a ten day Daytona test involving Dunlop and riders Sheene, Lansivuori and Aldana.

WRIGHT 'The big problem at Daytona has always been the accessory items like tyres and chains. There's nowhere you can duplicate the conditions in a lab and the only place you *can* duplicate it is at Daytona. The problems relative to tyres, and to a lesser degree chains, is heat. So we ran a number of 200 mile practice events in December. Even then it was difficult because it was very cold, whereas when we raced there in March it was 90 degrees with about 90 per cent humidity, but it was the best we could do at the time.'

The factory provided new lighter XR11s for the test and Wright found that two of the machines were labelled for a new teamster.

WRIGHT 'It's not generally known, but Phil Read was supposed to appear for that test having made a factory visit with a view to riding the Suzukis in 1975, and there was a distinct possibility of it coming off because two of the bikes that arrived at Daytona for the December testing were designated for Mr. Read.'

By March all was clear; Read decided against Suzuki and signed an MV contract, but US Suzuki planned a Daytona onslaught and hired Dave Aldana, Hurley Wilvert (Daytona only), Pat Hennen and Teuvo 'Tepi' Lansivuori. Smart and Carr were axed whilst Nixon and Sheene were retained. Despite all the December tyre testing there was much concern when Sheene crashed at

Above Factory test rider Ken Araoka aboard an XR11 during a pre-Daytona 1974 test at Ryuyo where, later that year, he and Nixon crashed whilst testing the new 500 cc XR14 *Wright*

Above right 'Going around corners with only his toe-nails left on the bike.' Paul Smart during his short-lived Suzuki debut at Daytona 1973. Ignition problems side-lined him *Archives*

170 mph during a private Suzuki practice session. Were tyres to blame?

WRIGHT 'I can honestly say we never found anything wrong with the motorcycle, and I'm not implying that there was anything wrong with the Dunlop tyres. What we *did* find were marks on the back-side of the swing-arm which theoretically ought not to have been there. What undoubtedly happened was that chunks of the tyre came off, but whether they made that mark or whether the tyre 'grew' to such a degree that it was dragging on there has never really been established. The next morning the tyre had 30 lb of air in it; it never went flat.'

After Sheene's accident the machine was dismantled and inspected under official supervision. George Vukmanovich—Hurley Wilvert's mechanic—was involved.

VUKMANOVICH 'Everything stopped. Everybody thought maybe the gearbox was locked up or it seized, or something broke. So I took apart Barry Sheene's motor and there was nothing wrong; it was absolutely 100 per cent. Every part of the running gear was in perfect mechanical condition.

'What was *my* conclusion? Well, they had these trick chain tensioners—a spring-loaded roller—and I think that the chain tensioner spring broke first, the chain tensioner was able to drop, and the side of the tensioner, which was steel, dug in the side of the tyre. And that's what ripped the tyre off the cords. The tyre never went flat—there was always air in it—but the tread came off.

'The spring *was* broken but it wasn't possible to be sure if that was cause or effect, but I would rely on my better judgement that it *was* the cause of the accident. Once the tread was broken from the tyre, it would jam between the tyre and the swing-arm.

'One of the springs had previously broken on another bike but nothing happened to that bike. Maybe it broke as it came into the pit lane.'

George Vukmanovich's theory sheds new light on Sheene's famous prang, and whilst it cannot be tested now, he claims that after the incident, the tensioners on the other Team bikes were modified just in case. . . .

The track itself bore out both theories; the tyre was momentarily jammed each revolution of the wheel.

WRIGHT 'There was a black strip, ever increasing in length and going a considerable way down the track which was obviously put down at each wheel revolution indicating that a chunk of tyre was coming off and *as* it was coming off, making this mark. Theoretically, the back wheel did not lock—the motorcycle did not mechanically seize—but at 150 plus mph with something like that going on at the back-end, it's not surprising that Barry and the bike ended up going down the road separately . . .'.

As in 1972, the Team reluctantly changed to Goodyear tyres for the race, but only Aldana finished, in 10th place. Tepi led for some time but crashed when his chain jumped the sprockets. Wilvert seized on lap 17, probably weakness caused by fuel shortage—he was due to refuel on lap 18. Hennen crashed when his *front* tyre punctured! Nixon, bravely overcoming the pain from his broken arms, qualified 29th but withdrew before the race commenced.

As always, refuelling jinxed the Team.

VUKMANOVICH 'It was a joke. We practiced on Saturday night and it was a joke; nobody could do it right and all they could do was laugh. There was enough people, it was just that nobody could do their job. Just nerves. In the race, they only screwed up Aldana's fuel-stop.'

One report says that Aldana had been 'given a gas-bath at one of his pit stops'.

By now, Sheene was prostrate in Daytona's Halifax Hospital with a broken thigh, broken ribs, cracked vertebrae and multiple cuts and bruises. He was later air-lifted to Heathrow and from there by helicopter to his Wisbech home. Within a few weeks, he was back in the saddle.

With only four scheduled National Championship events for 1975, it was clear that road-racing was low priority for the AMA and when the June Atlanta meeting was cancelled, the result was a five month lull before the second round at Laguna Seca in August. There, Aldana had gained 3rd place when a spark plug electrode broke and he retired. Hennen, with handling problems, finished 5th.

The third and final National meeting of 1975 at Ontario, saw a full team of Suzukis—apart from Sheene. After recovering from his Daytona accident, he then broke his other leg on a paddock bike! The other riders were in bad shape too; Lansivuori with a broken hand and foot—Ontario practice accident, Nixon with a broken shoulder—Ontario practice accident, and Aldana, bruised and battered—Ontario practice accident. Only Hennen was fit and he started the first heat in pole position. Aldana couldn't find neutral gear on the start line and was removed, but Hennen took an early lead which he soon lost to Kenny Roberts. Then Lansivuori's engine blew and he retired. Nixon and Hennen battled for 2nd place with Nixon prevailing, whilst Roberts was winner of the first heat.

Hennen had a poor second heat, finishing 12th overall. Nixon's clutch release bearing failed but Erv Kanemoto made a temporary fix and Nixon re-joined the race. Finally, when he couldn't engage sixth gear, and flames were shooting out of the carburettors, he retired; three laps from the flag. Nixon epitomised the courage of American riders—the specification hadn't changed since 1966—they were still tough, gritty and determined as were Mann and Hammer a decade

Above Preparing for the 1974 Talladega 200 *Cycle World*

Right Englishman Cliff Carr, who joined the 1974 Team, calmly waits whilst the mechanics and riders sort themselves out at Talladega. L to R: Sheene, Lunnis, Buck, Erv Kanemoto and Ken Bailey *Cycle World*

before. Nixon's supreme effort was in vain, however, for 1975 marked the last real year of AMA participation in road-racing events, and that too meant the end of the line for US Suzuki's involvement.

WRIGHT 'There was a certain sadness about Ontario; it was pretty much the last race for US Suzuki.'

A year previously the AMA decided to develop US road-racing and they approached the 1974 promoters asking for increased contributions if they wished to stage 1975 National Championship rounds.

WRIGHT 'Some of the out-of-the-way places like Atlanta and Loudon — which are very, very rural places — got a mediocre turnout of spectators and barely broke even, so this new fee would literally put them out of business. The effect in 1975, was that we ended up with just three road-races. For the pure road race specialist riders — and for Suzuki factory participation — this new arrangement was financially unfeasible. That was really where the decline set in.

'Frankly, US Suzuki were never really pro-racing anyway, and the logistics of maintaining a Team — although there were only three races — made it unviable. So the factory with some regret, decided that as of 1976, we would no longer participate.'

Ontario was an ignominious end to a decade of Suzuki's US racing efforts but it wasn't the end of the machines themselves, nor of young Patrick Hennen; both headed across the Atlantic in the early months of 1976 to renew the battle in Europe.

Nor was it the end of Merv Wright; he too flew to Europe and success far beyond his wildest dreams.

Above Merv Wright (left), and Barry Sheene share a joke with Peter Starr, director of the motorcycling film *On the Limit*, during its shooting at Ontario 1974 *Wright*

Below Dave Aldana, paddock wit and extrovert, gingerly opens the throttle of his XR11 *Archives*

9 Battle of Britain:
Sheene takes command (1970 to 1975)

In 1967, when Suzuki's UK concessionaire Associated Motorcycles collapsed alongside many other British motorcycle manufactures, Hambros Bank stepped in and conducted a holding operation. Two years later, with Suzuki sales at a low ebb, the franchise was secured by the Lambretta-Trojan Group. Chairman Peter Agg had watched Lambretta's sales falling after the early 1960s boom, as supplies from Italy dried up. To him, the acquisition of Suzuki GB was a lifeline. He already realised the marketing benefits of racing, having nurtured Lambretta competition and even manufactured Trojan go-karts alongside McLaren Formula racing cars, but during 1969, in spite of his personal aspirations, racing was low priority; he was too busy sorting out the mess after the take-over.

In these early days, Suzuki GB relied heavily on their dealers' expertise, and Eddie Crooks, a long-standing Suzuki dealer, was often contacted. It was in early 1970 that Crooks—a dedicated racing man—rang Suzuki's technical manager, Rex White, with a proposition.

> WHITE   'Eddie asked me if there was any chance of getting an XR05—as used at Daytona—to race in the Isle of Man. I put the question to Maurice Knight, our sales manager, and he contacted the factory. What we eventually obtained was an XR05 engine, fuel-tank and frame, but fitted with roadster forks and wheels. There wasn't even a seat on it.'

The chassis was designed for Daytona use but with Eddie Crooks' help, White rebuilt the machine ready for its debut in the Isle of Man TT four weeks hence, fitting Ceriani forks and rear brake with a Fontana eight leading-shoe front anchor. A new seat and fairing completed the project.

On Crooks' recommendation, ex-Suzuki factory rider Stuart Graham was enlisted as pilot, agreeing to meet White and Crooks for the Tuesday morning practice on the Island. Rex White arrived on Monday with the XR05 and a few spares—jets and sprockets—meeting up with Crooks and his mechanic Frank Whiteway.

> WHITE   'On the Tuesday morning, Stuart hadn't turned up so rather than waste time, Frank took it out for a practice lap. When he came back he said, "If Stuart Graham can ride that machine, he's a better man than me. It's frightening!"'

When Graham arrived Frank had a word with him.

> GRAHAM   'He said to me, "You can keep that, it's a real pig!" Well I got

on the thing and it really did frighten me to death. It was an absolute sod, it wriggled all over the place. For the time, it had a *lot* of horsepower—it was all low-down stuff—and it certainly was the original wheelie king.'

After just one day on the Island, Graham packed his bags and went home thoroughly disenchanted with the machine. But was it really *that* bad?

GRAHAM 'The wheelbase was nearly four inches shorter than the T500 road bike and the engine was stuck up high in the frame—a typical Daytona banking special. It was totally unsuitable for the Isle of Man. Anyway, we fiddled with dampers and suspension and after literally wiping myself off every wall in the Island, I realised then and there that there was no way that I wanted to be a motorcycle racer. I remember going through Kirk Michael trying to miss the doors on the wrong side of the road to where I should have been, and thinking, "What *am* I doing here?" I told Eddie that I just couldn't manage the machine and I came straight home. I was bitterly disappointed; I have never felt so sick in all my life as I did then. This was the last time that I ever rode a racing machine.'

To improve handling, the swing-arm was lengthened by Manx engineer Des Collins, and in the Senior TT, the machine was ridden by Malcolm Uphill. During the race a broken gear lever was hastily replaced with a vice-wrench but Uphill retired one lap later. He too disliked the handling, but after fitting Norton Roadholder forks he rode the machine at the Ulster GP. Lying 3rd towards race-end, the throttle jammed open and Uphill fell, breaking his thigh. His racing career was over.

The battered machine was returned and lay in Suzuki GB's workshop until September when a youngster and his dad showed some interest. They were Barry and Frank Sheene and they asked to see Maurice Knight, Suzuki's sales manager.

KNIGHT 'They asked if they could look at it, but came back and said it was in a hell of a state and would I let them repair it and send me the bill; Barry said it wouldn't be too much. So I agreed and they turned it into a very nice racing machine, and sent me a bill for £36. From that moment we were truly into the racing scene.'

The XR05 was rebuilt to original specification using Ceriani forks. Sheene's mechanic, Don MacKay, renovated the battered expansion chambers and the completed machine was tested at Snetterton. There, Sheene and Paul Smart agreed that the handling was doubtful and remarked on a power deficiency which was later discovered to be the result of the pistons being assembled back-to-front.

The Sheenes suggested using a Seeley chassis and Suzuki GB agreed to finance the operation. The Seeley Suzuki was to debut at the 1971 Easter Match Races, but Colin Seeley couldn't make the deadline and the machine didn't materialise until May.

A new TT debut was planned, this time with Frank Perris aboard, for although Barry Sheene was racing in the 125 cc and Production TT races he wasn't keen to ride the 500 there. Perris' 3rd place in the Senior TT confirmed Sheene's confidence in the Seeley chassis, and at the post-TT Mallory Park event

Right 'Trying to miss the doors on the wrong side of the road at Kirk Michael', Stuart Graham during 1970 IoM practice *Kirton's*

Far right The rebuilt Seeley Suzuki on which Perris finished 3rd in the 1971 Senior TT, was later raced with a vengeance by Barry Sheene *MCN*

Sheene brought the crowds to their feet with a masterly ride, finishing 2nd to Agostini's TT-winning MV 500. It was a brilliant Suzuki 500 debut for Sheene.

During the remainder of 1971, whenever Sheene rode the Seeley Suzuki, he was the equal of most 351 cc Yamahas in open or 500 cc class racing, and he soon built up a GP reputation aboard his ex-Graham RT67 125 cc model.

In 1971, Jack Findlay, Keith Turner and Rob Bron contested the classics on XR05s and Findlay won the Ulster GP—Suzuki's first 500 cc GP victory. Overall, Turner, Bron and Findlay were 2nd, 3rd and 5th in the World Championships. Over the winter, Sheene successfully raced the Seeley Suzuki in South Africa, where he met a local riding ace, Mike Grant—not to be confused with Yorkshireman *Mick* Grant—and because Sheene had accepted a 1972 Yamaha contract, he recommended Grant to Suzuki GB as his replacement.

By then, Suzuki GB had decided to field *two* Suzuki 500s for 1972 and Frank Perris agreed to ride one of them; a reincarnation of the original 'Daytona' frame fitted with a new XR05 engine. But before the machine was completed, Perris joined Norton as Racing Manager, and the rolling chassis was sold to Eddie Crooks. It was Perris who discovered the cause of the 'Daytona's' ill-handling; the Ceriani forks were two inches too long!

Mike Grant arrived in April intent on contesting the 500 classics with the Seeley Suzuki, then fitted with TR500II engine equipped with 'T'-ports—Suzuki's latest power-boosting inlet port design. Unfortunately, Grant crashed in a Dutch race whilst aboard a Yamaha and he returned to South Africa without having raced the Seeley, which was hastily retrieved from his lock-up garage and returned to Suzuki GB.

For the Easter Match Races, Rex White became involved with the US Suzuki team and their new XR11s. News of their brutal power has been widely reported in the press and the English crowds were impressed by their spectacular speed and frightening wheelies, and Suzuki GB requested a TR750 from the factory. All were already spoken for but Suzuki Japan suggested that they may be

able to borrow one from the Italian Team Europa, who possessed the only TR750 in Europe. The Italian Suzuki concern agreed that Jack Findlay could ride their machine under Suzuki GB supervision at the TT races.

Meanwhile, Roger Sutcliffe agreed to ride the Seeley Suzuki 500 in the Senior TT and Rex White enlisted Suzuki sales representative David Bardsley to help with preparation. Bardsley's brother Bran, a stalwart TT sidecar racer, helped Rex White solve an XR11 braking deficiency noted by Findlay during practice.

During 1971, Sheene fitted a disc rear brake to his Seeley Suzuki (and personalised the seat!) White

WHITE 'We couldn't get the brakes to work but then I realised that the front disc pads had a spherical face and the marks on the discs showed that they hadn't bedded-in properly. I faced off a spare set of pads in Bran Bardsley's lathe, and then early one morning we took the bike up on the mountain and Jack tested the brakes; they were 500 per cent better.'

The Seeley Suzuki was also troublesome, with regular seizures of the right-hand cylinder, and Sutcliffe was lucky to qualify.

SUTCLIFFE 'I *did* qualify on it late in the week—I did two laps on it. We'd pushed the jet sizes up really high and I took it steady just to be sure I qualified. I never gave it maximum revs because it was still rattling a bit. . .'.

Suzuki's garage was a rented mortician's workshop and it was here that Bardsley and White worked on the Suzukis, finally fitting the Seeley with a new cylinder and piston, exhaust system and ignition unit, in their attempt to cure the seizures. Unlike Bardsley, White was uncomfortable working in these morbid surroundings.

WHITE 'All the spare coffins were put on the first floor and Eddie Crooks' lads stored all the spare fairings and screens in them. I never did go up there. They knew I was a bit funny about this and I came into the workshop one day to find coffin handles taped onto my toolbox!'

In the Senior TT, Sutcliffe's Suzuki seized at Kirk Michael but in the F750 race Findlay had a good ride with excellent pit-work by David Bardsley at the two fuel stops—XR11s were *very* thirsty—and collected 3rd place. It was an incredible Island debut for the 'flexi-flier' although Findlay's machine was strengthened by an additional bracing tube in the rear sub-frame.

Findlay and the XR11 returned to Italy whilst the Seeley Suzuki 500 had a few mainland outings in the hands of Stan Woods, Charlie Williams and Kevin Cowley during the remainder of the season.

At the end of 1972, the Seeley Suzuki was eventually bought by Des Collins — Roger Sutcliffe's racing sponsor. In later years Sutcliffe raced the machine in Island events and at the Ulster GP. Collins still owns this machine.

For 1973, Sheene rejoined Suzuki GB with Stan Woods as team-mate. The factory agreed to provide a new XR11 for Woods, and arranged to forward an ex-US Suzuki XR11 engine which Suzuki GB planned to install in a Seeley chassis for Sheene. The factory also supplied twelve new TR500II engines; ten for sale to privateers and two for Team use in new Seeley frames. Seeley himself bought one of the engines and using his Brabham Formula One car chassis development experience, designed and built an all-aluminium monocoque

Barry with father Franko during the amazing £36 transformation of the ex-Uphill Suzuki into the successful Seeley Suzuki of 1971 *MCW*

chassis, the prototype of which was first tested by Woods and Sheene in January 1973. Suzuki GB placed an immediate order for two of these monocoques but Seeley's Formula One committments delayed the project so tubular types had to be supplied instead.

In fact Sheene *raced* the prototype Seeley monocoque at a March Mallory Park event and confirmed the excellent handling, being in a winning position until water in the fuel forced an early retirement. A few days later the new Seeley tubular chassis arrived and mechanics Don Mackay and Dave Hall quickly installed the engines in readiness for the Match Races. The two machines were identical except Sheene's had a drum rear brake, whilst Woods' used a disc.

The objectives of the new Shell-sponsored Team were ambitious; the FIM F750 'Prize' series, and the MCN Superbike and Shellsport Championships, in that order. In early-season short circuit events Sheene and Woods had mixed results with their Seeley Suzuki 500s and eagerly awaited the arrival of the 750s. Sheene's Seeley 750 was tested at Brands Hatch on 28 March where the engine's age became apparent, as first an oil pipe burst and later Sheene had gear selection difficulties. Workshop examination revealed a cylinder without oil drillings, and completely worn out small-end bearings. It was hoped the gear selection would ease with further use.

To gain race experience with the 750, Sheene and Rex White contested the Rouen 200 mile event, but in the first 100 mile leg, the ignition failed and a new unit borrowed from Findlay's Japanese mechanics was fitted. In the second leg Sheene retired when he lost all five gears. A gearbox strip-down indicated the cause; a missing circlip!

After a short spell in England the Team raced at the first F750 round at Imola where Sheene reached 6th place in both legs before retiring, the first retirement caused by clutch trouble, the second due to chain-jumping caused by the lack of a rear hub cush-drive in the Seeley 750. Back in England, White and engineer Ernie Hall worked all night incorporating a cush-drive in readiness for the imminent Match Races.

Sheene's Suzuki 750 UK debut was disappointing, his best result during the Match Races being a 3rd at Oulton Park, but a week later, Sheene broke the lap record at Clermont-Ferrand in winning the French F750 round. Stan Woods finished 4th (aboard his new XR11) without incident.

Following the 'King of Brands' meeting where Sheene was crowned 'King' despite having fallen heavily, Stan Woods contested the TT finishing 5th in the TT Formula 750 event. In the Senior TT—won by Findlay on an XR05— Woods retired after just one lap on his Seeley Suzuki 500. The Suzuki pair then added to their MCN Superbike and Shellsport Championship points by contesting a couple of UK Internationals before leaving for the Swedish F750 round at Anderstorp. There, Sheene took an early lead shadowed by Findlay and Woods who both passed Sheene when his 750 blew an oil seal causing an ignition fault. Sheene hung on to 3rd which hauled him to a 5 point lead in the series, whilst Suzuki Italia's XR11 rider, Guido Mandracchi, finished 4th.

A week later Sheene had his 500 cc World Championship baptism at Imatra in Finland, but whilst holding 4th place he was forced to retire when a piston seizure resulted in a broken con-rod. Within three days the Team raced at Hameenlinna for the Finnish F750 round.

The rare Seeley Suzuki *monocoque* at a Brands Hatch test in January 1973. L to R: Rex White, Barry Sheene and Stan Woods *MCN*

WHITE 'It was such a Mickey Mouse circuit that Barry felt he'd be better off on the 500 but Stan used his 750, and I had to make a new rear sprocket to lower the gearing for the tight circuit. The local Suzuki dealer took a sprocket off a brand-new road bike and we bored out the centre and welded to it a new outer ring with more teeth. Stan did well in that race but the sprocket weighed a ton!'

On his Seeley 500, Sheene finished 2nd to the Finnish rider Lansivuori, with Findlay 3rd, Mandracchi 4th and Woods 5th. Sheene's place consolidated his overall series lead.

Returning to England Sheene then won the important 'Mellano' Trophy at Brands Hatch, despite coming to grief twice on the wet track, and the following weekend the Team arrived at Silverstone for the British F750 round with Sheene in a strong position. In the first leg Sheene finished 3rd and when the head gasket of his Seeley 750 blew whilst warming up for the second leg, he climbed aboard his Seeley 500 and still finished 6th! His aggregate placing was 4th but the FIM jury decided that changing machine—effectively mid-race—was against the rules, and despite official Suzuki GB protests the matter wasn't finally resolved until three weeks later when the ACU ruled that Sheene's score should be discounted. This put Findlay in the overall series lead.

The Team added to their British Championship scores by contesting a handful of UK International events before setting out for the West German F750 round at Hockenheim. Findlay won the first leg followed by Sheene and Woods, whilst Woods won the second leg with Sheene 4th and Findlay out of the points. Woods won on aggregate with Sheene in 2nd and Findlay 5th. Sheene thus regained a slender lead of one point over his team-mate Woods with only one more round to contest.

After the two day drive to Barcelona the Team attempted to cure (permanently) a season-long problem concerning the expansion chambers which were always fracturing. Assistance came from an unusual quarter.

WHITE 'We went to the Bultaco factory and they rebuilt all three of Barry's exhausts — being two stroke experts they were very good at that — and they installed extra rubber blocks to prevent vibration reaching the exhausts.'

The race, held over the twisty Montjuich Park circuit, was won by John Dodds with Mandracchi 3rd and Findlay 4th. By finishing 2nd, Sheene clinched his first major title, whilst Woods — 6th in Spain — secured 4th overall place. Sheene was overjoyed.

SHEENE 'My achievement in winning that Formula 750 title in my debut season on the superbike against quite experienced opposition tends to be overshadowed. I thought I had done rather well but most of the hullaballo was centred on the 'proper' World Championships and I don't think I truly got the recognition I deserved, although that's not meant to sound like sour grapes.'

At the final Brands Hatch meeting, the Team scored well; Sheene narrowly won the overall MCN Superbike Championship in which Woods was 4th, and the overall Shellsport Championship with Woods lying 2nd. In the BP 'Bill Ivy' Championship Woods, Sheene and Paul Smart were equal victors, and to complete his triumph, Sheene's devoted British fans overwhelmingly voted him their MCN 'Man of the Year' later that year.

Despite Castrol sponsorship, Suzuki GB's plans for 1974 were not quite so ambitious nor expensive; Sheene and Woods were recontracted but with Sheene's heavy contractual arrangements with the factory (developing the new RG500) *and* US Suzuki (riding the XR11s) he had little time for anything other than retaining his British Championships. Furthermore, an FIM move early in 1974 reduced the number of F750 Prize rounds to three, removing its prestige.

The two Seeley Suzuki 500s were sold and replaced with a brace of factory TR500III water-cooled machines. The two 750s were retained and Sheene returned from Daytona with the latest factory XR11 which was more powerful and lighter than before.

After dashing all over Europe in 1973, Rex White was disappointed with the Team's objectives and resigned his position with Suzuki GB.

WHITE 'The reason I left was that I was hoping that we'd be able to build on the experience and success we'd achieved in 1973 when we'd been struggling for parts and having to make them and do everything ourselves. But it was decided that for 1974 we'd effectively give Barry and Stan their machines and let them get on with it themselves.'

White moved to North Wales and set up business with Barry Hart whose engineering workshop had helped keep the 1973 Team together. Graham Malyan, Suzuki's service manager took over responsibility for the Team after Rex White left in April 1974.

Woods contented himself by mainly competing in the ACU British Road Racing Championships and other UK Internationals, although he did venture to West Germany for a non-series F750 race which he won. By season-end, Woods had clinched the ACU Championship on his Suzukis, was 2nd in the MCN Superbike Championship, and 4th in the Shellsport series.

Above Sheene powering his 750 cc Seeley Suzuki to victory during the French round of the 1973 FIM F750 Cup Series *MCW*

Above right Riding mainly in UK events during 1974, Stan Woods became a familiar sight aboard his XR11 Suzuki superbike *Archives*

Regularly racing on both sides of the Atlantic, Sheene was fortunate in retaining the MCN Superbike and Shellsport titles, and somehow managed to finish 2nd to Woods in the ACU Championship! With such a busy season he didn't have *time* to contest the F750 Prize series.

Superficially the results weren't too bad, but Suzuki GB decided to exercise more team control for 1975, and when Rex White returned to Suzuki GB in December 1974, plans were laid on a new basis.

WHITE 'When I came back it was with the prime objective of setting up the 1975 race team on a professional basis. We started by recruiting a three man team; Barry and Stan were recontracted and joined by John Newbold. We had three new XR05s, Barry a new XR11, Stan had a 1974 XR11 and John had an XR11 that was built from old bits and pieces.

'During the winter period, we'd ordered two GMC motorhomes which, together with a Bedford 3-ton transporter, were painted in the new Team's livery. Transport wasn't going to be a problem.'

Interest in John Newbold commenced during 1974.

NEWBOLD 'Maurice Knight first approached me about riding Suzuki machines and I had a test on Stan Woods' bike at Oulton Park. But before this test ride, Barry asked me to have a go on his bikes at a Silverstone private practice session although I never rode his bikes there because it was too windy.'

The Team—again with Castrol backing—intended to contest the 500 cc World Championship, the FIM F750 Prize series and defend their MCN Superbike and Shellsport titles. It was a tall order, but the Team commenced with the first F750 round at Daytona, where Stan Woods had a disastrous race finishing in

42nd place! Sheene, riding for US Suzuki, crashed in practice. A Mallory Park spill badly damaged Woods' hand which was further damaged by a crash at the Imola F750 round. Newbold, however, ran for most of the race without a front brake and finished 15th, in this his first F750 event.

Back in England, Heron Corporation had taken control of Suzuki GB—now named Heron Suzuki GB—and for the Mettet round in Belgium, the machines were repainted with an additional yellow stripe and small 'Heron' decals added. There, Sheene teamed up with Newbold, finishing 2nd in the first leg but retiring with broken exhausts in the second. Newbold was placed 6th overall in spite of a broken gear lever and cracked exhausts—a problem that would haunt the Team during the 1975 F750 series. In France at the Magny Cours round, Sheene started in pole and decimated his rivals despite broken exhausts but Newbold had a refuelling problem and lost time whilst the equipment was sorted out. He finished 5th with Sheene the victor.

Stan Woods, though not fully recovered from his injuries, entered the Swedish round at Anderstorp—held the day prior to the Swedish GP—but when other F750 riders forced the organisers to pay them more start money, Woods' entry was refused and he remained in England. Sheene won the first leg and was 2nd in the second leg, taking the overall laurels, but Newbold suffered from the exhaust problem and in the second leg, a crankshaft oil seal blew and he retired, scoring no points. The Team returned to England for the Silverstone round, where Sheene captivated his fans by winning the second leg and the overall round despite a lowly 4th place in the first leg. Delayed by start-line marshals in the first leg, Newbold retired when he realised he was out of contention, but finished 6th in the second leg, again missing out on points.

Johnny Cecotto—a friendly Yamaha rival—won the first leg, but when Yamaha refused to loan him a replacement engine for the second leg, he caused a sensation by coming to the line on Tepi Lansivuori's spare XR11. Cecotto's Suzuki debut was short-lived when he pulled out with a leaking head gasket.

With three outright wins from three starts, Sheene led the series with 45 points against 2nd man Findlay's 29, but at Assen for the Dutch round, Sheene's XR11 misfired in both legs whilst Findlay finished 2nd overall, whittling away Sheene's lead to just 4 points. Newbold finished 3rd overall whilst Woods was disappointing in 11th place. Sheene's mis-fire had been caused by a damaged carburettor which allowed the slide to rotate and over-richen the mixture.

With the title in the balance Sheene couldn't afford to miss the final West German round at Hockenheim, but two weeks before the event, Sheene broke his right leg in a Cadwell Park paddock-bike spree and ended his F750 season as it had commenced; lying in hospital. Suzuki GB went to extraordinary lengths to help Barry win the F750 title; John Williams was recruited to ride Barry's XR11 just for this race and it seemed that if Newbold, Woods and Williams could ensure that Findlay finished lower than 3rd overall, Sheene would capture the title. In the event, Williams had a glorious debut ride, finishing 2nd to Patrick Pons in both legs. Newbold finished 3rd in the second leg—keeping Findlay in 4th—but in the first leg he made a bad tyre choice.

NEWBOLD   'The weather wasn't too good—black clouds and everything—and I ended up putting treaded tyres on and the back one just broke up completely and Jack Findlay beat me. Before the second leg, I was told that

Heavy sponsorship for Suzuki GB's 1975 Team enabled the purchase of two 27 foot GMC Motorhomes, used for support-team living quarters and for general hospitality *Archives*

Injuries baulked Stan Wood's style during 1975 when he again rode the XR11s under the Suzuki GB banner *Archives*

if I beat Findlay it would be alright and I did beat him, but it wasn't so. Barry lost the Championship and I was blamed for choosing the wrong tyres . . .'

Despite the tyre problems Newbold finished 7th in the first leg and 5th overall, and upon his return to England, he immediately visited Barry in hospital to personally explain what had happened, but it wasn't Noddy's day:

NEWBOLD 'There were so many people there it was impossible so I left him a note. When I came back down from seeing him the van was gone. It had been towed away—it hadn't been pinched—it'd been towed away by the police.

'It took a while to smooth it over with Barry . . .'

SHEENE 'I was hoping for a better effort from the other Suzuki Team riders when it came to the final decisive round in West Germany. Findlay did enough to get the points to win with a 4th placing and so that was that. Good luck to him.'

The final F750 tally showed Sheene and Newbold as 2nd and 5th in the series.

Whilst the F750 Prize was being fought in Europe, the three teamsters also contested the *MCN* Superbike and Shellsport Championships. Newbold and Woods finished 4th and 8th in the *MCN* series and Newbold was 8th in the Shellsport series. The final *MCN* Brands Hatch round was dramatic for Suzuki in that Sheene needed support here too, and Suzuki GB fielded no fewer than five riders on Team XR11s, in their attempt to prevent Sheene from finishing lower than 2nd place in the overall results. Mick Grant had already out-scored Sheene before his Cadwell incident and nobody could take points away from Grant or give points to Sheene at Brands Hatch. All they could do was ensure that no other rider out-scored Sheene during the final round. Williams, Newbold and Woods were joined by Percy Tait and Phil Read on the Brands Hatch grid, but at the very first corner—Paddock Bend—virtually the whole field collapsed like a deck of cards in front of millions of TV viewers and the race was restarted with a depleted entry minus Phil Read. It was impossible to prevent Barry Ditchburn winning the race which pushed Sheene down into 3rd overall place in the series. In the classics, Newbold finished 8th overall with Woods 16th—valuable experience nonetheless.

Unfortunately Sheene failed in his Shellsport title attempt, but he could at least look back on a good season; he'd shown GP form that would prove beneficial in 1976 and had won many prestigious events such as the Mallory Park 'Race of the Year'—for the second year running—and furthermore he was again voted the *MCN* 'Man of the Year', undoubtedly due to his gallant and courageous recovery from his horrific 170 mph Daytona spill, which further endeared him to his many fans.

Similarly, taken in isolation, the 1975 results didn't appear to be a fair reflection of the financial support and sheer physical effort poured into the project by Suzuki GB, but taken in context over their six year exposure to the racing scene, they were acceptable. In addition, Suzuki GB's racing experiences would stand them in good stead for the following season when their resources would be stretched to the limit and they would be out to prove themselves not only to the British and Europeans, but to the rest of the motorcycling world.

10 Invasion of Europe: the XRs attack (1971 to 1975)

For 1971, Suzuki agreed to supply semi-factory TR500 (XR05) machines to certain Suzuki importers including those in Italy, Holland and New Zealand. In turn, they sponsored Jack Findlay, Rob Bron and Keith Turner (respectively) to contest the 1971 500 cc World Championship.

Against all but the invincible Giacomo Agostini and his MV Agustas, the Suzukis were highly competitive and Turner became runner-up in the overall series with 2nd places in Austria, East Germany and Sweden amongst his results. With consistent performances, Rob Bron was placed 3rd overall whilst Jack Findlay achieved 1st place in Ulster and finished 5th overall.

Suzuki were elated that with such little effort they had been rewarded with such good results, especially their 2nd place in the World Manufacturer's Championship, So pleased in fact that for 1972, with the new FIM 750 cc class in the offing, Suzuki offered one of the new XR11 machines to Suzuki Italia, whose new rider, Guido Mandracchi, planned to contest the new series. For the 500 cc classics, Suzuki provided him and Rob Bron with the new TR50011 (XR05).

The 1972 500 cc World Championship results were relatively disappointing; Bron finished 13th overall, with Mandracchi 11th, but Mandracchi's XR11 carried him to a 4th place at Misano. For the Isle of Man TT races, Suzuki Italia's XR11 was loaned to Jack Findlay who raced it under the wing of Suzuki GB (see Chapter 9).

The following year, Suzuki Italia were supplied with a new XR11 for Mandracchi who, with Findlay, would also ride new water-cooled XR05s in the classics. Supporting them were factory mechanics Yasunori Kamiya and Shoji Tanaka who bought a Mercedes-Benz truck in which to carry the machines and spares. Their objective wasn't to *win* the 500 cc classics, but to get the measure of the opposition and during the season Makoto Hase, Suzuki's race designer, received many field reports identifying the areas in which the factory MVs and Yamaha excelled over the XR05s.

The power-bonus of the XR05 was produced at higher revolutions, leading to crankshaft failures, but by mid-season, new crankshafts solved the problem. In France, Mandracchi and Findlay were 6th and 10th and at Austria, Mandracchi finished 4th—his last points-scoring ride that year. Findlay won the Senior TT and with a 3rd in Belgium and a couple of 5ths, he finished 5th in the World Championship. Mandracchi was 14th.

For 1974, Barry Sheene was offered three independent race contracts. Suzuki GB wanted him to race the XR05 and XR11 machines in the UK and contest the F750 series with the 750. US Suzuki needed him to race XR11s at Daytona

The 1972 Suzuki Italia squad surround their first XR11. L to R: Patrignani (manager), Gilardi, unknown, Sandro, Emilio, Mandracchi, Findlay, unknown and Miyakawa (director) *Archives*

and other US National Championship meetings. But his biggest commitment was his factory contract to develop Suzuki's 500 cc square-four racer, the XR14 or RG500, in the classics.

Early in the year, Sheene was invited out to Japan to test the new 500 cc machine. There, in spite of its handling deficiencies and its habit of seizing, he reduced the Ryuyo lap record by $1\frac{1}{2}$ seconds!

Suzuki Japan hedged their bets in 1974: veteran GP racer Jack Findlay offset the relatively inexperienced, but quick Barry Sheene. US Suzuki teamster Paul Smart was also signed.

The XR14 made its debut at the French GP at Clermont Ferrand where the Italian MVs of Read and Bonera were threatening, whilst Agostini and Lansivuori were not to be discounted on the factory Yamaha YZR500s! Sheene qualified 4th fastest but experienced plug-oiling in the race and slowed whilst holding 2nd place. However, urged on by a pit signal he swept forth at greater speed, retaining his position only five seconds behind race victor Read. Lansivuori finished 4th, but the Yamaha crew knew then that Suzuki meant business. Smart, who'd broken his arm nine days previously, managed only one painful lap before retiring.

A rider's strike meant that none of the Suzuki teamsters competed at the West German GP but it was business as usual for the Austrian GP at the Salzburgring. There, after a poor start Sheene and Findlay slogged it out in 4th and 5th places until 3rd man Michel Rougerie retired, but by then both the Suzuki riders had been lapped by Agostini's Yamaha and Bonera's MV, such was the pace of the front-line battle. Sheene and Findlay finished 3rd and 4th at the flag putting Sheene and Bonera on equal points in the Championship. After a poor start Smart didn't figure in the results.

Two weeks later, the onslaught was renewed for the Italian classic round at Imola. But here, the factory Suzukis were not on form and Sheene and Findlay qualified in 5th and 6th positions behind the factory MVs and Yamahas. Mixed fortunes befell both Yamaha and Suzuki in the race; Ago's OW20, set a new lap record and then ran out of fuel on the penultimate lap, and Sheene was lying 3rd when his gearbox locked up (a shaft broke) and he went sliding up the road, a regular experience as RG development continued. This accident affected Sheene's eyesight and broke his ankle but after specialist treatment he was soon back in the saddle. Meanwhile, Findlay pressed on, finishing 4th behind Bonera, Lansivuori and Read.

Barry Sheene had requested his factory bosses to give his friend and US Suzuki team-mate, Gary Nixon, a GP ride on the new XR14. The factory agreed that Nixon could test in June at Ryuyo. Nixon and Ken Araoka, a race-shop test rider and another of Barry's US Suzuki team-mates, were lapping on a brace of RGs when Nixon's engine seized a piston. Araoka was riding directly behind and couldn't avoid running into the stricken Nixon. Bikes and riders flew in all directions with the result that Nixon spent most of the remainder of 1974 in hospital.

Sheene was effectively 'psyched out' by the knowledge that the Suzuki could seize so dramatically, and with the memory of his own close inspection of the Imola tarmac fresh in his mind, he started the Dutch TT at Assen with not a little caution. In addition, the Suzuki had exhibited some strange handling traits that the fitting of lower rails to the open-frame design—suggested by Team

mechanic Mitsuru Okamoto—had not totally eradicated. Sheene experimented with tyre brands and compounds, but at Assen, he was not particularly happy with the situation. Nevertheless, he had claimed 4th fastest practice time and in the race scorched through the field to 5th place, but when he thought he heard grating sounds from his gearbox and felt a slipping rear tyre, he decided to retire rather than repeat his Imola act. Findlay had qualified 5th fastest but fell during the early stages of the race, whilst Smart managed one lap before retiring.

The following weekend at Spa Francorchamps, Sheene was back on form, and during the race improved his best practice lap time by 12 seconds. Agostini was out on a new lighter and lower factory 500 Yamaha but couldn't catch the flying Read. By lap 6, Sheene had fought his way to 2nd place when the Suzuki's gear lever fractured and fell off. Sheene retired disappointed, but Jack Findlay finally secured 5th place.

The XR14s were being maintained by a small team of factory mechanics; Yasunori Kamiya—still with the race Team after 15 years—was aided by his old colleague Tadao Matsui, whilst 'Mitsi' Okamoto was enjoying his first year with the Team. This was a hectic period for the mechanics, parts being flown back and forth to Hamamatsu as Suzuki learned of new problems. Each time the machines were raced they were constantly improved and it was clear that when the machines were reliable, they could compete with the best of the opposition. Suzuki *must* win their first grand prix soon!

The Swedish Grand Prix on July 21 became another disappointment for Suzuki. Hopes of victory when Sheene topped the practice leader-board sagged when Lansivuori gained pole position in a last-minute practice session. The race itself had barely settled down when Sheene's water pump failed whilst in the

Above Findlay and Mandracchi shared the 1973 Imola '1000' ride using an XR11. One mechanic is about to add lubricant, another refuels the machine *MCW*

Right Early 1974 XR14s had wire wheels, vertical rear shock absorbers and 'open' frames with the engine supended from the upper frame rails by a cast lug *MCN*

lead. The boiling coolant spilled into the bottom of the fairing and when it splashed onto his tyre, down he went, thrown over the bars and into the catch-fencing. Ago, too, fell in trying to avoid the aerobatic Suzuki rider.

At Imatra, Finland, the Suzuki Team were reduced to one rider, Sheene too sore to ride. Jack Findlay came home 4th in the race that clinched the World Championship for Phil Read.

The Suzuki 500's first race victory came at the August Silverstone International when the now healthy Sheene clawed to the front from a poor start, even though hampered by a lack of rear brake! Sheene's many fans went wild as their hero crossed the line. Now the factory were confident of future GP success.

The final round of the 1974 500 cc classics was at Brno, Czechoslovakia, where the Team were back on full strength. The excitement was provided by the fight for 2nd place in the Championship between Bonera and Lansivuori. Nobody showed interest in Suzuki's efforts to eliminate the handling problems still present. In the race, Sheene's XR14, as well as handling badly, was hampered with plug-oiling trouble, and again his rear brake expired. It was still quick enough to finish 4th with Findlay 7th. It was Sheene's first points-scoring ride since the Austrian GP three months before! The score-sheet shows that when Sheene was able to finish, he averaged 10 points, against Findlay's $6\frac{1}{2}$. To win, however, first one has to finish. Sheene was faster, but possibly harder on the machinery than Findlay.

The final 1974 GP tally showed Sheene in 6th and Findlay 5th, and in addition, Suzuki were 3rd in the 500 cc World Manufacturer's Championship. Not so bad for a development season.

Over the winter, Suzuki improved the machines, pinning their hopes on Barry Sheene and Tepi Lansivuori—both US Suzuki riders for 1975. Neither Jack Findlay nor Paul Smart were re-signed. Suzuki also agreed that Suzuki Italia's Roberto Gallina and Armando Toracca, and Barry's Suzuki GB team-mates, Stan Woods and John Newbold, could have occasional rides.

But Suzuki showed interest in Phil Read—1974 500 cc World Champion—and he was invited to test the 1975 model at Ryuyo. According to Read, Suzuki wanted him as their number one rider, but he eventually declined the offer.

Supporting the riders was a strong team proving Suzuki's commitment to the project. Mitsuo Itoh, Ryosuke Matsuki and Etsuo Yokouchi were successive managers during the season supported by chief mechanic Kamiya and Matsui, Okamoto, Yasuhida Kita and Shoji Tanaka.

The 1975 GP season commenced at Paul Ricard, but Sheene's Daytona spill meant only Tepi started. In pole position! He led eventual winner Agostini by four seconds until a broken gear linkage ended his victory charge. Despite this disappointment, it was clear to the Suzuki squad that the new XR14 wasn't lacking speed.

Sheene was aiming to be fit for the Austrian GP but despite qualifying 6th fastest, and showing track officials medical certificates and his ability to bump start the Suzuki, he was not allowed to start. Whilst Sheene fumed, Lansivuori had a tremendous race finishing 2nd behind Kanaya's Yamaha.

At Hockenheim, Sheene *was* allowed to start, but whilst Tepi blasted towards the front Barry suffered an ill-handling machine that misfired from the start. He stopped for new plugs but shortly retired. Tepi finished in 3rd place and Stan Woods, having his 500-4 debut, placed 5th. Barry's machine was later found to be grossly over-jetted, hence the misfire.

For the Italian GP Suzuki fielded four riders; Sheene, Woods, Toracca and Gallina. Lansivuori had broken a collar bone in a practice spill, but in the race both Gallina—who later retired—and Woods, suffered from misfires. Whilst Sheene was scrapping with leaders Agostini and Read, Woods—finishing 5th—

Below left Sheene kitted out for a wet stint with his 1974 XR14 *MCW*

Below By late 1974, the XR14 frame was of full loop design and Campagnolo cast magnesium wheels were fitted. L to R. unknown, Shoji Tanaka, Saitoh, Kamiya, Murai and Matsui *Gruber*

was lapped, and when a vital screw within Sheene's gearbox came adrift he was left with only one gear and retired. Ex-MV rider Toracca—the fastest Suzuki qualifier in 3rd—finished 4th in his Suzuki debut ride.

This unreliability of a machine that would be dominating the classics within a year may seem incredible, but the Yamaha 500 took two years of development before *its* first World Championship. Thrashing a machine around Ryuyo is no substitute for the white heat of grand prix competition where missed gears burst engines, swift changes of line viciously over-stress chassis components and knuckle-white braking is left to the last micro-second in order to gain the advantage. Such fire cannot be simulated at Ryuyo. Only when a machine can pass the supreme test, the grand prix test, can it lay claim to victory. Suzuki were barely out of the development phase by mid 1975....

The five week lull before the Dutch TT enabled more permanent modifications to be made to the machines. Sheene raced to a convincing win at Chimay in Belgium, whilst the mechanics sorted out the bogies.

John Newbold had been campaigning his XR05 in the GPs with little success, but at Assen, his fortunes changed overnight.

NEWBOLD 'The factory said they'd got a spare bike so I just went to Assen and the 500-4 was there for me to use. It performed like a 750 but was so much lighter, even lighter than the 500 twin. On the twin, I thought that if I finished in the first half-dozen, I was having a good ride: when I got onto the four I knew I'd got the best bike in the race, so I *had* to get a good result.'

Three factory machines went to the line; Lansivuori, Newbold and Sheene, the latter in pole position. Sheene and Ago drew away from the battle for 3rd, dicing around the track to the delight of the crowd. Sheene was learning that races are often won by tactics, and by employing a ruse, fooled Ago into thinking he knew at which point, and on which side of the Yamaha, he would pounce for the lead. Further back, Newbold was having the race of his life and passed Tepi whose

Below right Lansivuori at speed on his XR14 in 1975. Tepi was Sheene's team-mate on both sides of the Atlantic that year *MCW*

Below Sheene was in devastating form and claimed victory at the 1975 Swedish GP. Compare the fairing design, swing-arm and rear suspension mountings with that of the 1974 XR14 opposite *MCW*

steering damper had broken its mount. On the final lap, Sheene launched his attack, surprising the Italian star, powering his Suzuki to its first—and his first—500 cc World Championship victory. Newbold and Lansivuori were 4th and 5th. It was Newbold's best GP result to date. Suzuki's celebrations went on until the early hours when the Japanese relayed the full story to Hamamatsu.

Suzuki's historic win hit the headlines of the motorcycle press, and the pundits gambled on a repeat at Spa the next weekend, where Newbold was again offered an XR14 ride. Sheene was determined to prove the journalists' intuition. In the race he stalked leader Read, but Sheene could lap quicker having already smashed the lap record in practice, and was choosing his moment as with Ago at Assen. With two laps remaining, Barry decided to move. He was just entering the longest straight when he felt his engine vibrating. He knew the primary gear fixing bolts were shearing and had to make a tough decision; to continue and risk his neck, or retire. He retired. . . . Newbold on the other XR14 flashed by his stranded team-mate to inherit 2nd place whilst Read grabbed the winner's laurels. Lansivuori retired with a seized engine.

But for Newbold, it was the end of his Cinderella life-style. He was not to ride the four again that year, (except at a Brands Hatch International) and returned to his faithful XR05.

NEWBOLD 'I was riding it better afterwards; I'd got some points in the Championship so I thought I'd better do as well as I could.'

Newbold's XR14 results proved the benefits of the power and acceleration of thoroughbred factory machines. Only in Holland and Belgium did he finish in the first six places during the 1975 classic season.

Sheene's failure galvanised the Team into action. Yasunori Kamiya rushed back to Japan with the broken primary shaft in his bag. A few days later he returned with four re-designed one-piece shafts machined from steel billets, which were fitted to four of the five Team XR14s. Such was the pace of development that year.

Two weeks later, sitting in pole on the Anderstorp grid, Sheene was even more single-minded. He decimated his rivals winning at record speed, whilst poor Tepi crashed in the early stages. Newbold had hoped for a third factory ride, but with the old type primary shaft in the spare machine, he had to ride his XR05 Last away, he was up to 4th when Alex George fell, bringing him down as well.

Sheene's elation was short-lived. At Imatra his XR14 was too rich, and misfiring, he retired, whilst Tepi, racing on home ground, raised the roof by finishing second. At the final round in Czechoslovakia, Sheene retired again when his XR14 rumbled. Lansivuori, in 2nd place, also retired when on the last lap, his XR14 suffered clutch problems. Toracca, having his final factory Suzuki ride, didn't figure in the results.

Suzuki's final World Championship tally put Lansivuori in 4th overall, and Sheene 6th—as in 1974. Already rumours of an improved Suzuki GP machine for 1976 were circulating. Some even spoke of a 750 cc version of the XR14 for F750 use! It was no secret that Suzuki intended to produce an over-the-counter version of the 500-4, and in 1976 virtually every GP rider worth his salt campaigned an RG500 MkI.

But before the end of the year, Suzuki Japan made an announcement that rocked the racing fraternity, not the least, Barry Sheene.

11   Masters of technology:
Champions of the World (1976 and 1977)

Suzuki's massive research programme to produce the four stroke GS roadster trimmed Suzuki's 1976 racing budget. It was impossible to provide the support to GP racing that riders had previously enjoyed, and rather than settle for second best, Suzuki reluctantly announced their withdrawal.

Peter Agg, Heron Suzuki GB's chairman and managing director, was horrified. Having enlisted the financial backing of Gerald Ronson, Heron Corporation's chairman, he flew to Japan to attempt a salvage operation. He argued that Heron Suzuki had persevered in fielding a professional racing team against all the odds and that they certainly had sufficient experience.

In Hamamatsu, he consulted the UK board who agreed to finance a full-scale racing team themselves. Peter Agg, a long-time racing enthusiast, privately bolstered the racing budget but Suzuki Japan would need to supply the machines and spares.

AGG   'We were disappointed that Suzuki had chosen to withdraw from racing, but we understood and accepted their reasoning. We were flattered that they had such confidence in Suzuki GB Racing that they entrusted us to run a full grand prix Suzuki Racing Team in 1976.'

Peter Agg commenced by recruiting a new Team manager, Merv Wright.

WRIGHT   'In November 1975, Gerald Ronson and Peter Agg stopped by at Los Angeles, and I met them at the Beverley Hills Hotel where we kicked the idea around and it eventually transpired.'

Merv Wright temporarily left US Suzuki, joining Heron Suzuki GB in January 1976. Whilst Wright totally controlled Team organisation, rider recruitment wasn't his responsibility. Stan Woods was dropped whilst 'Noddy' Newbold was retained, to be joined by John 'Willy' Williams whose 5th place in the 1975 500 cc classics had bettered Sheene's. But there were problems.

WRIGHT   'Barry liked to have on the Team people who were physically incapable of beating him, and I think he knew damn well he was going to have an awful lot of trouble on the racetrack with John Williams. Barry was distinctly worried about that.'

Moreover, Sheene wasn't keen on a trimmed contract fee.

SHEENE   'I wasn't at all happy with the original offer made by the British set-up and would have been prepared to have ridden independently if that was their last offer. . . . Happily, the fee was upped one hell of a lot and so I signed for them.'

For mechanics, Barry chose his father, Franko, and Don Mackay. Williams relied on Bob White whilst Noddy's tuner was Martyn Ogborne. With the race-shop re-housed at Beddington Lane, Croydon, the mechanics gave the interior a new coat of paint, and Peter Agg again personally supplied the Team with a lathe, pillar drill, and other equipment whilst Wright had brought with him almost the entire contents of US Suzuki's defunct race-shop, mostly XR11 spares and equipment.

> WRIGHT 'The first two or three weeks I was there, Peter Agg, Maurice Knight and myself were involved in some heavy-duty negotiations with Texaco and Forward Trust; organising colour schemes for the bikes, leathers, and transporters. We had a literal face-change in the entire organisation and it all occurred in the space of about four weeks, at which point we hit the road for Daytona.'

This was the factory's first involvement with sponsored racing and the resultant stickers; they didn't want travelling bill-boards running around the racetracks and there was much discussion over whose name should go where without upsetting others. A compromise was reached and the Team was named 'Texaco Heron Team Suzuki'.

Their objectives were the 500 cc World Championship, *MCN* Superbike and Shellsport series and the FIM Formula 750 series. The latter took the lowest priority because the XR11s were uncompetitive (being old 1975 models) and some F750 events clashed with World Championship rounds.

> WRIGHT 'We had hoped to share the laurels, but logistically—without having four sets of vehicles and personnel—we couldn't make it to all the races. As it was, our itinerary was really mind-boggling; we seemed to be doing every bloody race on the face of the earth!'

At Daytona, the XR11s were reliable in training, but the riders knew that Daytona's unique terrain imposed abnormal strains on 'bolt-ons'—items such as tyres and chains—but duplicating Daytona's conditions anywhere else was difficult.

> WRIGHT 'Racing is very, very much psychological—probably as much as 80 to 85 per cent—and the rider has got to feel totally confident when he goes out on that racetrack, and if he's got any concern in his mind whatsoever regarding such safety items as tyres, I would prefer that choice to be *his*.'

Daytona 1976 was the first occasion when Suzuki's fuel-stops went smoothly, mainly because Wright had trained each mechanic to concentrate on only one role.

> WRIGHT 'This was never possible in the past; there'd be bloody people all *over* the pits. It was like a Chinese fire drill with people literally falling over each other.'

In the race, Sheene's chain gave up on lap 48, Newbold's on the same lap, and John Williams fell on lap 35. Three DNF's....

> WRIGHT 'Williams was very "dingy" when we picked him up—almost

Sheene looks nonplussed during a 1976 Daytona training period as Roger Saunders (Dunlop) inserts his pyrometer in the XR11's rear tyre. Others, L to R: Gordon Whitehead, Tony Mills (Dunlop), Don Mackay and Martyn Ogborne *MCW*

unconcious—and he couldn't recall what had happened; the brakes hadn't seized, neither had the engine.

'Daytona is the most *boring* race that I've ever been to, but it's always been very high priority for the Japanese and it's rather tragic that Suzuki has had so many near misses. They desperately wanted to win Daytona. .. .'

Meanwhile, some Venezuelans were offering travelling assistance to entice F750 teams to Caracus' first F750 event two weeks later. Wright obtained Croydon's sanction and three mechanics drove to Miami where the Venezuelans provided transport aircraft. Barry Sheene was already in Japan testing the new GP machines, whilst injured Willy was en route to the UK. Gordon Whitehead, a senior Team member, joined Wright and Martyn Ogbourne for the Ryuyo tests which proved anti-climatic to Barry Sheene.

SHEENE   'I went out to Japan . . . to have final test rides on the so-called "special" RG500 four cylinder jobs that Suzuki had modified for me. They went well but there was nothing to shout about. When I went around the track on the production RG500 I was lapping at only half a second slower, so, in a way, their development work hadn't been shattering. . . .
'My 1976 racers had a little more horsepower, were slightly lighter and were said to have better handling characteristics when compared to any other 500 cc Suzuki available. It was due to Hase's careful and shrewd work that this had been made possible.'

Wright, Sheene and Ogborne then returned to typical Venezuelan hospitality.

WRIGHT   'When we arrived, they took away our passports—and we were in a mildly hostile country anyway—and then we were shepherded off to a hotel in the middle of Caracus.'

Much worse, the machines had disappeared, but the local Suzuki dealer, Motolandia, solved this problem *and* let them use their workshop.
Super-fit Sheene coped well with the heat during the race at San Carlos, but broke a con-rod leaving Newbold to finish 2nd to Gary Nixon, a result that was later scrapped by the FIM after Steve Baker disputed the result.

WRIGHT   'Venezuela was a total fiasco, a nightmare from the word go!'

Merv Wright's policy was for each rider to contest the classics on identical machines, and he says Suzuki Japan agreed, but when the new 54-54 XR14s arrived his plans went awry.

WRIGHT   'Somehow or other, Barry was able to commandeer all three of the new machines. One as his main bike, one as a spare and the other became known as his "International" bike. As it turned out, Willy and Newbold both ended up with the old XR14s which were very, very tired.'

Each were supposed to have a spare, but Suzuki GB had only one so they went the entire season with one out-dated spare between them.

BOB WHITE   'In theory, it was supposed to be a Team, but then it really started to show that it wasn't. We just had to accept this. Barry was the number one which everyone accepted, but my philosophy in racing has always been that you beat the man on the circuit.'

The Team started its European trek with the Imola F750 meeting where Sheene and Newbold finished 3rd and 6th on aggregate. But Newbold fell at Paul Ricard and his back injury layed him up until the Italian GP. After the Easter Anglo-American Match Races where Sheene was top-scorer, the depleted Team arrived at Le Mans for the opening classic round. There, Willy fell after stuffing an expansion chamber into the French tarmac whilst Sheene went on to victory.

In France, the Suzukis met the new 110 dB(A) noise limit—at a 5 bhp cost—but were the only machines in compliance. The FIM extended the dead-line to July! Meanwhile, at the Austrian GP, Sheene's quiet Suzuki led his noisy rivals over the line again. Luckless Williams crashed into some straw bales injuring his foot when a crazy marshal jumped onto the track in front of him. At the hospital it was found that his foot had been broken since his Daytona prang!

After a Cadwell Park meeting the Team had another long drive to Mugello for the Italian GP where Newbold returned but had to retire with engine problems, leaving Sheene and Read to fight it out.

WRIGHT   'It was possibly the best *race* in the entire GP schedule.
Initially, Read, Sheene and Agostini had a three-way ding-dong until Ago's ignition went. Then, Barry and Phil got into a monumental race, but Barry finally pipped him by about half-a-wheel on the final sprint up to the flag.'

The Belgian and French F750 rounds at Nivelles and Nogaro followed. In Belgium Sheene retired and Newbold was 4th, whilst neither scored in France; Barry retired and Newbold didn't qualify.

Wright's Team logistics now came under strain.

WRIGHT   'That weekend, we raced in France on Sunday, a Bank Holiday

Encouraged by a determined fan, John Williams pushes home in the 1976 Senior TT, his XR14 transmission broken. Maurice Knight thought he'd run out of fuel *Manx Press*

Brands International on Monday, and at 5.00 am on Tuesday we were on the practice grid in the Isle of Man. People think that you go to a race Sunday morning, pull your shiny motorcycles out of a truck, rush around a racetrack, put them back in the truck, and go home to pick your nose until Saturday and then drive off for the next race. It's not quite like that . . . . After the Sunday race, we'd get out of the circuit on Monday and then face a long journey to the next race track. We'd arrive with a completely clapped-out bunch of motorcycles in the van which you've then got to tear apart and totally rebuild for the Thursday practice. This goes on week in week out, for seven or eight months. It's literally 25 hours a day, eight days a week.'

Other Croydon-based Suzuki staff didn't understand.

WRIGHT   'You'd come back to Beddington Lane and everyone would say what a good time we must have been having. It gets to you after a while.'

But Wright was about to become embroiled in a problem involving his relationships with Williams and Sheene. The TT was to be contested by Williams whilst Sheene preferred to race at Chimay in Belgium—an unscheduled Team-event—but the TT was more prestigious and Wright went with Williams.

Below Williams commences the last lap of the 1976 Belgian GP closely followed by teammate Sheene. Within seconds, Sheene's XR14 faltered and he was lucky to finish 2nd *Castricum*

WRIGHT   'I think this is where the first rift with Team Sheene—as opposed to Team Suzuki—occurred. There was a colossal amount of shit-stirring went on about the spare parts we took for Willy. I didn't load the truck—Bob White did that—and possibly did shovel the shelves into the truck. If that was indeed the case, I'd say with good cause.'

WHITE   'We took everything we could possibly think of needing to the Isle of Man, and I've been going there for a very long time. You need everything bar the kitchen sink. As for spares, there was nothing Barry needed, he carried all his own spare wheels and engine spares.'

During the Senior TT, Williams broke the lap record set by Mick Grant, but from the start couldn't disengage the clutch. Meanwhile, Suzuki GB's sales director Maurice Knight was concerned about the Suzuki's fuel-stop schedule. At the planned half-distance pit stop, Williams reported his clutch problem which caused re-starting difficulties; another good reason supporting Wright's fuel plan.

WRIGHT   'I distinctly remember Maurice pointing to the weather vane and saying "If you run out of petrol, your balls are going to be hanging from that weather vane!"'

Meanwhile, Williams has a very healthy lead but then a gear selector spring broke causing unpredictable gear selection. On the final lap at Governor's Bridge dip, he couldn't find a low gear, or disengage the clutch, and stalled the motor. It was impossible to restart and with a superhuman effort, he pushed in to 7th place. Everyone thought he'd run out of fuel, but examination showed there were $1\frac{1}{2}$ pints in the tank.

In the classic race Willy made amends, winning by well over a minute from Alex George's Yamaha.

Sheene returned from Chimay triumphant, and the whole Team raced with success at the Mallory Park Post-TT meeting before leaving for Assen.

At the Dutch TT Sheene was 22nd off the line from pole position but his powerful XR14 took him past 14 riders in the first lap! Sheene was 2nd on lap 2 and took the lead after 4½ laps. If that performance didn't demonstrate Sheene's mid-range power-bonus, nothing would and he was in devastating form in spite of the freak heat-wave which caused other riders to retire through heat-exhaustion. Assen was Sheene's 4th successive GP win. Newbold retired with chassis problems and Williams finished 6th.

It was now theoretically possible for Sheene to clinch the Championship at the Belgian GP the following week but by now, Wright was becoming concerned at Sheene's involvement with personal sponsors who were attracted by his flambuoyant lifestyle and, of course, his GP victories. But Heron Suzuki GB relied on their *own* sponsors; Texaco, Heron, Forward Trust and Suzuki Japan who supplied the hardware.

WRIGHT 'These people were paying very substantial sums of money for the privilege of having their names on the motorcycles. Then at the racetracks, Barry would come out with "Mashe" jeans stickers on the motorcycle, and I would be two paces behind ripping them off because they were not supposed to be there. It clearly stated in absolute terms in the contract to that effect.'

SHEENE 'Mashe may have been splashed all over the bike and my leathers that season but that was nothing to do with Suzuki. That was a private contract of my own with the French jeans company for whom I had to promise to wear their products when in the public eye. I always did as well!'

But Sheene's *Suzuki* contract required him to wear *Suzuki* clothing—a point of conflict on a number of occasions. How does Maurice Knight see these problems?

KNIGHT 'There certainly was some agony with the fact that very seldom would he wear Suzuki clothing; very seldom would he promote the name Suzuki. In fact, we once fined Barry £5000 for wearing a Yamaha tee-shirt in public! I think Barry lost sight of the fact that the machine was as important as he was—it had done an awful lot to get him where he was.'

At Spa-Francorchamps, Sheene had his two 54-54 XR14s whilst Noddy and Willy persevered with old XR14s.

WRIGHT 'Williams and Newbold were never allowed near Barry's bikes, even though he always vehemently denied there was any advantage in the bikes, but he sure as hell protected them whilst saying this. The fact that Barry guarded them so jealously made you realise that there *was* something worth guarding.

'What turned into a potentially ugly situation at Belgium was that in the latter stages of practice, Michel Rougerie, who was running a private RG500, went through his last set of pistons and was out of the final qualifying session. I suddenly looked out onto the racetrack and there was Rougerie thrashing around on Barry's spare 54-54! Not only did he come back with eyes like the proverbial soup-plates, shaking his head in disbelief, he was 4th fastest and ended up on the front row of the grid! You don't climb onto a strange bike and go around *that* quickly, if there isn't something exceptionally good about that motorcycle.'

Newbold and Williams and particularly Bob White, weren't impressed.

WHITE 'We got a bit upset over that. Other people could ride the factory bikes but our riders couldn't.'

Rougerie wasn't allowed to ride the XR14 in the race—Wright saw to that—but finished 4th on his private RG500.

During the race, which Barry had had shortened by two laps, Sheene and Williams battled for the lead whilst Newbold had primary shaft problems and eventually finished 9th. Williams led towards the latter stages, whilst Barry's engine misfired with fuel problems.

Motocourse 1976–77 'John eased off on the last lap of the race, intending to let Sheene go into the lead and collect the victory that would put his Championship beyond all doubt. John waited, and waited, and waited, but Barry did not overtake. When Williams glanced over his shoulder, Barry was not there! And as John just dawdled towards the flag Barry, with a persistent misfire that looked as though it might oil the plugs and stop him altogether, crawled home 2nd . . . Williams, the reluctant winner, was almost embarrassed by his success. . . .'

As if by ESP, Williams had forseen this situation.

WHITE 'Before the race, John told a reporter called George Turnbull, that if he found himself in a position to beat Barry, he would stop on the line and let Barry cross in front of him. John never used to say much— deep down he always wanted to beat Barry. He knew in his own mind that he had the ability to beat him. On equal bikes there would have been no two ways about it, but he wouldn't have ridden to beat Barry, but ridden to back him up. He would have been a good team man. We were a team. . . .'

By finishing 2nd at Spa, Sheene needed only a further 10 points (3rd place) to clinch his Championship.

The following weekend at Snetterton, Barry's Championship hopes were almost ruined when a mechanic omitted to fit the front brake pad retainers to his XR14. At the end of a straight he had an accident when the pads flew out.

SHEENE 'I hurtled into the banking and went end over end. Sheer luck prevented it from being a bloody major spill . . . I felt decidedly secondhand. . . .'

Ironically, Fabergé—a sponsor for Barry Sheene—were shooting footage for a TV commercial, and the incident was captured on film!

Amazingly enough Barry had further problems in Sweden.

WRIGHT 'Just prior to practice, Barry and I were looking over the bike and Barry said, "Look at that!" The pads were all in place with the screws, but one pad on one side was in back-to-front with the metal backing plate against the disc! To my surprise Barry thought it amusing and laughed.'

And more problems:

SHEENE 'My number one bike had to be rebuilt after the Snetterton mishap and . . . we noticed there were the wrong triple clamps on that particular machine. There were other problems too — we had no record of the right pressures to use in the air forks and my number two bike had been given the wrong gearbox.

'It was difficult to lay the blame at anyone's feet but somewhere there had been a right cock-up. Don and Franko weren't at fault; it was a case of being sent the wrong parts from the stores at Croydon. Michelin had also sent me the wrong tyres.'

In the race, after a poor start, Sheene eventually cleared the pack, gaining the lead six laps from the chequered flag. He raced on to win the Swedish GP and his first — and Suzuki's first — 500 cc World Championship. Newbold finished 10th.

In spite of their rivalry, Barry almost certainly saved the life of John Williams during practice for the Swedish GP when Willy again crashed and Sheene stopped to clear his blocked throat.

Meanwhile, with Willy again in hospital, and Barry having withdrawn from the remaining GPs, Newbold contested the Finnish GP alone. Merv Wright joined him.

WRIGHT 'Imatra was a classic case of mind over matter. Noddy was pottering around and I put out a fairly rude sign to him, to the effect, "Get your finger OUT!" at which he promptly broke the lap record and improved his race position.'

Newbold finished 4th in the race which saw the unscheduled debut of a new Suzuki rider.

WRIGHT 'We actually gave Tom Herron a ride on Willy's 500. He acquitted himself rather well in practice, but in the race, his plugs fouled.'

The Team now raced on home ground. First at the Brand's 'Hutchinson 100' event where Barry scored a hat-trick of victories delighting his many fans, then at Silverstone for the British F750 round. Sheene was 2nd in the first leg but a broken crank in his aging XR11 forced retirement in the second, dismaying the crowds and upsetting Barry himself. Newbold, however, had a good ride and finished 4th.

With Sheene no longer contesting the classics, and Williams still injured, Newbold made a valiant attempt to improve his own World Championship standing on his 1975 XR14. At Brno, Czechoslovakia, he lay 2nd to Lansivuori who on the last lap, ran out of fuel and Newbold swept by to his first classic victory. At the Nürburgring in West Germany, he was placed 4th.

The classic season had been a Suzuki demonstration; the first 12 places were filled with Suzuki riders, mostly on production RG500s. Newbold placed 5th and Williams 9th but for Suzuki and Barry Sheene, it had been a record year. Suzuki had won the 500 cc World Championship *and* the World Manufacturer's Championship in a clean sweep.

At Sheene's Wisbech home, Franko had converted one of Barry's special XR14s into a 'Superbike' by fitting larger 56 mm pistons, upping capacity to 532 cc. With this machine, Sheene eventually won the *MCN* Superbike Series

Rapid changes in fairing design improved performance and the 'Donald Duck' type of Sheene's 1977 XR14 was soon superseded. In the quest for lightness, Suzuki even modified the chain-adjusters to single-bolt types *MCW*

overall after a hard battle with Mick Grant.

In the Assen F750 round, both Newbold and Williams competed—Sheene raced at Scarborough that day—but whilst Willy was placed 13th, Newbold finished in 4th. At the final F750 round at Hockenheim, West Germany, Newbold again finished 4th overall having won the first leg but crashed and remounted in the second. Williams finished in 7th overall, still not on top form after his many tumbles. In the final count, Newbold was 3rd in the F750 series aboard his 'bitza' XR11.

Crowning a successful year, Sheene claimed the Shellsport title with Williams 4th and Newbold 5th, the latter pair claiming 5th and 10th in the *MCN* Superbike Series.

After a tough season for Merv Wright, who had commenced the year with such high personal aspirations, it was the end of the line.

WRIGHT   'I looked upon the first year as an exploratory thing so that in the future, we could look into running it realistically as a business venture. It became apparent as the year went on that racing was indeed a business although *we* weren't engaged in it per se as a business. We were supposed to be in it for the sport, but there was really no sport. It was just a great big back-stabbing affair.

'On paper we had a very successful year too; of the four Championships that we attempted to contest, we won three, and finished 3rd in the F750. We had contested 103 races in 17 countries in $7\frac{1}{2}$ months. . . .'

'In a nutshell, it was no *fun*; nobody was really enjoying it. At the end of the year there was just so much unnecessary aggravation that I wasn't sure

that I wanted any more of it. And then the proposal was made that for the next year it would be organised differently—by persuing this independent Team thing against which I'd been battling all year—I could see that there was no way in holy hell that something like that could work. So we mutually agreed that it's been fun, thank you very much. Sayonara.

'It was just one of those once-in-a-lifetime opportunities that may or may not have been silly, but in retrospect, something I wouldn't have missed for the world.

I've always been a road-race freak. . . .'

With Merv Wright back in Southern California, Rex White was reinstated as Team coordinator. Sheene signed his contract knowing that for 1977, he would be responsible for his own 'team'—transport, hotels, mechanics—and his retainer adjusted accordingly. Newbold and Williams left the Team for their own reasons, replaced by US rider Pat Hennen and British Champion Steve Parrish. Martyn Ogborne stayed with Heron Suzuki to become the Team's chief technician and to coordinate the riders' efforts at each meeting where they would assemble as a composite Team.

The Team were provided with four RG700 XR23s—two for Sheene, one each for Hennen and Parrish—and new XR14s for the GPs. With no homologated 750s—the XR11s were pensioned off—Suzuki dropped out of the new F750

World Championship, the new XR23s to be used in UK 'open' events. The Team hoped to retain the 500 cc World Championship and their *MCN* Superbike and Shellsport Titles.

Sheene's team consisted of Franko and Don Mackay whilst Hennen employed New Zealander Mike Sinclair and American Frans VandenBroek, all managed by brother Chip Hennen. 'Big' Martin Brookman prepared Parrish's mounts.

Despite the Venezuelan's poor record of 1976, the FIM granted them classic status for 1977; the season opened at the San Carlos track where Sheene took top honours with Hennen and Parrish in 3rd and 9th places.

The new 652s arrived and Hennen went to Snetterton for private practice.

HENNEN   'The handling seemed to pose a problem with a wobble.
Everyone was immediately worried that this was a permanent feature of the bike but as soon as we took them to Brands Hatch, it was no problem at all. The bikes were quite good. Afterwards, we realised the problem was actually caused by the treaded tyres.'

Using these machines, the Team contested the Anglo-American Match Races where Hennen became top-scorer over the six race series. The Brands round was run as a UK National meeting, and slick tyres were banned. Many riders, including the Suzuki teamsters boycotted the *MCN* Superbike race.

HENNEN   'Putting the new RG700 on a rain or intermediate tyre was really crazy. Even in a short race, you'd be lucky to have half a tyre left by the time you got back. It was just in the interests of safety.'

At the next Cadwell round of the *MCN* Series, the Team, using their 652s, scored a hat-trick; Sheene, Hennen and Parrish!

The three riders then packed their trucks at Croydon ready for the Team's first slug at Continental GP races. The key to classic victory seemed to lay with spares availability and Chip Hennen decided to mastermind the spares material, his Bedford transporter becoming the Team stores.

The Austrian GP saw the riders in revolt after a practice fatality and the teams moved north to Hockenheim and the German GP. There, Sheene romped home at record speed with Hennen and Parrish in 2nd and 4th. Steve Baker's Yamaha OW35 was seen as *the* threat to Suzuki—he'd split the Suzuki Team. Maximum points again for Sheene in Italy put him 17 points ahead of Baker, whilst Parrish was 11th, but here at Imola, Hennen fell badly.

HENNEN   'I'm still not really convinced it was purely pilot error, because of the fairings we were using—the area of them. They were quite sensitive to side-loads from the wind, and my riding style meant I was dependent on the front wheel, and at the Grande Curve, it was obviously light, and suddenly, *no* steering!'

Hennen's low-crouching style was suggested by his brother Chip to move the centre of gravity forward and thus assist steering. It seemed to work
MCW

As explained elsewhere, many fairing developments were progressing in 1977 and this was just one of them. Hennen's painful knee was treated by GP medical specialist, Dr Costa but Pat wasn't really fit for the French GP. In the race won by Sheene, he finished 10th, with Parrish 6th.

HENNEN   'At Paul Ricard, I wasn't in that good a condition physically, but after Imola, I wasn't really sold on the tyre I was using, so we spent a lot of time in France experimenting with different brands. In the race I just cruised around.'

After the traditional pre-TT Brands Hatch event a small private aeroplane piloted by Manxman Dennis Brew, lifted off from a field behind the circuit. Inside were Hennen and his crew, off to their TT debut. As usual, Sheene went to Chimay, winning the 750 race on his 652 and finishing 2nd in the 500 cc event. Hennen had already ridden around the Island in February but now he was determined to put in as much practice as possible.

> HENNEN 'The TT's quite fun, you don't mind the natural hazards so much if you can learn where you're going, and the only thing is it takes a real long time to truly learn the course. If you stayed there a month, your lap times would continue to fall every day, so I just kept working on that base and covering as much ground as I could before the race.'

John Williams, a TT expert, agreed to ride a Team XR14 in the Senior and classic races and Phil Read, making an Island return rode a factory-engined private RG500.

The history of Read's engine is quite remarkable. Martyn Ogborne recalls its engine number immediately, 1011. He first saw it in 1975 in Lansivuori's factory machine. When Newbold's 1976 XR14—a 1975 model—arrived in Croydon, he was pleased to see the engine number was 1011. During the winter of 1976–77, Hennen was loaned the engine to contest the 'Marlboro' series down-under which he won. Now at the TT, Read would also use this same old engine—now an XR14 museum-piece—to win the Senior.

In that event, Williams' machine seized on lap 1 but Hennen finished 5th in his first ever TT, with Parrish 16th. During the classic, Hennen, astride his 652 cc machine, lay second to Mick Grant whilst Williams had to stop to remove a rag from his radiator. Riding eratically as he tried to catch the leaders, Williams crashed and retired. Then Hennen's crank broke, leaving Grant an easy winner.

At the Post-TT Mallory International, Sheene cleaned up whilst Hennen had trouble in becoming re-accustomed to short-circuit scratching after his TT safe-riding technique, a TT rider's occupational hazard.

At the Dutch TT, the crowds went wild as Dutchman Wil Hartog led the field until Christian Estrosi passed him. Sheene and Hennen were behind waiting when Estrosi fell on the damp track leaving Hartog to take the flag ahead of Sheene and Hennen. The partisan crowds went wild!

One week later at Spa, Sheene had a record-breaking dice with Michel Rougerie who eventually retired leaving Sheene an easy winner from Steve Baker and Pat Hennen, with Parrish 5th. Then it was back to England where Hennen won the Snetterton 'Race of the Aces' before sailing over to Sweden. At Anderstorp, Sheene again had to work hard, raising the lap record by 2 seconds in his long battle with Cecotto's OW35 works Yamaha—his first GP since his Salzburgring accident in May. Parrish was 4th with Hennen 10th. Sheene, with 102 points, led Baker by 34 points but with 45 points still available in the remaining rounds, he had to race at Imatra, a natural circuit he disliked, to defend his position.

During the race, Hennen retired when his clutch bearing broke up. Sheene slowed, *his* Suzuki overheating. Later, Sheene and Parrish held 5th and 6th but then Sheene saw a pit-board telling him that Baker was out of the points in 12th place. Realising that 6th place would clinch his title, Sheene helped his protegé's overall position in the Championship by letting Parrish pass by to 5th place. Sheene was jubilant at his victory and returned to England whilst Hennen and Parish went on to Brno for the Czechoslovakian GP where they finished 4th and 7th respectively, both suffering machine problems.

With the TT no longer a World Championship event, the British round was fought out at Silverstone and Sheene was determined to show the home crowds the form that had made him a double World Champion. But Sheene's XR14 — still suffering from overheating caused by cylinder head bolt weaknesses — retired with a blown head gasket, and Parrish took the lead ahead of John Williams and Hennen. Then Parrish fell followed by Williams, leaving Hennen a surprise winner of the miserable wet event. His win pushed him to 3rd in the World Championship — the same as the previous year — and ensured Suzuki's retention of the World Manufacturer's Championship, whilst Parrish was 5th in his classic series debut year.

In the late-season home internationals, Hennen was on top form; in the five remaining rounds of the *MCN* Superbike Series, he scored 71 points to Sheene's 46, but because of Sheene's early successes, he retained this title too, with Hennen and Parrish in 3rd and 5th. Similarly, in the three final rounds of the Shellsport Series, Hennen outscored Sheene 51 to 35 but again, Sheene retained the overall title, from Hennen and Parrish, a hat-trick for Texaco Heron Team Suzuki!

After a hectic season, Suzuki had met their objectives, and whilst Suzuki Japan were delighted with their World Championship victories, Heron Suzuki were also pleased at the Team's home performances.

During 1977, there were few in-Team bickerings, probably because each rider was allowed, to an extent, to 'do his own thing'. Furthermore, Sheene and Steve Parrish were the best of mates whilst the quiet-spoken American was just too pleased at his first factory contract to become involved. With such a good season behind them, great things were expected of the Team for 1978, when the brand-new Suzuki XR22 would make its grand prix debut.

An 'all-nighter' in progress at the 1977 Austrian GP. Ogborne (right) takes notes as Franko Sheene and Taddy Matsui work on Sheene's XR14s. Note the new style fairing and seat for the XR14 at left *Gruber*

12 Licking the wounds:
Suzuki retreat (1978 and 1979)

Yamaha were determined to wrest the 500 cc World Championship from Suzuki in 1978, but they needed a top rider hungry for the title. They found him in the States; Kenny Roberts, whose racing pedigree was blemish-free. Roberts was no stranger to Europe but had never before contested a full grand prix season. Aboard his Yamahas, Roberts could be devastating although Suzuki hoped his unfamiliarity with GP life would be reflected in his results. Nobody seriously thought he could win the Championship; in his first year, on a new machine, in strange places. Everybody was wrong. . . .

To meet this threat Suzuki's riders were carefully selected. For more concentrated effort, Parrish was dropped, Sheene and Hennen retained. Their main objective was to retain the 500 cc World Championship and their British titles; the tools were new XR22 GP and XR23A 652 cc machines.

But Barry Sheene wasn't overkeen at Hennen's inclusion.

VANDENBROEK 'Our Team always thought that Barry was afraid of Pat, that he was capable of stealing the lime-light away from Barry. When Barry was consistently beating Pat, everything seemed to be going quite smoothly; when Patrick started beating Barry at the beginning of '78, then a very distinct rivalry started to develop.'

The Italian Suzuki distributors also fielded a 'factory' team; Yamaha defector Steve Baker rode for the Olio Nava Fiat team, managed by ex-GP rider Roberto Gallina. Baker's mount, until the Italian GP, was a 1977 factory XR14.

The first classic round was run in the blistering heat of Venezuela at the San Carlos circuit where Sheene and Hennen split the Yamaha teamsters in the practice leaderboard; Cecotto, Roberts, Sheene, Hennen, Baker and Katayama. After two laps of the race, Roberts' engine blew and the expected Sheene-Roberts probing-match never materialised. Sheene had a bad start, but taking advantage of his super-fitness, and sipping 'Gatorade' glucose mixture as he circulated the track, he reeled in his rivals—including Hennen—to take 1st place, followed by Hennen and Baker. Cecotto retired and Katayama crashed. . . .

With a 15 point advantage over Roberts, Sheene's prospects looked good, but at Jarama in Spain, Hennen took an early lead and although Roberts eventually pulled past him he was forced to slow when his throttles jammed. With Sheene in trouble, Pat Hennen took the flag ahead of Roberts, Katayama, Cecotto, Sheene and Baker. Hennen's win really upset the formbook; he now led the Classic series from Sheene with 27 points to 21. Sheene could see a pattern establishing itself, for Hennen was leading the Shellsport and *MCN* Superbike

Right Hennen guns his No. 1 XR22 to victory at the Oulton Park round of the 1978 Match races. Wings on the fairing increased the front wheel down-force

Far right Same race, same corner. Sheene is more comfortable looking *over* rather than through the screen *Nicholls*

series too at this point, and had been top-scorer in the Match Races at Easter with 92 points to Sheene's 65. It looked as though Sheene's threat came not from Roberts, but from his own team-mate Patrick Hennen. Pat's mechanics felt uneasy.

VANDENBROEK 'Before the Spanish GP, Barry came up to Mike Sinclair and myself who were working on the bikes and said, "I want you guys to realise this aggro between Pat and myself has nothing to do with you." He was definitely trying to be nice to us. Between Mike and myself and everybody else there *was* no problem, it was the rivalry between the two riders. . . .'

At the Salzburgring, Roberts pulled out a lead with Sheene and Hennen duelling for 3rd place behind Cecotto. Instead of attacking the Yamahas, the Suzukis were fighting themselves, but suddenly, Hennen's XR22 suffered ignition failure leaving Sheene to take 3rd place behind the Yamaha pair. Now Sheene led the series with 31 points, with Hennen and Roberts equal 2nd on 27 points.

Before official practice commenced for the French GP at Nogaro, Sheene track-tested his tyres, eventually choosing Michelin rear, and Goodyear front. The Hennen squad usually arrived later than Sheene because they had to pack the Team's spares into their transporter. Time was short for the Hennen equipe.

VANDENBROEK 'We tried Michelins ourselves but Patrick thought we'd try a Goodyear on the front. We'd also played a lot with suspension fork-oil at the front, to improve the bike's handling.'

In the race, Hennen took an early lead whilst Roberts closed on 2nd man Sheene, passing on the 3rd lap and taking Hennen's lead 2 laps later. At the flag Roberts led Hennen by 10 seconds, who in turn led Sheene by 19 seconds. Roberts' brilliant riding had obliterated Sheene's initial 15 point lead, and he now led the Championship on 42 points to Sheene's 41 and Hennen's 39.

VANDENBROEK 'After the race Barry was angry with Patrick for having

copied his set-up for the race, when in truth, we used a completely different set-up and the only thing we had copied was the use of the Goodyear.

'Barry instructed his mechanics that at the next racetrack, he wasn't going to park anywhere near Pat Hennen. At this point, this was just a rumour to us, but when we got to Mugello, Barry's mechanics had already arrived and set up all their gear. We were under Suzuki instructions to present a Team effort and everybody had to look like they all worked together—and Mike said to Don Mackay, "Rumour has it that if we park next to you, you have to move 100 yards down the paddock," and Don kinda looked sheepishly down at his feet, and hemmed and hawed, so Mike said, "We'll save you the trouble." Since we hadn't unpacked, we parked ourselves further down the paddock.

'So we got on OK with the mechanics, but the rivalry between Barry and Pat carried over into our section in this way.'

At Mugello, Sheene was instrumental in securing an XR22 for Steve Baker, but ironically, Baker beat Sheene to the post; 4th to Sheene's 5th. Ahead, the familiar pattern developed with Hennen close to race-victor Roberts with Marco Lucchinelli in 3rd. Roberts had extended his Championship lead to 6 points over Hennen's 51 and Sheene's 47. Whilst Hennen was almost matching 'King' Kenny, Sheene was clearly 'psyched-out' and out-classed by the two Americans. Sheene said his poor performances were the result of a bug he'd caught in Venezuela; but nevertheless his rivals grasped the advantage of Sheene's lack of form.

Sheene then contested, and won the Chimay event in Belgium, whilst Hennen returned to the Island. Some said that with his GP prospects he was foolish to risk racing on the dangerous circuit. So why did he go?

VANDENBROEK 'Pat only went to the TT for the money. I know that his retainer wasn't enough to pay his expenses through the year and to pay the mechanics. Consequently, he had to add to his income by riding races that paid a lot of start-money, so there was some financial incentive to go.'

But did he *enjoy* racing in the Island?

VANDENBROEK 'He *learned* to like it; he thought it was fascinating. He'd return from practice almost euphoric saying, "Gosh, I wish you guys could come with me and sit on the back of this thing and see what it's *like* to go around this racetrack."'

In 1978 it became a challenge to Hennen; he liked the bonhomie, he liked the course.

HENNEN 'As far as atmosphere goes, my mechanic sums it up saying, "It's gotta be the biggest club race in the world!" Everyone seems to be in a really good mood, and you've got the garage just a couple of steps downstairs. You get up in the morning, put your leathers on, walk down and hop on the bike, drive up through town for scrutineering and you're on a racetrack! When practice's over, you bomb back to the garage, get changed and then you're in for breakfast.

After Hennen's TT crash, Hartog (right) joined Team Suzuki inheriting Hennen's mechanic Frans VandenBroek (2nd from left), who is smirking at something said by either Sheene or his mechanic Wes Pratt *MCW*

'I think it's pretty neat; it's a great time and that's for sure.'

For the Senior, Hennen had two signalling points; in Ramsey and the pits. He was out to win on his XR22 despite the changeable weather, and unlike his rivals who chose slick tyres, Hennen played safe, selecting intermediates.

HENNEN 'Wet roads; dry roads. One lap it'll be wet and dry about fifteen times, then it'll start to rain the next lap, then the next lap it *won't* be raining.'

After one lap, Hennen was 3rd behind TT specialists Tom Herron and temporary team-mate John Williams—both later sacrificing their lives in Ulster's 'genuine' road races—all three aboard Suzuki fours. On lap 5, Williams' XR14 expired but Herron and Hennen riding together—although Herron was 20 seconds *ahead* on corrected times—were having a battle royale during which

Pat broke the lap record with the first sub-20 minute lap. 19 minutes 53.2 seconds; 113.835 mph! But Pat's riding became untidy as he scratched around the dangerous Island circuit. He started the last lap in 2nd place: it ended at Bishop's Court.

There, on the tricky Glen Helen section he struck a kerb at top speed. Nobody really knows the cause of Pat's tragic accident, least of all Pat, but his crew, after recovering from the initial shock, later returned to Bishop's Court.

VANDENBROEK 'I talked to two witnesses who saw him come through that section with one hand on the handlebars and the other on his visor. They saw him clip the kerb as he was going through the corner and the bike was going at a very high speed—it was in top gear when we disassembled it, which is probably over 150 mph—and when we retrieved his visor, which the police at first impounded, it had splotches on it. He either hit a bird or a bug—there was yellow goop all over it. My own theory is that he either tried to clear his visor or was hit in the face and startled. That's my own personal opinion.'

Hennen knew the dangers of distraction, and in a previous interview with the author explained his Island strategy.

HENNEN 'Every time around, the track gets quicker and quicker. The bends that first look like turns start straightening out. *Around the Island you just need pure concentration and anything that blocks or disturbs that for me is no help.* [Author's italics] I need to constantly talk myself through each lap; what's coming up next bend? Next bend? Next town? Jump?'

Pat's accident was certainly not caused by a mechanical defect.

Upper left Hennen, Sheene and Roberts (Yamaha) at Brands Hatch. During the early 1978 GPs, Hennen proved a good match for Roberts *MCW*

Upper right During his debut ride, at the Nürburgring in 1978, Virginio Ferrari aviates his XR22's front wheel. His win clinched Suzuki's 3rd successive 500 cc World Manufacturer's title *MCW*

VANDENBROEK 'We disassembled the bike and there was absolutely nothing wrong with it, and the police were there checking to make sure the bike was OK. Nothing had locked up: nothing had seized.'

Hennen was air-lifted to Nobles Hospital, Douglas, in a coma from which he didn't recover for months. Later he was transferred to Liverpool's Walton Hospital where he lay constantly surrounded by his team, brother Chip, girlfriend Karen and mechanics Mike Sinclair and Frans VandenBroek, who coaxed Pat by playing his favourite records and, when there was a flicker of response, talking to him. Gradually, he came around, his team restoring the dormant muscles by exercising his limbs. The Team PR man, Garry Taylor, a long and close friend of Pat, spent his weekdays maintaining press interest in Pat, and his weekends in Liverpool. Slowly, Pat improved but his racing days were clearly at an end, and when he returned to the States, the team disbanded; Chip became US Suzuki's PR manager, Mike Sinclair joined Wil Hartog's team and Frans VandenBroek took a motorcycle engine development job with US Kawasaki. Pat still works with motorcycles.

GP experts acknowledge that, but for Hennen's accident, he could have become the 1978 World Champion. So what enabled Pat to consistently beat the reigning World Champion?

VANDENBROEK 'The secret to Pat's success was that he was a very analytical person; being very mechanically perceptive, Pat was very very good at setting up motorcycles and Mike was very good at correcting the complaints that Pat had. We would try modifications that were his idea and he would go out and try it, and maybe ten laps later would come back and say, "I know it was a lot of work doing that, but I don't think it works. Unless you guys see some improvement on the lap times, it's no good." And this was his *own* idea! There were other riders on the Team who wouldn't admit that; they'd try something and say it was better even when it wasn't.

'Chip would talk to him about riding style. He'd say, "If you stay down on the tank you'll be able to go faster through the corner," and Pat would try it and it did work and his style changed.'

With Hennen *hors de combat*, at least Sheene was relieved of some pressure, but it didn't reduce Kenny Roberts' brilliant form and Wil Hartog was drafted into the Team with specific Team orders to 'help' Sheene overcome the Roberts' threat. Hartog's first factory ride was in the Dutch TT at Assen. Sheene had already proclaimed that he had now shaken off the mystery Venezuelan virus that had previously plagued him, but had also said that his XR22 was slower than Roberts' YZR500. Hennen had already proved that the XR22 *could* live with the YZR. Could Hartog?

From the start, Sheene and Roberts pulled away in a private battle whilst Hartog had problems and soon lost contact with the leading bunch. Cecotto surprised Roberts and Sheene by taking the lead, positions that were held to the flag. Hartog's 5th place didn't answer the questions; Sheene had rediscovered his form but was it too late? Roberts led Sheene by 12 Championship points.

At Belgium, the question was unequivocally answered. By then, the Team had recruited Michel Rougerie to further shield Barry's title. The Frenchman startled all by qualifying 2nd fastest, followed by Hartog and Sheene. Even with three factory XR22s on the front row of the grid, it would be difficult stemming the Roberts tide.

> *Motocourse* 'It wasn't a question of whether Hartog could beat Roberts at Francorchamps; it was a question of whether Sheene could beat him at all. . . . What he (Roberts) had to do . . . was to beat Sheene and of course neither Hartog nor Rougerie would be able to prevent it. That was up to Sheene; and Roberts.'

Hartog and Sheene moved quickly to the front as rain squalls fell, but later with Roberts pressurising Sheene for 2nd place, Hartog pulled away from Sheene — of little concern to Roberts; Hartog was out of *Championship* contention and Roberts' goal was to beat Sheene. Hartog then slowed, waiting for Sheene to speed up and pass him at the finish as Team orders dictated, but Sheene's race was run and Hartog was signalled 'GO!' On the last lap, Roberts powered past Sheene whilst Hartog extended his lead to the flag. New teamster Rougerie was 4th. . . .

> *Motocourse* 'There was a great deal of jubilation, but later, when it had all died down, Hartog was standing in the paddock looking blank. He had just been told off. Sheene was furious with him for taking the points when he should have been getting in Roberts' way. Hartog was puzzled and evidently upset. He had done as his team manager had told him, most professionally and to great effect. His account was simple; "I waited for Barry but he couldn't keep up. They told me to go, so I had to leave him to sort out his own problems."'

Karlskoga is a Suzuki circuit. It twists and turns, bumping its way around Sweden. Here, handling, suspension and acceleration are more important than outright speed. Nevertheless, Cecotto took pole position but during the race, neither he nor Roberts — who was physically in poor shape — were in serious contention. Hartog accepted Team orders again, shadowing Sheene who led from the early stages. With no Yamaha threat, Sheene led Hartog over the line by just 0.05 seconds. Roberts' 7th place scored 4 points to Sheene's 15, putting Sheene on 82 and Roberts on 85 points. Close, but not impossible.

Over the season, Sheene had been complaining to his mechanics about specific machine faults and at many of the GPs Martyn Ogbourne, Heron Suzuki's chief mechanic and Mitsuru Okamoto had performed an 'all-nighter' checking out the Champion's complaints; often finding everything perfect. After final practice at the Finnish GP, Sheene suggested they replace a crankshaft main-bearing — another 'all-nighter'. After checking the machine for excessive vibration and finding nothing amiss, they decided against changing the cranks.

On the fourth lap of the race, Sheene's prediction was ironically proved correct and he retired with a broken main bearing. It was Sheene's first grand prix failure since the start of the 1976 World Championships; 23 successive classics without a breakdown! Sheene was livid, openly remonstrating his mechanics to the pressmen, and annoying his English boss.

> KNIGHT 'When that happened, he put up the biggest black mark with Japan that he could ever have done; he'd made that quite public and Japan

Okamoto, lap-timing at Brands Hatch in typical pose relaxes with chief designer Hase. Mechanics Dave Johnson and 'Radar' Cullen are smiling too!
Brandmark

didn't like that at all. I think that was the beginning of the end as far as Japan were concerned.'

Meanwhile, the race had ended in Hartog's favour and fortunately for Sheene, Roberts also stopped when his ignition system failed. So with two classic rounds in hand, the outcome was still in the balance.

Silverstone literally went off like a damp, very damp, squid. The race commenced with dry roads, but rain was already falling heavily nearby. Roberts blistered into the lead with Sheene in 6th and Hartog 2nd but then the Silverstone skies opened and instead of stopping the race, the organisers allowed the teams to decide how to overcome the problems facing their riders. Soon, the riders began to pit, changing to grooved 'wet' tyres. Roberts' YZR had a quickly detachable front wheel and he pitted for just $2\frac{1}{2}$ minutes. Normally, QD wheels aren't fitted to GP machines; a rider changing a wheel mid-race may just as well retire. But at Silverstone, everyone changed wheels. Except Steve Manship who'd fitted intermediate tyres from the start and thus had the advantage. Sheene's pit-crew scrabbled, his XR22 was stationary for $7\frac{1}{2}$ minutes. . . .

With so many riders pouring into and out of the pits, most team lap-scorers became confused and after the farcical race was over, *everybody* claimed victory. Despite the confusion, the official lap-scorers were correct in declaring Roberts the rightful winner with Manship 2nd and Sheene 3rd. Sheene had lost the race in the pits; in wet weather he was certainly superior to Roberts, and had lapped Roberts twice after his tyre-change, simply to unlap himself!

Roberts started the West German GP with 110 points to Sheene's 100 and to retain his Championship, Barry needed to win with Roberts placed 4th or lower; only if Roberts finished 10th could Sheene afford to finish 2nd. On a track that both Roberts and Sheene denounced as too long (over 14 miles) and too dangerous (no run-off areas) Roberts had a decisive advantage; he could cruise whereas Sheene would need to scratch.

As always, Suzuki Japan were most intent on winning the 500 cc World Manufacturer's Championship—as they had in 1976 and 1977—but at the Nürburgring, Yamaha and Suzuki were level-pegging, and to improve Suzuki's chances, Virginio Ferrari was provided with a Texaco Heron Team Suzuki XR22—he normally rode an XR14. Ferrari joined Rougerie, Hartog and Sheene who qualified 3rd, 4th, 5th and 6th in practice respectively. Hartog crashed on the 1st lap but Ferrari and Cecotto—Yamaha too wanted the Manufacturer's Title—cleared off with Roberts in 3rd followed by Sheene. They finished in that order; Sheene seemingly didn't *attempt* to win, whilst Roberts admitted he'd ridden like an old woman, his strategy to *finish* the race and claim his first World Championship. Sheene was relying on a Yamaha break-down, but Roberts never strained his motor.

Bitterly disappointed at finishing 2nd in the World Championship, Sheene declared that his title had been lost in Finland when his mechanics hadn't replaced the faulty crankshaft. But Sheene's title wasn't lost in Finland; it was lost in Spain, Austria, France, Italy, Holland, Belgium, Britain and West Germany, where, for various reasons Sheene had failed to shine. Despite Sheene's criticisms of XR22, Hennen, Hartog and Ferrari all managed to beat the unbeatable Kenny Roberts on *their* XR22s.

The factory weren't as disappointed as Sheene; they hadn't raced for nothing having won *their* Manufacturer's Championship. Sheene also retained his Shellsport and *MCN* Superbike titles which pleased his British followers and Heron Suzuki at least.

Sheene's PR attractions became a major factor in Heron Suzuki's deliberations regarding riders for 1979. It was too risky to lose his association: Sheene and Suzuki were synonomous.

KNIGHT 'Japan, who were keen to go ahead with Barry in 1978, were doubtful for 1979. But Barry was still a top-line publicity man, despite the results.'

Maurice Knight re-signed Barry Sheene. After his one-year absence, Sheene's protegé Steve Parrish was signed, whilst new blood came with Ulsterman Tom Herron, a wily GP campaigner of old.

But Suzuki Japan were under pressure again to widen the supply of factory machines to the Dutch and Italian racing teams. The Riemersma-Nimag and Olio Nava Fiat team riders, Hartog and Ferrari, were invited to Japan with Sheene to test the new XR27B machines; the factory had succombed. They also tested a 500 cc development machine with the radiator mounted in the fairing nose—the XR27BFR (Front-Radiator)—which Sheene preferred despite its weight penalty, much to the astonishment of Hartog and Ferrari who disagreed.

The Venezuelan GP was too expensive to contest and didn't appear in the British Team's contract terms but the riders still contested it. Roberts, the defending World Champion, was absent due to injuries sustained whilst testing Yamaha's new 'Power-Valve' YZR. Sheene overcame Hartog's early lead in the race and whilst Herron suffered from heat exhaustion, Ferrari passed him snatching 2nd place behind Sheene. Hartog fell at the hairpin and at the flag it was Sheene, Ferrari and Herron.

At the Brands Easter Match Race round, Herron fell on his XR23B, damaging his left hand, but not before he'd sampled Sheene's newly-arrived XR27BFR which Sheene had ridden in practice and slung to one side in dismay. On the new XR23B—the 'pregnant duck' 652—Sheene won three of the six races but the British Team were trounced by a Roberts-less American team.

Barry Sheene again tried the XR27BFR in practice the following weekend at the Salzburgring, where the factory fielded Hiroyuki Kawasaki, a development rider and motorcycle racer in Japan, on another XR27B in the factory's blue and white livery. In practice he was 5th fastest with Sheene 6th and Herron 2nd. Hartog was 8th and Ferrari 15th! Kawasaki was said to provide a Japanese communication link between XR27B deficiencies and the Japanese technicians. Unofficially, he was the Team's bench-mark; the factory were becoming increasingly confused by the riders' comments concerning power and particularly handling. Whilst Ferrari and Hartog pronounced satisfaction with the XR27Bs handling at Ryuyo, neither were happy at Venezuela. Was it really the machine at fault? Kawasaki would provide the answer—privately—in Japanese. His Austrian practice times established Kawasaki's GP credit-rating.

In the race Roberts chased early leader Ferrari and soon took an unchallenged lead whilst Sheene was struggling mid-field with a front disc running out-of-true and having to pump the lever when braking. Tom Herron, followed by Kawasaki, almost caught 3rd man Hartog, whilst Parrish and Sheene finished 7th and 12th.

Chatting with 1979 teamster Tom Herron (wearing Sheene's helmet!), Maurice Knight at an early-season Brands Hatch event *Brandmark*

The powerful factory personnel demanded a post-race inquest into Sheene's brake problem. They found a washer—normally under the disc bolt-head—sandwiched between the disc and wheel!

Roberts, still sore but riding-fit, had wiped out Sheene's pre-Austria 15 point advantage in just one race and went to Hockenheim tying with Sheene in 3rd place. But unless he could sustain his winning performances it seemed that overall leader Ferrari, with 24 points, could threaten his chances. In West Germany, even Roberts failed to catch Hartog by a narrow margin. Ferrari was 3rd and Parrish was 9th but Herron and Sheene both retired with crankshaft problems whereas Kawasaki crashed on the last lap whilst in a good position.

The points table showed a distinct pattern; the Suzukis were definitely superior to Kenny's Yamaha, but Suzuki's lack of international Team discipline could mean that their successes were spread amongst too many riders to achieve the individual Championship. To date, Hartog and Sheene had one win each whilst Ferrari's consistency put him on top with 34 points to Roberts' 27. Sheene had scored only 15.

At Imola, Roberts led almost from the start. Both suffering tyre problems, Herron and Sheene dropped to 3rd and 4th places whilst Hartog crashed. Ferrari finished 2nd and Mike Baldwin, a relatively unknown American, finished 5th on his Suzuki with Parrish finishing 11th.

Sheene fell in Spanish GP practice; his elbow visibly swollen, but Baldwin took pole! After a poor start Sheene couldn't catch the leaders, retiring on lap 10. Early leader Ferrari was passed by Roberts, but Hartog and Baldwin were knifing through the field to attack Roberts, who promptly stormed off to win the race with Hartog, Baldwin and Ferrari behind. After a crash in practice Herron left Jarama early to contest the North-West 200. Parrish—11th in Spain—followed.

Some say that Tom shouldn't have raced in Ireland with his damaged hand but courageously, he couldn't disappoint his patriotic fans. A tough character, Herron had many years of GP experience as a privateer and wished to show his countrymen the form that resulted in his first factory contract. In the 1000 cc race, Herron lost control in attempting to take 4th place from Parrish. He later died of his injuries.

Hartog (XR27B) leading Roberts and Randy Mamola (Suzuki RG500 Mk IV) during the 1979 French GP at Le Mans *MCW*

Herron was the first Suzuki factory rider to give his life since their first competition in 1953. Suzuki had been proud of their safety record. Herron was a family man *and* a brave competitor—a rare combination.

At the TT, Mike Hailwood rode an XR22—specially built for the occasion and in his own red white and gold livery—to victory in the Senior, setting a new lap record of 114.02 mph. In the Classic, Hailwood was 2nd, 3.4 seconds behind Alex George's 1000 cc Honda. The results were better than Hailwood had originally expected.

HAILWOOD   'I was a bit wary of it (the XR22) but after a couple of laps at Donington I thought it wasn't that bad; a few laps later I thought it was pretty good. It turned out to be *really* good—a lot better than the Yamaha I rode in 1978—the handling was much better, although engine performance was about the same. I didn't have any problems; it went like a dream for the whole race.'

Left Sheene riding the 138 bhp 652 cc XR23B at a UK International event in 1979. The seat fairing was specially widened to accommodate the long, bulbous mufflers prompting its 'pregnant duck' nickname *MCW*

Roberts led the Yugoslav GP, constantly hounded by Ferrari. Sheene retired when a stone struck his steel-plated knee, causing unbearable pain. Roberts won with Ferrari 2nd; Hartog was 4th and Parrish 9th. Roberts led the Championship with 72 points to Ferrari's 66. Hartog had 45 and Sheene 23.

At Assen, Roberts took pole and stalked the Hartog, Sheene and Ferrari pack. Hartog fell back changing places with Ferrari, and Sheene then passed the Italian to lead the race. Ferrari re-passed Sheene on the last lap to take the flag with Hartog 3rd, Roberts 8th (suffering monoshock problems) and Parrish 10th Another new American, 19 year old Randy Mamola, was 13th in this, his first 500 cc GP.

Sheene had been undecided about passing Ferrari; with no inter-Suzuki Team orders and Ferrari, Suzuki's Championship prospect, should Sheene let him win or improve *his* own status? According to Sheene, he *could* have won, but decided to support Ferrari instead. Sheene was later instructed by Heron Suzuki GB, to race to *win*; he was contracted to *them*. Sheene was relieved; Team orders were anathema to him.

Ferrari went to Belgium, six points ahead of Roberts in the Championship, gaining factory credibility for Team Gallina. The Spa track incorporated a new link-road, but it's oily surface was like a skid-pan and all the leading riders boycotted the event on safety grounds.

At the Karlscoga Swedish GP round, Roberts again had monoshock problems and never challenged. Conversely, Sheene blistered through the pack, inheriting Hartog's leading position when the Dutchman crashed on lap 19. Then, 2nd man Phillipe Coulon also fell, leaving Dutchmen Jack Middleburg and Boet van Dulmen in 2nd and 3rd. Mamola was impressive on his RG500 Mk IV, finishing 6th behind Parrish. Ferrari's chances expired on lap 1 when he retired with a suspected seizure, but Sheene had won his 2nd GP that year, though still 33 points behind Roberts overall. Scoring no points this time, Ferrari was lying 2nd, two points behind Roberts.

Few riders like the Finnish Imatra course—a 'road' circuit with natural hazards. In the wet, Imatra is lethal. It rained prior to the race, but consistent riders could 'ride the strip'—a dry line left by previous events. Roberts was inconsistent, riding off the strip—and off the track—relegating him to 10th place by lap 3. From pole position, van Dulmen took an unchallenged lead. Mamola soon took Sheene's 3rd place, and then began attacking Hartog with Sheene in his wake, but Hartog's XR22 throttle was sticking, and he finished 10th. Van Dulmen's victory established the production RG500 as a GP winner; similarly-mounted Mamola was 2nd, followed by Sheene and Middleburg. Parrish finished 11th, and Ferrari 15th after crashing and remounting. Sheene was closing the gap on Roberts in the Championship; As Roberts' and Ferrari's late-season performances sagged, Sheene's improved. Now 3rd in the Championship, to win, Sheene needed two victories whilst Roberts would have to score zero in one and finish 10th in the other. It was a very, very long shot.

The dogmatic attitude of the FIM heirarchy had annoyed the riders in their disciplinarian handling of the Spanish, Belgian and Swedish rounds. In Spain, Roberts' start-money was cut and he 'donated' his trophy to the organisers from the podium, to bolster their funds. After the Belgian riders' boycott, the FIM imposed heavy fines and suspended Roberts' and Ferrari's racing licences, whilst in Sweden the riders — notably Ferrari — expressed dislike of the Mickey Mouse Karlscoga track and its low safety standards. At Silverstone, the riders' 'World Series' answer was officially announced, and the paddock hummed with gossip.

Hartog took his customary lead, followed by Ferrari, Sheene and Roberts, but Roberts and Sheene relegated Hartog to 3rd and gradually drew away in a personal duel for the lead. They slowed when neither were prepared to take the initiative — nor the leadership pressure — and Hartog closed. On the final lap Roberts and Sheene were neck and neck when a back-marker baulked Sheene, giving Roberts a significant lead. Sheene's task looked impossible, but drawing on his vast GP skills — and more besides — Sheene raised the outright lap record and entered the final fast Woodcote corner — flat-out to the courageous — in Roberts' slip-stream, and attempted an outside pass around Roberts. Sheene's tyres skirted the grass but Roberts' line was quicker, and he won by a wheel. If nothing else, this proved that riders don't lose their skills, only their confidence to use them. It was possibly Sheene's best race during his Suzuki career.

With a 4th place at Silverstone, Ferrari could still just win the Championship if he won at Le Mans with Roberts not scoring. It was impossible; the pressure on Roberts was non-existent. Sheene *couldn't* finish higher than 3rd overall, and Hartog could even relegate him to 4th. The La Mans race saw Roberts cruising around in 4th with Mamola tailing him, whilst Sheene and Ferrari banged fairings contesting the lead. But Ferrari crashed badly — handing Roberts the Championship — and with nothing to lose or gain but his GP reputation, Roberts surged into the lead with Mamola still on his tail. Mamola briefly took the lead but Roberts and Sheene passed him, and on the final lap, back-marker Roberto Pietri crashed causing Kenny to fall in avoiding him. Sheene took advantage — Mamola was distracted — and swept into the lead whilst Roberts re-mounted finishing 3rd. Roberts had retained his World Championship and Suzuki their 4th 500 cc World Manufacturer's Championship. Additionally, Parrish had won the Shellsport Series which Sheene didn't contest, although he had finished 3rd in the World Championship in which Ferrari was 2nd and Hartog 4th. On their XR23Bs Parrish and Sheene claimed 5th and 6th in the *MCN* Superbike Series, a low Team priority.

For Barry Sheene it was a time of forward planning; he wanted to run his own Suzuki team, but Suzuki were dead against the plan. The end came one day when Sheene had a meeting with Heron Suzuki's Maurice Knight who'd been considering Sheene's recent results. It appeared that Sheene had lost some of his aggression, having publically stated his reluctance to risk his neck for race victory. Perhaps after 1977, Sheene had become complacent. Knight made Sheene a final offer that day, and was called away to another scheduled meeting. Sheene decided against signing a further Suzuki contract; if Suzuki raced in 1980 it would be *without* Barry Sheene. It marked the end of an era.

13 Regaining lost ground: Suzuki's deathblow (1980 and 1981)

For 1980, Barry Sheene formed a Yamaha-based 'Team Akai with Texaco'. Suzuki lost more than Sheene; £300,000 was trimmed from Texaco's Suzuki sponsorship and Heron Suzuki considered a racing withdrawal. Peter Agg and his directors responded by ploughing another £$\frac{1}{4}$ m into the budget and began searching for Sheene's successor. In America they talked to Mike Baldwin, still bed-ridden after his Loudon spill in June 1979. That looked risky, so what about this Mamola kid? His manager, Jim Doyle, negotiated with Heron Suzuki and Mamola signed an expensive contract.

But the factory—and British race spectators—were interested in F1 racing, and during 1979 Heron Suzuki had asked Paul Dunstall to run a brace of factory Yoshimura GS1000 F1 racers in UK F1 events. These had had little success, apart from Sheene's 2nd place at Oulton Park, and the factory agreed to supply new Yoshimura-powered XR69s for the 1980 F1 Championships. Heron Suzuki needed a versatile rider able to support Mamola in the GPs. Eventually, New Zealand's Graeme Crosby signed the contract. Mamola mistakenly agreed to ride the XR69s too; he thought 'F1' referred to the 652 cc XR23B! He rode the Suzuki F1 once—at Mallory Park—achieving 4th place.

With new XR34s for the GPs and XR69s for open and F1 classes, the XR23Bs were rarely used due to spares shortage, and were returned to Japan. Randy's mechanics were George Vukmanovich and Gerry 'Blossom' Burgess. Croz relied on Mick Smith and Dave 'Radar' Cullen (GPs) and Dave 'Junior' Collins—the Team's F1 specialist with part-timer Steve Moore. Team manager Rex White, and chief technician Martyn Ogborne, ordered a new Team transporter—with seats in the front and workshop storage space in the rear. An awning clipped on to the coach to create a large private working area.

A reformed Olio Nava Fiat Team had two new riders, Marco Lucchinelli and Graziano Rossi, whilst the Riemersma-Nimag Team continued with Wil Hartog. All used factory supported XR34s despite 1979's tactical problems.

The Austrian GP was cancelled when heavy snow fell. In the Salzburgring paddock, Mamola's new motorhome exploded; a gas leakage was ignited by the 'fridge. Fortunately, Randy had just stepped outside.

At the Italian GP 'Lucky' Lucchenelli qualifed fastest with Roberts and Mamola 2nd and 3rd. All three lapped Misano in formation during the early stages of the race when typically, Roberts blasted off, trailed by Mamola. But Mamola, Lucchinelli and Hartog retired with main bearing failure: Crosby with a seizure. Roberts won with Rossi 3rd. Mamola was philosophical about his factory GP debut.

MAMOLA 'Nobody was to blame; it's machinery and it can break down any time. I get along really well with the Japanese; they're there for *their* purposes, and they know *my* purpose, and when something happens to the bike they're really apologetic, always saying they're sorry, and I say, "Hey, it's not your fault. You build a good bike that'll finish and I'll try my hardest to win." '

Misano was Crosby's first GP and he sensed some personal pressure.

CROSBY 'I felt I had to prove myself. Being given a factory bike was the opportunity to prove that they'd made the right decision.'

Self-sufficient Crosby had to adjust to his new role.

CROSBY 'I'd load up the bikes and Martyn would say "No, no, the *riders* don't do that!" So I'd try to change a wheel, but I shouldn't do that either. So I was sitting around twiddling my thumbs doing nothing, thinking that it wasn't much fun, which it wasn't.'

The Italian XR34s always used 16 in. front wheels but the British Team preferred the greater tyre-choice of 18 in. wheels, (only Michelin produced 16 in. tyres). At Jarama for the Spanish GP, Mamola, Hartog and Rossi used XR34Ms; Crosby and Lucchinelli XR34Hs. Both Rossi and Hartog crashed during the race which Roberts won, followed by Lucchinelli and Mamola. Crosby was 12th. Hartog reverted to his old XR34H and gave Mamola his XR34M chassis.

At Paul Ricard, Lucchinelli clashed with Roberts and Mamola for the lead, but a misted helmet visor slowed Randy who finished 2nd to Roberts with Lucchinelli, Rossi and Crosby in 3rd, 4th and 5th.

Outta sight! Mamola's XR34M antics astounded even seasoned race-fans throughout 1980. This Donington Park shot is typical *MCW*

CROSBY 'The French GP was my turning point because I got into the swing of it right from the start. I really enjoyed that race; my bike went like a rocketship!'

Graeme Crosby contested the Senior TT on his XR34H, and the Classic and F1 events on his XR69, attended by Pops Yoshimura, his family and mechanic Asakawa-San. The TT F1 event ended on a political note; Crosby finished 2nd and as he followed winner Mick Grant across the line, Crosby reported seeing Grant dent his Honda tank, a dodge to overcome the 24 litre fuel-tank size regulations; Honda may have obviated a fuel stop to their rivals' disadvantage. Gordon Pantall—sponsor of 4th man Alan Jackson—lodged a protest but the Honda had been released from the post-race inspection, and despite an FIM investigation confirming Grant's win, suspicions ran high. Crosby had a superb ride to victory in the Senior, but retired on the first lap of the Classic, his 1084 cc XR69 suffering carburation problems.

Shortly after the Dutch TT commenced, Mamola led Roberts around the damp Assen track, but again his visor misted over and he slowed, whilst Lucchinelli, in similar trouble, retired when the visor he'd lifted blew off completely. Roberts also retired with a punctured tyre leaving Middleburg to win from Rossi, Uncini, van Dulmen and Mamola, with Crosby in 8th place.

At the Belgian GP Randy felt good on the Zolder circuit.

MAMOLA 'In practice, the bike was working really well on the circuit, but it was a hard one to get around really quick because it was so rough.'

On the grid Mamola was confident of victory.

MAMOLA   'I *knew* I was going to win it, but I wouldn't say it to anybody.
To me, that brings bad luck.
'At the time, Martyn was saying, "Just go and do it like Donington; go
straight for the thing and win!" But I wasn't going to listen to *anybody*
because I had enough pressure on me; I was the fastest qualifier. Zolder
was probably my most keyed-up race.'

Mamola took the lead at the second turn and never looked back. Rossi fell on lap
4 but at the finish Lucchinelli was 2nd, with Roberts, Crosby and Hartog
behind. Instead of shadowing Roberts, Mamola had raced *himself*.

OGBORNE   'Most riders have a funny thing about beating their heroes;
it's a mental barrier that Randy broke through at Zolder. He told me that
he thought he'd been riding too fast if Roberts couldn't keep up, then,
when he noticed his lap times — 1 minute 41 seconds — he *knew* he could
beat Roberts; he'd *qualified* at a higher speed! He'd passed through the
barrier. . . .'

For Crosby too, it was a break-through.

CROSBY   'Zolder was a new circuit for *everybody* and I had a race-long
dice with Kenny and Hartog and that made me feel as if I was one of the
boys. Since France, I'd begun to lose all that feeling of inadequacy and
inferiority; now I'd be able to talk to the boys on the same level.'

Mamola was 12 points behind Roberts overall, and needed to win the Finnish
GP. What were his chances?

MAMOLA   'Slim. I *needed* Kenny to break down because I needed extra points just to beat him. There was a chance. I was so close to doing what I wanted to do. I decided to try my hardest in the next three races. There was a lot of pressure building up for Finland and my chances were good there, because Kenny didn't *like* the circuit because his bike didn't handle on it, and I *knew* my Suzuki would.'

Randy had already considered his Imatra action plan.

MAMOLA   'If Kenny was right behind me or he was ahead of me I'd *definitely* try to go for it. If there was a chance of me winning, I'd push it to 105 or 110 per cent of my riding ability.'

But during Imatra practice, Christian Estrosi pulled across his path into the pits. At 150 mph, Randy hit the machine amidships, flying between some trees before landing on the lake shores, spitting gravel. A deep wound in his right — braking — hand was his most serious injury. The broken down-tube of the Suzuki frame was repaired by Ogborne and Vukmanovich; frames were rare, even to a factory team!

In the race Hartog took the lead after Lucchinelli retired, his XR34M spewing petrol. Rossi also retired with a blown head gasket, leaving Roberts 2nd behind Hartog, whilst Mamola diced with Uncini for 3rd, his right hand throbbing. Hartog took the flag from Roberts, Uncini and Mamola. Crosby was absent, racing at Suzuka in Japan.

Roberts and Mamola were equally determined to win at Silverstone, so often the decisive Championship round. Soon after the start, Roberts, Lucchinelli and Mamola were dicing for the lead, but Lucky slowed with tyre trouble, and Mamola eventually overwhelmed Roberts with consistent lap times to win the race. Earlier, whilst battling for 4th place, Crosby's rear tyre deflated and he finished 13th. Lucchinelli was 3rd and Rossi 4th, but Hartog retired with main bearing failure. As Randy took the flag, tears rolled down the cheeks of his personal manager, 'Jumbo' Jim Doyle. He yelled out 'That's *my* boy out there!'

Croz was disappointed.

CROSBY   'Whilst Daytona was the most gratifying race, Silverstone was the most disappointing, but it was made half-right by the Formula 1 result.'

In the F1 race, Crosby had thrashed the factory Hondas again, whilst new team-mate Joey Dunlop finished 2nd.

At the Nürburgring, Roberts and Mamola agreed not to race if it rained. Race day dawned dry . . . A Suzuki win would clinch their 5th successive 500 cc World Manufacturer's Championship, but Yamaha fielded Cecotto aboard the latest 'Power-valve' model to foil Suzuki's efforts, thus relieving Roberts of additional pressure; as in previous years, Roberts need only cruise to secure *his* title. In the race, Roberts lay 5th, with Mamola and Lucchinelli in front, followed by Crosby and Hartog, but a broken oil seal slowed Mamola who finished 5th, Lucchinelli winning from Crosby, Hartog and Roberts. Cecotto secured 6th place and Rossi — demonstrating against the dangerous track — retired after one lap.

Thus Suzuki retained their prestigious World Manufacturer's title and Roberts the individual Championship. Mamola, in his first factory-supported

Far right Graeme Crosby's hard-riding style suprised even Robin Drury during Croz's bid to catch eventual winner of the 1980 TT F1 race, Mick Grant *Bailey*

Right Croz was equally at home on the XR34H towards the end of 1980 *MCW*

season, was a close 2nd to Roberts. Lucchinelli was 3rd, Rossi 5th and Hartog 6th. Crosby, racing in America, Europe and Japan, still finished 8th in his *first* GP season and had already gained the TT F1 World Championship adding an Ulster win to his 2nd place at the TT. Suzuki's racing manager, Etsuo Yokouchi, sent him this telex:

> 'Dear Mr. G. Crosby, In honour of your great success in the 80 Tourist Trophy road racing World Championship we would like to say congraturations to your getting World Championship for your own and also for Suzuki Motor Company Limited.

> 'Your victory is highly appreciated and praised by the members of Suzuki Motor Company Limited, and also of Suzuki family in all over the world.'

Croz also won the Daytona 'Superbike' and the Suzuka 8 hour endurance race — partnered by American Wes Cooley — and came 2nd in the Forward Trust TT F1 Championship. Later in the year, he raced his trusty XR69 to victory in the Australian 'Swann' series.

Riding XR34s in the Shellsport series Mamola and Crosby were devastating, finishing 1st and 2nd. It was the Team's fifth successive victory. In the low-priority *MCN* Superbike series, Mamola was 5th and Crosby 12th.

It was no surprise that Randy and Croz signed Heron Suzuki contracts for 1981; Mamola to ride 500s, Graeme Crosby to ride 500s *and* F1 — as in 1980. John Newbold and Mick Grant signed to partner Croz in F1 events whilst Hiroyuki Kawasaki — Suzuki's Ryuyo test rider — joined the British Team for the early-season GPs riding a blue and white factory XR35.

After Texaco's part-sponsorship of Heron Suzuki in 1980, and the subsequent paddock references to the Team as Texaco's 'B Team', Heron Suzuki began the search for a new major sponsor. The result was 'Ingersoll Heron Team Suzuki' with additional Shell support. Martyn Ogborne became Team manager with Rex White the Team coordinator. Randy added Belgian Thierry

Left Mamola used the aluminium-framed XR35 Gamma for the 1981 Mallory Park Race of the Year, but a broken footrest slowed him considerably. The race inquest involves L to R: Gerin, Vukmanovich, Mamola, Burgess, Ed Mamola and his manager, Jim Doyle *Author*

Right Vukmanovich warms up Mamola's XR35 Gamma for the 1981 British GP which the American won. Roberts' Yamaha crew were pit neighbours at Silverstone *Author*

'Terry' Gerin to his support team whilst Crosby retained his 1980 GP squad, and Stewart Bone joined Dave Collins to maintain Crosby's F1 equipment. 1980 Team part-timer Steve Moore became Newbold's full-time mechanic in 1981.

In Italy, Roberto Gallina's Team Suzuki-Nava signed only Marco Lucchinelli to ride the new XR35s; Ton Riemersma's Dutch-based team comprised Wil Hartog.

Crosby was elated at qualifying fastest during the Austrian GP's final practice, but Mamola suffered a high-speed practice spill on the fastest bend.

MAMOLA 'I was really down. After tearing off two finger nails, my hand was really sore. Everyone said take pain-killers. Instead, to prove to myself that it was *my* fault, I went back out and qualified fastest. The next day was when the pain really showed up.'

During the race Roberts (aboard his new square-four Yamaha) retired and Lucchinelli crashed, whilst Mamola, Crosby and Kawasaki crossed the line in that order. An impressive debut for the Ingersoll Heron Team Suzuki squad.

One week later at Hockenheim rain effectively halved practice, but during dry sessions Mamola compared his Suzuki with Roberts' Yamaha.

MAMOLA 'Kenny was *still* the man to beat; shit that thing was haulin'.'

In good conditions a titanic race-battle developed between Roberts, Mamola, Lucchinelli and Cros who gradually fell back.

CROSBY 'We had a gearbox problem, apparently caused by slight seizure of the selector drum due to a lubricant problem. I ran off the track trying to change gears and on the last lap, the engine seized and I retired.'

Randy was suffering.

MAMOLA 'It was one of my most disappointing races; I know I *could* have

won it, but I hit a bump under hard braking and it jarred my wrist enough so that I couldn't move it. I was almost $1\frac{1}{2}$ seconds down on the last lap and when I made my last lap charge, I ended up 2nd. That really got me down . . .'

Last lap charge?

OGBORNE 'Randy did a sling-shot on Marco but he didn't get past Kenny and he was on the *outside* of the final corner.'

Roberts held a tight line whilst Randy slowed to avoid running wide, leaving Kenny to win from Mamola and Lucchinelli, with Croz out of the points. Hiroyuki Kawasaki forged ahead of Sheene and finished 5th. Overall points were: Mamola 30, Roberts 15, Kawasaki 14.

The new Yamaha aroused Suzuki's curiosity. Its higher-pitched exhaust note indicated a shorter-stroke engine and by watching the pre-race technical inspections, its stroke and weight were revealed. The 7500 rpm noise test speed of the Yamaha indicated a 51 mm stroke. Obtaining the weight was more difficult.

OGBORNE 'Mitsi and I got up at 6 o'clock to observe the weighing of the Yamaha. I don't think Yamaha expected us to get up quite so early. Kenny's mechanic refused to get off the bike when he saw us watching, but I noted the weight anyway. Then two big Germans lifted the mechanic onto the weighing machine to weigh him alone and I subtracted the two figures. The Yamaha weighed 136 Kg—nowhere near the magical 120 Kg on the paddock grapevine.'

The Suzuki gear selection problem was subsequently solved by changing the lubricant grade but other problems arose at the Italian GP.

CROSBY 'It took four days of practice to set these new 37.5 carburettors spot-on—they're really difficult to tune because of the low venturi air-speed. Then my bike threw a rod and I asked a spectator to watch the bike but when we returned to collect it the carburettors were missing. All four had been stolen.'

Race-day, unlike the hot practice periods, dawned cool, wet and misty, with heavy rain forecast; the machines were adjusted accordingly.

OGBORNE 'This means softening the suspension, slightly richening the mixture, and changing the tyres. On the warm-up lap Randy's engine seized, but he went through the motions of starting. We knew from the flat exhaust note that it was hopeless and he retired after one lap.'

After a tactical race Crosby finished 2nd to Roberts, with Lucchinelli in 5th place having started the race in pole. His problem? A small piece of tyre rubber lodged in a carburettor causing a race-long misfire.

The FIM regulations permit any pump fuel, and the 101 octane fuel available in the USA and Japan is commonly used. At the French GP, Ingersoll Heron Team Suzuki's fuel bowsers were empty and consequent use of 98 octane gasoline caused detonation problems. From two tune-up kits sent to Paul Ricard by Suzuki for Lucchinelli and Mamola, the pistons of higher silicon-content with anodised crowns provided the solution.

After an inspired race, Lucchinelli, Mamola and Crosby scored for Suzuki another XR35 hat-trick! In the overall points Mamola now had 39, Roberts 36, Crosby 34, with Lucchinelli and Sheene each with 31. Mamola was losing ground. . . .

Mamola drove to Rijeka for the Yugoslav GP hungry for victory, especially after a private Imola test-session en route proved that fitting Mikuni VM36SS carburettors solved the detonation *and* low-speed response problems of the VM37s. Furthermore, Ogborne had organised some race-fuel from Belgium.

At Rijeka, Mamola concentrated on gearing, (see Chapter 15) which enabled him to decimate his rivals, but track temperature was also critical.

Above After switching camps from Honda, Mick Grant took the 1981 Senior TT laurels ahead of Donny Robinson (left) and TT newcomer Newbold (3rd) *MCW*

MAMOLA 'We were all afraid our tyres wouldn't hold up for the race distance. And the track's really tight, and it makes you work for it. At the start, I wasn't sure I could last—my wrists were still hurtin'—because I was running a 3 inch by 18 inch front wheel—not a 16—and it was the biggest front we ever ran. It was really hard to push around. I spent all my time there figuring out a really good gearbox and I had Lucchinelli beat out on a gearbox! He had to ride his ass off to stay with me through the corners. That was a good victory for me; I really liked that one.'

The heat was so intense that Crosby changed his normal black helmet to an all-white version to keep his head cool! But Yugoslavia opened Graeme's eyes in other ways.

CROSBY 'Yugoslavia was a real hard race it was so hot. That's where I realised that my physical condition wasn't really good enough.'

At race-end it was Mamola, Lucchinelli — who rode brilliantly to stay with Mamola — Roberts and Crosby, a result extending Mamola's overall lead.

For the Dutch TT, Mamola's spare XR35 had been rebuilt using an aluminium frame which Taddy Matsui had brought with him from Japan. (Mitsi Okamoto had already returned to begin Suzuki's 1982 preparations) Masaru Ikegami, a Mikuni technician, visited Assen to solve Suzuki's carburation problems. (By now, the hot-tip was VM36SS.)

The race commenced in heavy rain. Crosby and Mamola both failed to finish.

MAMOLA   'I crashed. . . .'

CROSBY   'C-R-A-S-H! One of the most dreaded DNFs you can have . . . Rider error. . . .'

Roberts' Yamaha wouldn't start and Sheene soon retired but it was Lucchinelli's experience and skills that took him to victory, with Van Dulmen 2nd and Kork Ballington (Kawasaki) 3rd.

Lucchinelli deservedly became overall Champion leader with 58 points to Mamola's 54, with Roberts on 46 and Crosby on 42.

MAMOLA   'Things just started going downhill from that point on. . . . Every race after that, I had a problem; a certain problem.'

Mamola tried the new aluminium-framed XR35 in Dutch training but decided to race it at Spa-Francorchamps.

MAMOLA   'The Belgian GP was the first time I ever raced the aluminium frame. And it wobbled like crazy.'

The race started dry, but after a shower — which allowed van Dulmen to snatch a short-lived lead — order was restored; Roberts led, trailed by the Lucchinelli, Mamola and Sheene trio. Where was Crosby?

CROSBY   'Belgium was one of those races where sometimes you go good, sometimes you don't. And I just couldn't get to grips with the whole circuit.'

Crosby finished 7th whilst the brilliant Lucchinelli stormed through to snatch victory from Roberts, Mamola and Sheene.

Lucchinelli travelled to Italy for the San Marino GP at Imola, speculating on his fortunes with a home crowd *and* a 9 point lead over Mamola! Could he make it a hat-trick?

But Randy faced a difficult decision; his aluminium-framed XR35 (after much testing) now handled best, but his steel-framed model had the better engine. He chose the latter, despite the difficulties of heaving it through the chicane and during the early stages of the race he lay 4th with Sheene leading a fierce Lucchinelli-Crosby battle for 2nd place. Mamola decided to move.

MAMOLA   'I passed Crosby and Lucchinelli on the same corner and started to catch Barry. Then the rear tyre spun on the rim — about a third of a revolution — and it went so far out of balance that I couldn't really ride and I dropped back into 4th, and that's where I finished.'

Above Suzuki's 1981 World Champion Marco Lucchinelli mirrors Mamola's style aboard his Team Gallina XR35 Gamma. Lucky used a 16 in. front wheel *MCW*

OGBORNE 'As Randy accelerated past the pits, it made this terrible "wurbling" sound as if the engine had gone off. The rear wheel was bouncing off the road, and Randy later told me that it vibrated so bad, he couldn't even see where he was going.'

Following Randy's tyre problem, Dunlop effectively 'glued' the tyres on to the XR35's Dymag wheels! Meanwhile, Crosby had problems.

CROSBY 'The skies opened, but it only rained on one side of the circuit and the track was like glass—it was unreal. I was trying for 2nd place—Barry— and I passed him going into the corner, then the front wheel slid sideways, the back wheel went the other way. It was like a semi-trailer in a spin. Bikes and wheels were everywhere. I was thrown off the bike but held on with my hands. My arms broke the screen into bits. So that was real close; I was lucky to get 10 points out of that one!'

Kenny Roberts was too ill to start, but in the race (stopped eight laps short because of rain) Lucchinelli rode superbly to a well-deserved third successive victory, extending his overall score to 88 points, 16 ahead of Mamola.

Sheene was the favourite at Silverstone's British GP, but from the start, Croz led the field with Roberts and Sheene on his tail. Soon, Mamola and Lucchinelli joined in to form a five-man breakaway squad but as Croz led into Stowe corner on lap 3, his front wheel broke away and under panic-braking Sheene fell and retired alongside Crosby. Also falling in the mêlée, plucky Lucchinelli eventually re-started but was out of contention and finished 13th. Of the favourites, only Roberts and Mamola remained, but Kork Ballington and Jack Middleburg (on his Suzuki RG500) had tremendous rides to catch the American pair. In tight formation, all four jostled for the lead. Eventually, Ballington retired with a broken disc-valve, and three laps from the flag, Mamola's XR35 slowed and he finished 3rd. On the last lap, the Dutchman took the lead as they approached some back-markers giving Roberts no opportunity to regain it.

But what had caused Croz's embarrasing prang?

CROSBY 'I remember the front went, then it gripped again but by then the back had started to come round. It was a pretty straightforward crash.'

And Mamola?

MAMOLA 'I was set to win when the crankshaft nut backed off, punched a hole in the cover and weakened the mixture, which eventually burned a hole in the piston.'

At Imatra for the Finnish GP, the pressure was on Mamola but whilst 'Lucky's' Gallina-prepared XR35 ran perfectly, both Crosby and Mamola suffered major misfiring problems with theirs, probably due to the problematic 37.5 mm carburettors.

MAMOLA 'It would only run on three cylinders and then you'd hit a bump and it'd fire up on four. It was the hardest thing ever to ride because in some corners it'd go onto three, then kick onto four and it'd just go sideways because of the horsepower difference.'

Likewise, Sheene and Roberts shared problems with 'power-valve' breakdowns;

Sheene retired, Roberts slowed, his Championship chances dashed. It seemed that Imatra's notoriously bumpy surface was the culprit.

From pole position Lucchinelli led the race throughout, the drama in his slipstream, where Roberts held 2nd place until the last-lap, Sheene retiring mid-race. Crosby nursed his misfiring Suzuki to 5th place, whilst after Roberts' retirement Mamola's 'last-lap charge' enabled him to snatch 2nd place from Ballington.

And so to Anderstorp and the Swedish GP. Lucchinelli needed only a 6th place to win the Championship for Suzuki: Mamola to win *and* with the Italian 7th or lower. Run in semi-wet conditions, tyre choice was crucial. Lucchinelli and Roberts fitted full 'wets' but 'intermediates' proved wisest, and both Sheene and van Dulmen benefitted from them. After the warm-up laps, Roberts and Mamola *knew* they had problems; Roberts' tyres were worn out and Mamola's XR35 had a broken front fork seal. Roberts retired on lap 6 and Mamola struggled around and finished 13th. Lucchinelli was riding cautiously on his 'wets' too, but when he passed Mamola he knew the title was his. Meanwhile, Sheene and van Dulmen pulled away and it was the British rider who took the chequered flag ahead of van Dulmen with Crosby (suffering from a spongy front brake) in 5th, and Lucchinelli 9th—but WORLD CHAMPION!

What a party there was in Anderstorp that night! Lucchinelli and Mamola had taken 1st and 2nd places in the Individual Championship whilst Suzuki had retained their Manufacturer's title for the sixth successive year.

Mamola's immaculate Suzuki XR35M glistens in the Rijeka sun as he heads for the flag during the 1981 Yugoslav GP *Vogelzano*

Meanwhile, Ingersoll Heron Team Suzuki attacked the F1 World Championship with Crosby, Newbold and Grant. In the Island round, Grant retired with a bent valve—third gear had failed too—but Croz easily won the race with a new F1 lap record to boot—113.7 mph. Newbold, an Island newcomer, rode brilliantly to finish 4th.

The F1 race wasn't without its politics. After discovering a punctured rear tyre minutes before the start, Croz arrived at the line about 20 seconds late and was ordered to the back of the grid—a time penalty of about 5 minutes. Like a man possessed, Croz accepted the challenge but Honda's Ron Haslam was declared the winner. However, Suzuki had lodged a protest during the race—and told Honda—and the FIM jury later scrubbed Croz's time penalty and declared him the rightful winner.

In the TT Classic event, despite another bent valve, Grant finished 2nd, crossing the line with winner Crosby, with Newbold again in 4th.

The second and final F1 round at Ulster was run in cold, wet and misty conditions. Haslam won this muddy affair with Croz, Grant and Newbold in 2nd, 3rd and 4th places. With a 1st and 2nd at each of the two rounds, race times decided the F1 World Champion and Croz's Island dash earned him the title for the second year, with Newbold and Grant 4th and 5th.

In UK mainland events, Crosby was virtually unbeatable, crushing the F1 Hondas—Crosby won the *Motor Cycle Weekly* F1 Championship—and winning all but one of the Shellsport races (Mamola won the other) on his XR35 to retain the title for Suzuki.

Whilst 1981 was a good year for Suzuki, the immense cost of racing caused Heron Suzuki to reconsider their 1982 plans. Having spear-headed Suzuki's GP campaigns since 1976, the publicity value of GP successes was outweighed by the viability of UK mainland victories. Conversely, Suzuki Japan began to appreciate the customer value (especially in Japan) of Individual, as opposed to Manufacturer's, World Championship titles. It became preferable to promote a *rider* linked to the Suzuki brand rather than vice-versa. This new philosophy was an important factor in formulating Suzuki's 1982 racing plans.

In the autumn of 1981, Heron Suzuki's chairman Peter Agg, and commercial director Denys Rohan—a keen race enthusiast—flew to Hamamatsu to confer with Suzuki. A decision was reached and in October Rohan established a new Swiss-registered company, Suzuki Racing Promotions, a joint venture of Suzuki Japan and Heron Suzuki GB with the single objective of grand prix racing. Kenji Shimizu was chairman and Masao Tani—Suzuki's European marketing manager—was director whilst Denys Rohan became the managing director controlling the UK-based company. One rider had already signed up.

ROHAN   'The goal of the new company is to win the 500 cc World Championship, both individual and Manufacturer's. Randy Mamola has already signed a two year contract and will be leading our attack. In Randy, we have a rider capable of winning the 500 cc title in 1982 and for many years to come.'

Rohan also negotiated a £1m sponsorship deal with HB, West Germany's top-selling cigarette manufacturer and the new association became 'Team HB Suzuki'.

But what about Suzuki's incumbent 500 cc World Champion? Marco

The angled anti-dive units on the front forks show Newbold to be riding the 1981 Yoshimura-tuned XR69-S. Noddy finished 4th in the TT F1 Classic series that year
Archives

Lucchinelli had already signed a multi-million dollar Honda contract to ride their new two stroke GP machine. Lucchinelli's defection underlined the value of Suzuki's new racing policy; long-term rider contracts and GP dedication.

SRP considered potential team-mates for Randy, but most of the GP stars were already contracted and the short-list was short. But one talented rider had—for contractual reasons—lain dormant for two years; Virginio Ferrari, the 1980 runner-up in the classics aboard a Suzuki XR27B. Denys Rohan approached Ferrari who gratefully signed with SRP as number two rider to Mamola.

With riders and factory hardware confirmed, SRP's team manager Martyn Ogborne commenced the organisation; premises, transport, equipment and experienced mechanics. Mamola retained his 1981 support crew, but for Ferrari, who came without a support team, Ogborne went immediately to Mike Sinclair who was kicking his heels in New Zealand following Hartog's retirement. Ogborne had little persuading to do. Sinclair was joined by Steve Flaunty, another ex-Hartog mechanic.

Acknowledging the track record of Roberto Gallina's Italian Team, Suzuki also provided new XR's for Franco Uncini and Loris Reggiani and on past records, the Gallina squad is likely to be a force to be reckoned with in 1982.

With Suzuki's GP future assured, Heron Suzuki GB were free to exploit the UK racing scene with British riders on semi-factory production RG500 Mk VIIs, XR69s and Suzuki Katanas for the 'Streetbike' class. Rex White became the new team coordinator working from a brand new race shop incorporated in Heron Suzuki's Crawley headquarters.

Over twenty years road racing experience on four continents has raised Suzuki from relative obscurity to that of world leaders in motorcycle technology. For Suzuki at least, racing *has* improved the breed.

Chapter 14   Suzuki's arsenal:
XR rockets (1966 to 1978)

When US Suzuki decided to contest the 1966 Daytona event, they commenced a race-conversion of the recently-launched Super Six — 'X6' in the USA — 250 cc roadster. The porting was fettled, and expansion chambers and larger carburettors fitted, but many chassis items remained standard. A twin disc front brake was tested during the Carlsbad races after which it was replaced by the standard drum brake. Only its large fuel tank and humped-back seat spelt 'racer', the idea being to demonstrate to the Americans the durability of a standard Suzuki.

During 1967, GP commitments prevented factory developments but US Suzuki further improved the X6 racers; radical porting, Wiseco pistons, and 27 mm Mikuni carburettors fed by rubber-mounted float-chambers, together with a crankshaft-mounted US-made ARD magneto boosted power output. Cylinders with larger cooling fins improved engine cooling while bracing tubes around the steering head strengthened the frame.

Having withdrawn from GP competition in 1968, Suzuki's factory race-shop had time to develop their new T250 roadster into the TR250 'over-the-counter' production racer. The engine was based on the standard bottom-end, with power raised to a reliable 35 bhp at 9000 rpm. Driving through a six-speed gearbox, this was sufficient for speeds approaching 120 mph. Chassis components began to resemble GP hardware; the four leading-shoe front brake was ex-RT67 and a new GP-type fairing hid the totally new frame.

For 1968, Suzuki also developed the TR500, (XR05) a racing version of the new T500 twin roadster, but only the engine was common and *that* was heavily modified. In place of the generator, Suzuki fitted a Kokusan-Denki magneto and a brace of Mikuni VM32SC racing carburettors fed the special cylinders, but the XR05 retained the five-speed gearbox, wet clutch and CCI lubrication system of the T500, although the oil pump flow was regulated by handlebar lever. To withstand racing stress, the CCI system was supplemented by a lean pre-mix. The chassis was entirely new; a twin-loop cradle type with a rear sub-frame of smaller diameter tubing. The engine was mounted high in the chassis and the twin down-tubes were pinched to clear the exhausts. Maximum power was 63.5 BHP at 8000 rpm; dry weight was 297 lb (135 Kg).

For 1969, the XR05 was modified; becoming much lower and narrower, and with a 1 bhp increase, top speed was raised by 12 mph.

Until 1970, AMA racing rules favoured Harley-Davidson. Only side-valvers were eligible in the 750 cc class and Suzuki raced the XR05 against the Milwaukee thumpers. In 1970, the AMA changed their rules and at Daytona, OHC 750 cc Hondas and OHV 750 cc Triumphs vied with the Harleys. Suzuki took note of the growing interest in 750 cc class racing.

Upper The T250-based TR250
of 1968 used special sand-cast
cylinders and heads and twin,
remote-floats fed the Mikuni
carburettors *MCW*

Lower The 1966 X6 racer
closely resembled its roadster
brother, even retaining the
kick-starter. Dick Hammer
(wearing track suit) watches his
mechanics change plugs *Cycle
World*

Chris Young and Riichi Itoh about to drop the engine from an XR05 at Ontario in 1971. The cowl improved cooling until the model was water-cooled in 1973 *MCW*

The specially cast cylinder and head castings of the 1972 XR11 are evident here as are the oil pump, early-type clutch cover and the blanked-off main bearing enabling a shorter crankshaft to be used *Cycle World*

Winter development yielded a 6 bhp bonus raising power to 70.5 bhp for the 1970 XR05—VM34SC carburettors were specified, although other changes were minimal. 1970 marked Suzuki's last attempt at fielding a competitive 250 cc machine. Power was up to 41 bhp at 9000 rpm and the TR250 managed 122 mph (197 Km/h), but was still grossly overweight. US Suzuki teamster Jody Nicholas

NICHOLAS 'They were so big, they looked like 500s. In fact, the quickest way to tell them apart was to look at the expansion chambers; the 500's tail pipes were longer than the 250's. They weren't that slow, once you got them up to speed, but it took them forever to accelerate because they were so heavy.'

The 250s were withdrawn mid-season. Despite a decade of effort, Suzuki had never achieved success in the 250 cc category.

For 1971 the XR05 was only marginally improved, including the fitting of electronic ignition, but nevertheless, XR05s were 2nd and 3rd in the 500 cc World Championship that year. 'Daytona' porting was specified for the

Following the Atlanta protest, the XR11s were wheeled out at Talladega (1972) with street-legal cylinder and head castings. Note the improved clutch cover *Waaser*

following year, and the model became the TR500II although the factory coding was stil XR05.

After his initial involvement with the RS67 V4, Makoto Hase had designed Suzuki's little monoposto racing car, the Fronte. Powered by a 360cc three cylinder two stroke engine and originally air-cooled, Hase had converted it to water-cooling. In 1971 Suzuki announced the world's largest-ever two stroke motorcycle, the water-cooled GT750. Suzuki decided to race the triple in the USA and Hase became involved. It was coded XR11, or more generally, the TR750.

HASE 'The biggest problems with the TR750 were the crankshaft which was the standard component and was easily twisted, and the clutch. A wet-type clutch was not feasible and so we changed it to a dry-type but there was not a lot of room for the conversion. It was a big job.'

Shoji Tanaka joined Suzuki's race-shop in 1970. He now works at a Suzuki dealership in the USA.

TANAKA 'Cooling the clutch was a problem and we drilled the covers at one time. We made many different prototypes but we mostly used clutch covers with the large air tube.'

Generally, the GT750 lent itself well to race conversion. The key to power lay inside the cylinders and a racing cylinder was cast with modified porting incorporating a larger, bridged exhaust port.

TANAKA 'If you saw the inside, it would look the same as a GT750 cylinder, but if you modified a GT750 cylinder and you ground the exhaust port too much, then you will break through into the water passages. That's why we made a completely different casting.'

Below The 1974 XR11 'low-boy' frame, a nickname earned because of the reduced seat height *Author*

Bottom The 1973 XR11 chassis *Author*

To reduce weight, magnesium castings were used and titanium for the screws and other chassis parts. Carburettors, too, were special racing Mikunis (originally 32 mm but later 34 mm bore), but the basically standard crankshaft—modified to reduce engine width—proved satisfactory at that stage.

To house the 100 bhp motor, a new ultra-light chassis was made, but with tubing too small in diameter it became the achilles heel of the XR11 and led to it being nicknamed the 'Flexi-flier' by those who rode it.

During the early months of 1972, US Suzuki rider Jody Nicholas flew to Hamamatsu for an XR11 Ryuyo track test.

NICHOLAS 'I really didn't know what to expect and I was having so much trouble trying to figure out how to hang on that I didn't scratch around as hard as I could have: I guess I was a little afraid of it. With the tall gearing we were using—almost Daytona gearing—it was deceptive. It didn't yank your arms out of their sockets when you accelerated, because bottom was a 90 mph gear!'

On Ryuyo's long straight, that high gearing moved Nicholas through the speed trap at 173 mph. The subsequent poor handling wasn't apparent at Ryuyo.

NICHOLAS 'It wasn't so bad in Japan because the curves were more gradual and faster. The tyres *were* questionable and there was no sense in flinging it up the road. It didn't start to show its bad traits until we got to England for the Match Races.'

As Jody prepared to leave Japan, team-mate Ron Grant arrived, but Jody was then familiar with the tyre/sheer brute bhp combination.

NICHOLAS 'We were going around for the second time and we'd got about to the second turn, and I'd already told him, "You've got to watch it because you can break the rear-end loose!" Even though we were running Daytona gearing, when Ron whacked it on, the bike got sideways and spat him off.'

Suzuki never introduced the GT750 with racing in mind; until 1971 AMA rules forbade water-cooled machines, by which time the GT750 was already designed. The XR11 was a genuine roadster-based racer unlike the Kawasaki 750 which in later years became water-cooled to cope with escalating power.

As the XR11's first season progressed, handling was improved. Bracing tubes were added to the chassis and rear suspension experiments abounded but it was not until years later that the beast was tamed. Meanwhile, the riders had to formulate their own techniques.

Right Factory fresh and
straight from the crate, a
gleaming XR11 at Ryuyo in
1972. Compare the rear frame
design with those below which
were additionallybraced to
improve the squirming
progress of the 'flexi-flier'
Cycle World

NICHOLAS 'It was hard to ignore the handling, it was so bad! The TR750
was awfully big and heavy, but when you got on the power, the frame
seemed to bend in the middle. I finally figured out how to steer it; you just
aimed and squirted it—and hoped to get there wobbling around, especially
in the lower gears, even in a straight line. Once up to speed, if you didn't
make any fast manoeuvres, it was pretty stable.'

For 1973, it was decided to water-cool the XR05 engine, in line with the XR11
which shared the same bore and stroke. The new TR500III also had an air-
cooled clutch, and a six-speed gearbox was added in mid '73. It produced 73 bhp
at 8000 rpm—only a small increase—but was more reliable.Despite the addition
of a radiator and water-pump (which was installed in place of an oil-pump), the
use of exotic materials kept its dry weight down to 308 lb (140 Kg), little more
than its predecessor.

Handling and braking were vastly improved with a new, lower chassis and the
triple disc arrangement that had been proved on the heavier XR11. However, it
was plain that the 500 twin was at the peak of its development and would soon
need replacement.

For 1973, XR11 performance was boosted to 107 bhp by modified ports and
expansion chambers and larger, VM38SS carburettors. Handling was improved
by small changes to the frame.

TANAKA 'We had a little bit problem with the frame—it's not strong
enough I think—and around the rear end it was too weak. In 1973, we
changed the pipe size and we put in extra tubes around the rear, and
everything we made from slightly stronger tube.'

Incredibly the overall weight was reduced by 16 lb (7 Kg) to 352 lb (160 Kg).

By 1973, Masanao Shimizu, the engineer behind Suzuki's 1960 GP machines,
had become general manager of the engineering department, and agreed to back
a proposal put by Makoto Hase.

HASE 'The racing department obtained a budget from Mr Shimizu to
design a machine to beat Yamaha. The objectives were to win the 500 cc
World Championship and the World Manufacturer's Championship. The
budget was not small. . . .'

Hase's proposal was to revolutionise Suzuki's European prospects and become a legend on the world's grand prix racetracks, the RG500 or XR14.

HASE   'I started the RG500 layout in July or August 1973. Our target was 100 bhp because at that time, we thought that Yamaha and MV had around 90 bhp. There were two persons working on the engine, Makoto Suzuki my assistant, and myself. One person, Hisao Inagaki, was responsible for the chassis design.

'We started from nothing and designed a square-four—not the same as the RS67 because the RG500 had a primary shaft. I thought that the cylinders must be vertical for easy maintenance and to make it more small. We decided on a 500 because we had some chassis experience with 500s and 750s at the Daytona races and also the 500 cc class gives more publicity and prestige.

'We intended the RG500 to start racing in March 1974 so we had eight months to design and develop it, and one month for shipment to Europe.

'At this time we had no intention of selling a production version of the RG but I thought that in the future, maybe we could sell it so it should not be too complicated—very easy machining.

'To save time we developed the ports, disc valve timing and expansion chambers using a single cylinder 125 cc version.'

Nicholas and Grant made abortive attempts to tame the XR11 at Ryuyo by changing the rear suspension pre-loads and damping forces of these special units *Cycle World*

Expansion chamber design was still a chop-and-weld development and over 50 types were evaluated before Number 50 was chosen. This was used on all factory 500-4s up to 1978 when Number 116 was used. Production RGs up to MkIV used Number 50. Currently, over 150 RG expansion chambers have been tested on Suzuki's dynamometers.

Light weight was critical and in Japan, magnesium is difficult to cast due to the climate but Hase found the Kobe-Seiko Company capable of producing the intricate, though expensive, RG castings.

After machining, the first complete engine was assembled and soon the crisp Hamamatsu air rang to the sound of a square-four two stroke, the first time in almost ten years.

HASE   'The first RG500 engine ran at the end of November and we tested throughout December and January. On the dynamometers we checked the parts for durability and strength. The first problem we had was with the crankshaft gears; they kept breaking. So, we thought about materials, hardness and heat-treatment; everything we had to change. We had big-end problem in the early stages and we thought it necessary to use an oil pump. The oil pump fed oil direct to the big-end bearing which is the most important bearing. After more testing, we found an oil pump was no longer necessary.' (The pump was deleted for the 1976 XR14.)

Despite using four water-cooled cylinders, the first XR14 machine weighed 290 lb (132 Kg), less than its predecessor the XR05, and produced 95 bhp, just short of Hase's objective.

Whilst Hase and Suzuki struggled with the engine, Hisao Inagaki wrestled with the chassis and to save weight, designed an open-type frame, similar to that

Upper Findlay's 1973 water-cooled XR05 was fettled in Europe by Shoji Tanaka. Basically two-thirds of the XR11, it was developed in parallel. Note how the oil pump was deleted in favour of a water pump *MCW*

Left By late 1974, the XR14 was on its 3rd frame redesign. The full-loop chassis solved its early handling problems *Gruber*

Below Early XR14 crankshaft unreliability was overcome by forced lubrication via an oil pump mounted beneath the front carburettor. (Oil was carried in the seat tank—*see above*.) As usual, the radiator was made of aluminium *Gruber*

of the RS67 125-V4. During the 1974 season, this design was modified.

> HASE 'The original frame was not so stable in the corners so we used
> bolted-in tubes temporarily before we introduced a full-loop chassis.'

During this development period, little time was spent on the XR05, but a modified cylinder incorporating larger water-passages—in line with the larger water-pump—was introduced for 1974, boosting power and mid-range torque. Similar changes to the XR11 improved power to 108 bhp, whilst the oil pump was removed as big-end lubrication had improved by controlling con-rod side-thrust at the small end which exposed the big-end bearings to the pre-mix lubricant. A six-speed gearbox was specified and double-piston calipers improved the braking of Suzuki's fastest machine, which now had a lower chassis, the 'low boy'.

For 1975, the XR14 was still using five port cylinders—four transfers and a loop scavenge port—but power had increased to 100 bhp at 11,200 rpm. The chassis became a fully welded loop-type and handling was much improved. The lower mountings of the rear suspension units had moved back to a point almost above the rear axle, resulting in a more progressive action for soaking up circuit bumps, and a box-section aluminium swing-arm was specified.

Similarly, the XR11 was face-lifted for 1975 with an XR14-type swing-arm, 'lay-down' shocks and power increased to 116 bhp at 8250 rpm. Now, the handling was near-perfect, overcoming its power deficiency compared to Yamaha's new 750.

Reports from factory personnel in Europe during 1975 convinced Makoto Hase that to improve the XR14 for 1976, some basic changes were required. Out went the old cylinder dimensions and in came the classic 54 mm bore and stroke.

> HASE 'The 54–54 engine made for Barry Sheene in 1976 was different
> because the low and middle-range power was improved. Maximum power
> was only slightly improved, but with a longer stroke, we had bigger ports
> although rpm had to be slightly reduced.'

At the same time, the oil pump was deleted and the primary shaft—previously an unreliable two-piece unit—redesigned as a one-piece forging.

> HASE 'Everything was different compared with the original type. To
> improve power output, everything has to be considered: the carburettor,
> the carburettor air-funnel, the disc valve, the scavenge ports, the shape of
> the cylinder heads, expansion chambers. Everything.

> 'The porting has been developed: the original RG had only four ports plus
> the loop scavenge port, but by introducing a seven port cylinder, we had
> more low and mid-range power.'

The Suzuki seven port cylinder actually has ten holes. The bridged exhaust accounts for two, the loop scavenge a further two (one above the other), with three scavenge—or transfer—ports up either side. With the piston at BDC, there are actually seven ports transferring mixture to the cylinder. The secret lies in the *shape* of the transfers; the loop scavenge port may be directly opposite the open exhaust port but being angled sharply upwards, the swirling gases emitted from it effectively prevent the escape of the mixture down the exhaust port. Any that does is quickly pushed back inside the cylinder by the action of the expansion chamber. Hence Suzuki's efforts in developing their shapes.

Before changes are made, it is not only power, durability and strength that are considered, because ultimately, the rider must be able to tune his engine.

HASE 'If we make a small change to port timing or valve timing, it is necessary to change the air-funnel to obtain the best power curve and also to improve the rider's feel when he is setting up the carburation.'

Two of Sheene's three 'special' XR14s had new chassis, nick-named 'A' frames by the factory mechanics. In addition, the 'lay-down' shocks were moved forward on the swing-arm, a feature of the revised chassis. Kayaba, Suzuki's supplier of suspension components, contributed special pneumatic front forks—nitrogen-charged to about 1.2 Atm (17.5 psi)—further improving handling and adding instant adjustability. The legs were 35 mm in diameter with a 150 mm stroke, dimensions which would dramatically change as the XRs were developed.

With these improvements, the chassis could cope with the 114 bhp delivered by the new engine, a World Championship-winning package in 1976. Hase's goal had been achieved in just three years.

During 1976, Hase and his team were busy developing a larger version of the 500 machine for Team use in 1977, the 652 cc XR23. Basically an over-bored version with 62 mm diameter pistons, this monster produced too much power for the chassis and was detuned to a milder 135 bhp at 10,800 rpm! The unique feature of this engine was its 'stepped' cylinder layout.

HASE 'We went to the stepped cylinder design because it lowered the centre of gravity and moved it forward. Additionally, it was good for cooling because it freed the area just behind the radiator; if the front cylinders are high, there is less room for air-flow. It was also possible to remove the transmission from the right without the need to remove the engine from the frame.'

Air-flow through the radiator was also the subject of fairing development as Hennen's tuner of 1977 and 1978 recalls.

SINCLAIR 'A lot of experimenting was done to get the air off the front mudguard and the fairing and onto the radiator. A plastic divider was used from 1977 to provide a chute and the radiators were more effectively sealed.'

The XR23 design solved several problems; the changed centre of gravity reduced the 'wheelie' effect and improved handling. Furthermore, although previous models had interchangeable gear ratios, the ratios of the XR23 could be changed much quicker.

SINCLAIR 'Suzukis are easier to work on than most of the others because they build them with maintenance in mind. They do odd little things to suit the mechanics like the little tabs on the clutch case so that you can prise it off. Swapping internal gear ratios? I think the quickest it was done was about 15 minutes, but that was by throwing the bike on its side—no oil draining. Normally it's about 20 minutes. 75 minutes was the record to change the cranks, that's with two people, one handling the spanners, the other working. These times are much quicker than when working on a

Yamaha. If you have to, you can work real quick on these things.'

With Suzuki's old policy of dual-purpose employees such as designer-mechanics, the XRs were as quick *off* the track as when they were on it! If a rider goes to the line with *exactly* the correct gear ratios and suspension settings, he has a winning edge over his rivals who haven't the time or facility.

The purpose of designing the 652 cc machine was not a portent of a renewed F750 onslaught. Suzuki were simply pushing forward the technological barriers to learn of future problems when the 500 cc model produced the same performance. The XR23 was a mobile laboratory.

Some features of the XR23 were soon transferred to the 500s; the braced swing-arm, which according to Makoto Hase increased stiffness by over 50 per cent, and the sophisticated, $2000 Kayaba 'Golden Shocks', perhaps *the* most adjustable rear suspension system. They were totally hand-built, their bodies machined from an aluminium billet, and were fully adjustable. The volume of nitrogen gas, varied by the addition or removal of packing pieces, provided the sole springing medium. Pre-load varied according to the gas pressure—usually about 3.5 Atms (52 psi)—and damping force was adjustable in two ways: changing the oil viscosity for coarse tuning, and fine tuning by turning a knurled ring which introduced progressively smaller holes into the damping oil circuit. To reduce oil aeration and temperature, a remote reservoir connected to the main body by hose contained a fully-floating piston separating the gas and oil. Adjustment was a daunting task but Hennen soon mastered the art. The XR23 used pneumatic forks similar to those first seen on Sheene's 1976 XR14s.

The 1977 XR14 500 cc engine was similar to that used in 1976 but the chassis was modified. Golden Shocks controlled the rear end whilst pneumatic forks of larger diameter and shorter stroke, 36 mm by 140 mm, handled the front. The machine was consequently 10 mm lower.

Above Hennen's 1975 XR11 represents the zenith of 750–3 development. Morris magnesium wheels, plasma-sprayed aluminium discs and the liberal use of titanium nuts and bolts reduced its weight to 326 lb (148 Kg) *Bill Delaney/ Cycle*

Left Crankcase 'stuffers' maximumised the primary CR whilst straight-cut primary gears ensured minimal power loss. Clutch plates were sintered bronze, carburettors magnesium alloy. The extra gear ratio (6-speed) of the 1975 XR11 necessitated deletion of the oil pump *Bill Delaney/ Cycle*

During 1976, the factory investigated aerodynamics and frequently tested machines in the JARI (Japan Automobile Research Institute) wind-tunnel near Tokyo. Many advances resulted, the first of which was seen at the 1977 Venezuelan GP. There, the factory XR14s sported a small spoiler, integral with the fairing and positioned around its lower nose. (Factory mechanics called this fairing 'Donald Duck'!) At the practice for the abortive Austrian GP this was superseded by a new 'razor edge' fairing, with a sharp lower nose and dead flat bottom in the place of the former wide belly pan. Actually, two types were evaluated; one had a blunt lower nose whilst the other was quite pointed. Furthermore, each type was available to suit two widths of radiator, wide for hot days and large radiators, and vice versa. After much testing during the early-season GPs, the blunt-nosed version got the riders' votes.

Involvement with the World Championships left little time for other projects, but even whilst working flat out in 1976 on the new 652 cc models, Hase managed to provide time to satisfy a request from Suzuki's overseas marketing department to produce 100 and 125 cc models for racing in South East Asia. Suzuki were attacking this market with their smaller roadsters, but so was Yamaha, and sales hinged on local racetrack successes. A design team led by Yazukazu Fujisawa—with Riichi Itoh as dyno-technician—produced the XR21 and XR24 model single cylinder racers. Originally, these racers had horizontal cylinders, but handling problems prompted a redesign with inclined cylinders, with such large cooling fins that the crankcase appeared miniscule. A disc valve and front exhaust with under-slung expansion chamber was specified, together with a crankshaft-mounted magneto. Although similar in concept, the chassis was quite different; the horizontal top-rails of the XR21 resulted in a long flat fuel tank, whereas the top-rails of the XR24 ran straight from the steering head toward the swing-arm pivot. Thus the XR24 fuel tank was similar to those on the larger XR racers. Both models featured pneumatic forks and conventional rear suspension units, and the swing-arms were tubular steel fabrications supporting a spoked wheel with a 150 mm diameter single leading-shoe drum brake. A similar 18 inch front wheel mounted a 250 mm diameter hydraulic disc brake. Both fairing and seat units were based on the early XR components.

Designed for 1977 use, though not unveiled until 1978, the new XR22 GP model featured stepped cylinders, allowing the harvest of rapid gear-ratio changes to be reaped on the GP circuits. Power was raised to 122 bhp at 11,000 rpm and many XR23 chassis features were incorporated, such as the braced swing arm and 37 mm diameter fork legs—although stroke was further reduced to 130 mm. Golden Shocks were now mounted with their auxiliary chambers *above* the body, obviating the swing-arm cut-aways to clear the chambers as on the 1977 XR14.

Hennen's fierce late-braking techniques necessitated a more balanced system. Frans VandenBroek worked with Mike Sinclair on Hennen's machines throughout his European career.

VANDENBROEK 'Patrick didn't use the rear brakes too hard at all and we made a simple pedal modification that reduced the leverage on the rear brake. He liked to have his bike set up so that he could pull hard with his right hand and stomp with his foot and not have to modulate the two functions.'

SINCLAIR 'As a result of our experiments, the brakes were changed; bigger on the front and smaller on the rear. It was just development of tyres; front tyres got better and you could use more front brake. The rears were always over-braked. It took them a while to twig on that you didn't need that much rear brake.'

The XR22 front discs were 5 mm larger in diameter (300 mm) whilst the rear disc was 10 mm smaller (230 mm).

The XR22 fairing was redesigned. This time, it had sprouted a pair of 'wings' and its blunt nose was tucked further under the front tyre.

SINCLAIR 'The idea in bringing the nose more forward was that the air could come off the tyre and straight onto the fairing for good directional stability at really high speed.'

The wings needed modification.

Above This XR22 side-loading gear-cluster could be pre-assembled and installed within 15 minutes. The 'stepped' cylinders of the 1977 XR23 first made this possible. (See p 171) *Author*

VANDENBROEK 'The original stubby wings allowed the air to escape over the side, so we made some side plates out of a plastic food container and put it together and it *did* work. It gave us more down-force but knocked some speed off the top end. It also made the front tyre a little hotter.'

HASE   'The wings improved high speed stability and provided a down-force for good grip on fast corners. Now they aren't necessary because we have made more improvements to the cowling shape.'

By mid-season yet another fairing was used with larger carburettor bulges each side; the air-intakes were further from the fairing walls and power was increased. To reduce weight, carbon fibres were used in their construction, one of many spin-offs from aircraft and Formula One car development incorporated by Suzuki. In the quest for strength and light weight, certain *engine* components were made of this space-age material; engine top and bottom covers, and mounting plates.

The 1978 652 cc model, the XR23A, used an improved clutch operating mechanism.

HASE   'We changed the mechanism from push-rod type to pull-type system because the number of parts is less and we lost some weight. Also, we sometimes had the push-rod ends friction-weld together if the grease ever got out.'

Improved twin-float Mikuni carburettors with larger plastic air-funnels were fitted, which overcame a fuel surge problem under hard acceleration. 'Nikosil' plated cylinders not only reduced weight—previous cylinders used cast-iron liners—but improved cooling by way of better heat conduction. Chassis modifications were minimal although XR22-type fairing and seat units were used.

The press were never informed of these subtle modifications to avoid embarrassment if unsuccessful. Furthermore, the press never appreciated that technical advances in suspension technology were being made under their very noses. Unless armed with vernier calipers, they would never know of the changes in fork leg diameter and suspension stroke. Even such simple modifications necessitated other changes: fork legs needed new fork yokes, handlebars and fork sliders. Reduced stroke meant changes in steering geometry, fork dampers and fairing design. But always, the Team Suzuki machines came to the line in their familiar colours with the familiar stickers.

Meanwhile, the XR21 was completely redesigned by Yazukazu Fujisawa using all the knowledge gained in Europe on the larger race-ware.

More marketing pressure was applied.

HASE   'We designed the RJ100 (XR29) just for racing in Indonesia because the market is getting bigger and it became necessary to beat Yamaha for good publicity.'

The engine was an inclined single with forced water-cooling via a water pump, skew-gear-driven off the crankshaft. The traditional disc valve mounted a Mikuni VM32SS carburettor. Because both ends of the crankshaft were occupied, the Nippon Denso CDI magneto, sitting above the gearbox, was gear-driven from behind the air-cooled clutch, which was operated by push-rod via a mechanism similar to that on the early factory fours. The engine sat high in the compact full-loop chassis, which was a virtual replica of the later square-four types, with the lower mounts of the 'lay-down' rear shocks further along the aluminium box-section swing-arm. The shocks were lightweight aluminium coil-sprung units with remote reservoirs and were inverted to reduce unsprung

Above Cutaway flywheels were only used in the 652 cc 1979 XR23B. Note the independent cranks *Author*

Upper left The 1978 XR29 100 cc single cylinder racer was derived from the square-four brethren. The water pump and magneto were both mounted above the gearbox *MCW*

Hennen's 1977 XR14 used
Kayaba 'Golden Shock'
dampers. The adjustment ring
is beneath the main body; the
nitrogen valve on the auxiliary
chamber. The plastic tie-wrap
indicates suspension movement
and helps suspension tuning
MCW

weight. Wheels were 18 in. Campagnolo magnesium types, mounting
hydraulic discs; a sub-miniature 200 mm diameter rear and a 285 mm diameter
front. Pneumatic forks were still specified. The most radical change was the
carbon-fibre reinforced fairing which was the result of much wind-tunnel
development. Like the XR22 version, its leading edge followed the contours of
the front tyre, but below the engine, it was 'pinched' almost to a knife-edge. Seat
unit and tank were again similar to XR22 components, the seat being mounted
by 'Kamikaze seat belts'! Actually, these were small plastic 'tie-wraps' made by
the Kamikaze Company, but in Suzuki's parts inventory, the first description is
used. This elegant little racer produced 25 bhp and was raced with much success
on the Djakarta racetrack.

In spite of all the improvements to the XR22, during 1978 Kenny Roberts'
Yamaha YZR500 ruled the racetracks, but to Makoto Hase, it was evident that
engine performance was not the crucial factor; in the autumn of 1978, his
engineers concentrated on chassis improvement, a policy that eventually
returned the Individual World title to Team Suzuki.

15 Final developments:
Suzuki's full-floaters (1979 to 1981)

For 1979, Suzuki's 500 grand prix racers were re-designed. The new XR27B—there never was an XR27A—incorporated many ex-XR23A features: clutch mechanism, 'Nikosil' plated cylinders and 'twin-float' Mikuni carburettors. The cylinders were bolted down independently of the heads which now had six retaining bolts each. The XR27B and the new 652, the XR23B, shared the same brakes with 10 mm larger front discs, at 310 mm diameter, whilst the rear disc was correspondingly smaller at 220 mm. Both were fitted with a totally new front suspension device.

> HASE 'The anti-dive suspension system was designed by the racing department as a group and we asked Kayaba to make it. This system makes for more safety when stopping because during braking, the front is down more, so the rear is more up and this is not so effective, not so quick to stop. We just think about the cat and the dog; when the dog starts to run, his front is down and when he stops, his back is down. That is the ultimate system.'

This new system was misunderstood by the press and even some riders, but Suzuki developed it nevertheless.

> SINCLAIR 'When they first brought it out, there were mistakes made with it and the way we had to set it up meant that we were compensating for the design. It's quite easy to use now—it's like any new thing. It's definitely a must because we've tried bikes back-to-back with the same front fork but no anti-dive mechanism, and the bike definitely transferred weight too quickly.'

The anti-dive system reacts to front brake operation. A small pipe is tapped into the brake line and brake fluid pressure acts on a small piston, against a spring. The sealed piston supports a tapered needle running in a jet, similar to a carburettor needle and needle jet. The damping oil passes through the jet whenever the forks compress, and as the brakes are operated, so the needle restricts the jet and increases the damping force. Adjustment is made by packing-washers under the cylinder.

The new XR27B produced 124 bhp at 11,000 rpm, more than sufficient to win grands prix but the success formula still lay in superior handling. During 1979, so many frames were tried out that Tadao Matsui, a GP campaigner of old, recalls that year without trouble.

> MATSUI 'Frames? In 1979, so many try. . . .'

Before the 1979 season commenced, Barry Sheene was testing in Japan when he saw a 500 model with the radiator in the fairing nose. It was coded XR27BFR (Front Radiator). With more weight over the front wheel, wheelies should no longer be a problem.

But there were other benefits.

HASE 'We made a front radiator model because it is more effective for cooling and is also more lighter because the radiator is smaller. We just tested one but that machine is not completed yet—just tested—and on the straight it is not so fast because the drag forces are bigger. Now we finished to use.'

Makoto Hase didn't want a development machine in Europe, but Sheene insisted. However, when he used it at an early Brands Hatch meeting he was disappointed in its handling and passed it on to Steve Parrish to ride. Towards the end of 1979, the machine was rebuilt as a standard 652 cc XR23B; the special chassis and radiator returned to Japan.

The XR23B engine was little changed from the XR23A; in the engine, only the transfer ports were modified by siamezing the rearmost pair up each side of the cylinders, thus raising performance a little. Less restrictive, though longer, silencers were used and those serving the rear cylinders were contorted with two 90 degree bends to provide FIM-legal dimensions. (Exhausts are not allowed to project beyond the rearmost part of the rear tyre.) To accommodate these bulky mufflers, a much wider seat unit was fitted, and from the rear, the XR23B looked ungainly. 'Pregnant duck' was the common nickname.

The emphasis for 1980 was placed on chassis improvements; power didn't pose a problem.

HASE 'I know how to get more power but we are not using it yet because a racing machine is not only power; it's necessary to be simple and more reliability and easy to maintain and less weight. So we consider *total* performance.'

MATSUI 'In the sixties, engine power was the most important. Chassis and suspension was second or third priority. Today, suspension is more important than any other factor.'

Mike Sinclair, the Kiwi ex-Hennen tuner now working on Virginio Ferrari's factory Suzukis agrees.

SINCLAIR 'Everybody seems to think that you need a fast engine to win races but I think there's more to it than that now, because people are starting to concentrate more on frames. They've got more than 125 bhp and that's more than you can normally put on the floor, so if you can get the chassis better you can use it all. I think the big thing now, is being able to set the suspension up.'

The race department were searching for such a suspension package for the 1980 XR34 500 cc model.

HASE 'Both engine and chassis development are important, but for 1980, we introduced the 'Full Float' monoshock rear suspension system. If engine gets more horsepower, necessary more good handling, grip,

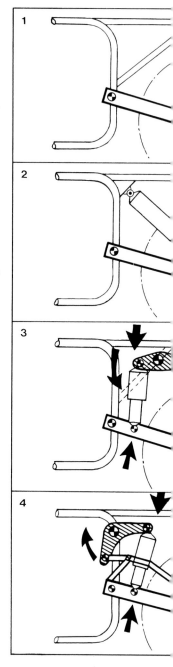

Rear suspension development from conventionally mounted rear shocks to advanced 'Full-float' (schematic only)

Vertical – up to 1974
XR05
XR11

Lay-down – 1975 to 1979
XR11
XR14
XR22
XR23,A,B
XR27B

Conventional Full-float – 1980 to 1981
XR34M
XR35Γ

Advanced Full-float
XR69-S

stability. All must be improved together. At the moment, work is more important on chassis.'

'Full Float' describes the movement of the suspension unit's mountings. Suzuki's monoshock is not fixed rigidly to the chassis; the lower end is connected to the swing-arm just behind the pivot whilst the upper mount is via a rocking beam pivoting about its centre. The rearmost end of the beam is also connected to the swing-arm via an inverted 'U' frame anchored in the same position as the normal 'lay-down' shocks. The geometry is fully adjustable, providing effective rate-changes of the shock. Pre-load is adjustable via a large threaded nut bearing on the upper end of the coil spring. The almost vertically mounted Kayaba suspension unit has a remote reservoir and adjustable damping forces. The system provides a good relationship between load and movement.

SINCLAIR 'The biggest advantage over Golden Shocks is a real progressive rise and the stiffness of the suspension at the rear tyre contact patch — because that's what the rider feels. They went to diminishing rates on the double-shock system to try to get that, but you can't beat a rocker set-up because you can really straighten out the progression.'

To satisfy Hase's 'cat and dog' principle, the rear brake calliper was underslung and its torque stay snaked forward but was anchored to the frame *above* the swing-arm pivot. Under heavy braking, the torque stay was tensioned, overcoming the effect of the rear-end raising by pulling down on the suspension. This reactionary force is always proportional to the braking effort but was adjustable to suit the circuit and rider; the chassis mount was variable. This rear suspension 'anti-lift' combined with the front's anti-dive ensured that the XR34s were rock-steady and sitting squat under braking.

For the early 1980 GPs, Randy Mamola and Graeme Crosby used machines designated XR3400, XR3402H and XR3403H, with conventional rear suspension springing although each had different steering geometry. They were the precursors of the Suzuki monoshocks and became the track development work-horses. The first monoshock Suzuki was the XR34M1, first raced in Spain but quickly superseded by the later XR34M2. The five different machines raced in the GPs that year indicated Suzuki's logical step-by-step approach.

HASE 'We changed the mounting positions of the rear suspension units many times to make it more progressive and compliant. The smoother the better; that's why we asked Kayaba for many types of suspension units.'

With a machine that didn't dive under braking, there was no longer the need to compromise steering geometry. Normally, under heavy breaking, the fork angle becomes steeper and the steering sharper and a compromise steering rake is selected. With the XR34M devices, this situation did not apply. But how big was the improvement of the XR34M over the XR34H?

MAMOLA 'I'd say 100 per cent. When we ran the bike at Paul Ricard, we used the softest compound tyre Dunlop had ever used; the XR34M is not that hard on the tyre. The way the bike's built, the suspension absorbs the horse-power and allows it to squat down when you accelerate and doesn't allow the wheel to spin that much. The tyre gets more traction; more of a drive.'

Mechanically, the XR34M was little changed, except for fitting larger VM36SS carburettors, but again, the front fork leg diameter and stroke were amended; leg diameter up to 40 mm, stroke down to 120 mm. In engineering terms, the fork's resistence to flex under load had improved by 50 per cent whilst stroke had reduced by 20 per cent. Steering head loading is proportional to its height from the road and the combined improvement exceeded 60 per cent as compared to Sheene's 1976 XR14.

Another similar development commenced in 1975. Then, Suzuki experimented with smaller 17 inch wheels, but racing tyre manufacturers were experiencing problems with their *larger* tyres and the project was abandoned. A smaller wheel lowers the steering head and reduces its stress under braking, and with a smaller frontal area higher speeds are possible. The idea was resurrected in 1979 when the tyre companies showed interest in Honda's NR500 GP racer shod with 16 inch wheels. In Italy, Roberto Gallina's Suzuki factory team reacted quickly and had some 16 inch wheels made for the XR27B. Then Suzuki showed an interest. They saw other advantages in this development.

> HASE 'The purpose of the 16 inch wheel is to reduce the gyroscopic forces so the handling is much quicker. Also the braking torque produced by the front tyre is less and the brake discs can be smaller. In addition, the machine is lighter and lower.'

The wheels were tested by the 1980 factory riders at a Ryuyo test session early in the year. All but Randy Mamola and Graeme Crosby used them during 1980 GP races.

When Suzuki launched their first four stroke roadsters in 1976, Hideo 'Pops' Yoshimura—a tuner of large-displacement four strokes—asked Suzuki if they would help him develop the GS750 into a competitive AMA racer, and Suzuki agreed.

Above left A cylinder from the 124 bhp XR27B. Contrary to popular belief, the secret of factory cylinders is inherent in the design *not* in hand polishing *Author*

YOSHIMURA 'Suzuki told me that they knew very little of four stroke engines for racing and accepted my help. There are no documents or contracts tying us to each other; it's just a gentleman's agreement. We just trust each other and never argue over policy.'

With this loose arrangement Yoshimura had soon established Suzuki as a dominant force on the USA's racetracks. When the GS1000 was announced, he was soon able to modify it, but found its chassis components couldn't cope with the power he'd produced. The factory agreed to help and the Yoshimura GS1000s were gradually transformed with XR chassis technology: a complete front end, then an XR type braced swing-arm and rear wheel. By 1979, the machine was virtually an XR1000!

With European Formula 1 events dominated by factory Honda RS1000s— Suzuki commissioned Yoshimura to produce the XR69. These machines were based on the GS1000 engine which was heavily modified by Yoshimura. A special crankshaft was used and new, forged pistons fitted. The cylinder head had a special bolt-in cam-chain idler-wheel and the camshafts provided exotic valve timing whilst enlarged valves were opened by lightweight tappets. Special titanium valve-spring caps located the adjustment shims between the valves and tappets. The reprofiled ports were highly polished and were fed by a quartet of

Above Specially converted aluminium camera cases were made to house the interchangeable gears for the XR27B transmission *Author*

Upper right Compare the fairings of Croz's XR35 Gamma with Hennen's XR22 (*below*). The upper/lower 'split' was repositioned for pit-lane convenience and Croz's pointed nose superseded the stubby variety. The XR35 tail unit is more enveloping (and the mufflers were not as splayed). Also, the XR35 fairing incorporated more carbon fibre *MCW*

29 mm Mikuni 'smooth-bore' carburettors. The electric starter and generator were discarded and the major castings lightened by liberal drilling. A new Nippon-Denso CDI ignition system, similar to those on other XR racers was used, but the transmission remained basically standard with a wet clutch feeding a five-speed gearbox. Finally, the whole power-plant was sprayed with a gun-metal heat-dispersant paint. The XR69 engine produced 130 bhp at 9500 rpm, even more than the factory 500-4s!

The chassis components were a carbon copy of the XR models and were produced by Suzuki. An XR-type frame was supported at each end by Dymag wheels mounted on XR27B forks—with anti-dive fitted—and an XR27B type swing-arm. XR34H type rear suspension units were specified. Factory-type fairings and seat units designed on the GP equivalents were fitted to reduce aerodynamic drag. Compared to other XR machines, the XR69 was overweight; at 367 lb (167 Kg) it was 50 lb (23 Kg) heavier, but its superior power gave it a similar top speed.

Occasionally, larger pistons were fitted to increase its capacity to 1084 cc and with Keihin Racing Carburettors fitted, power became 150 bhp at 9500 rpm! This same basic machine was used for endurance events, and to generate lighting power, a car-type alternator was fitted in line with the gearbox sprocket, from which it was driven. Handling was so good that Graeme Crosby often raced it against pure GP machines in open events and often left them in his wake. The Yoshimura-Suzuki combination is a powerful partnership which continues to this day.

In May 1980, Ryosuke Matsuki left the race team to lead the Katana project, being replaced by Etsuo Yokouchi, the engineer who had masterminded Suzuki's first four stroke roadsters, the GS series. Yokouchi applied his fertile brain to a complete redesign of the XR34 machines. He assigned the engine to Makoto Suzuki—nicknamed 'Big Mac' (Makoto Hase was 'Little Mac')—and a colleague, Shiro Yoshida. Martyn Ogborne, Ingersoll Heron Team Suzuki's 1981 Team manager, recalls their roles.

OGBORNE 'Shiro had the ideas about the cylinder heads, boost port, and

Above Bracing ribs for the cylinder head fixings were only used on the 652 cc models. This XR23B engine has 'funnel-type' Mikuni VM36SS carburettors with twin floats. The exhaust bands helped reduce noise levels. The XR23B had the highest power-to-weight ratio of any Suzuki, an incredible 1034 bhp/ton! *Author*

Upper left This XR35 16 in. wheel has 12.2 in. (310 mm) discs attached by 5 studs (one less than previously). Note that even the titanium bolts have been countersunk and drilled for lightness! *Author*

exhausts, but Big Mac worked out how to shorten the engine—clutch, gearbox, screws, covers, the lot; the difficult bits. They were a good pair.'

The first prototype XR35 was tested at Ryuyo in the autumn by Hiroyuki Kawasaki and Masaru Iwasaki but by October, Randy Mamola and Graeme Crosby were riding it at Ryuyo. Suzuki greatly respected Mamola's views; he'd been very helpful throughout that year.

> OGBORNE 'The XR34 chassis' were progressively improved due to Randy's efforts. At Ryuyo it was like a machine telling them; he gave them computer-like information: nothing airy-fairy. Nothing including the human element. Just understeer, oversteer, chattering, no chattering, fast steering, slow steering. The lot.'

In response to Mamola's requests, the XR35 chassis was even smaller than the XR34M2. The upper frame rails were 5 mm lower, the fuel tank was narrower and lower. After three days of testing, Mamola had lapped Ryoyu in a dead 2 minutes equalling the 'lap record', an impressive feat on this, his first visit to Ryuyo. (Hiroyuki Kawasaki subsequently lapped in 1 m 59 s.) Crosby too was lapping almost as quickly, but he was testing both Formula 1 and XR35s.

> MAMOLA 'Some people said I broke the lap record, some say I tied it, but I'm not bothered; I was really happy with the bike. It steered a lot better than before and it was a lot lighter, but when I attended a meeting there, I told them that I wanted the bike shipped to California so that I could test it. I said "It's fine here, but European circuits are so different." I also wanted changes in the frame; a smaller scale of that same frame and I said "Just make it for me, I don't know if it's gonna work, but I want to try it against this one."

Ogborne recalls that meeting with Yokouchi, Hase, Mamola and himself. Mamola was specific: the frame rails and engine must be dropped 10 mm, the engine moved 5 mm forwards. Suzuki wasted no time.

> OGBORNE 'Mitsi (Okamoto) made the frame using a blow-torch and hydraulic jacks to lower the engine, and repositioned the mounting lugs, but before it was finished, we had to leave Japan.'

Meanwhile, the Italian Team Gallina squad had arrived for their test session which included assessing new Michelin tyres of just 6½ lb (3 kg) weight—about 2¼ lb (1 Kg) lighter than others. The new 'Mamola' chassis was by then being tested at Ryuyo by Masaru Iwasaki and to conclude the Italian testing, Marco Lucchinelli rode the new machine. He was enthusiastic. Suzuki then took the gamble of supplying the new frame to all the factory teams. Mamola wasn't too pleased at the news:

> MAMOLA 'That sort of upset me; I was doing my development for *me* not for everybody else.'

In February 1981, the prototype XR35 was secretly tested in the USA at Willow Springs and Sears Point. Mitsi Okamoto joined Ogborne, George Vukmanovich, Peter Ingley (Dunlop tyres) and Randy Mamola for the three week session. The objective was to select tyres, tune the carburettors and suspension, and back-to-back test the XR35 against the XR34M2. US Suzuki supplied a truck

Left The front-radiator chassis was temporarily fitted with an XR23B engine and used by Sheene at Brands Hatch in 1979. It placed more weight over the front wheel but raised the centre of gravity too. See also p 178 *MCW*

and workshop space at their new Brea HQ, but despite the secrecy, the press managed to haunt the team across California. But how good was the XR35?

> MAMOLA 'It didn't even compare with the XR34M2. It was so much better. I was breaking lap records at Sears Point and Willow Springs so I was very happy. From then on, we made only detail changes before sending it back to Japan.'

After a two day respite in the UK, Ogborne jetted back to Japan with Dave 'Radar' Cullen to help build the team machines; four for Ingersoll Heron Team Suzuki, two for Team Gallina and two test-bikes for Suzuki Japan. Together with Robertine Polise, 'Jarni' and Tony of the Gallina squad, and the Japanese race-fitters, the eight machines were assembled.

> OGBORNE 'After each engine is built, we have to dyno-test them. Suzuki give us the target figures, including fuel consumption—the best indication of engine trouble. If the engine suddenly runs weak—fuel flow too low—there may be an air leak somewhere. If fuel flow is high, there's probably too much internal friction—piston seizure for instance.'

The new machines were finally tested at Ryuyo before shipment to Europe together with spare parts. Spares usage was colossal; Ogborne was carrying 15 spare sets of exhausts—60 pipes—by season-end! Furthermore, not a single XR34 component fitted the new XR35 machines.

In GP warfare, machines need to be 'tuned' to suit individual tracks and of the highly developed XRs, the XR35 was the most sophisticated. Adjustable suspension and steering geometry—rake and trail—were now prerequisites and fine pit-lane adjustments were catered for with the XR35 chassis which incorporated modified geometry to suit the 16 inch front wheels now virtually standard following Dunlop's design of tyres to suit. The fork legs, of larger diameter and less prone to flexure, were mounted in a choice of three yokes with 27, 32 or 37 mm offset to vary the trail (Suzuki provided Crosby with a 30 mm offset during the season). Rake was adjustable by raising or lowering the legs in the yokes. The suspension medium reverted to coil springs whilst nitrogen gas could be added to increase the progressive spring effect. An anti-dive system was specified which was lighter and simplified. At the rear, the full-float system was lighter and more progressive than that used on the XR34M2. (A *titanium* spring was tested during 1981 in the quest for weight-reduction). Light weight even dictated drilling the brake discs and using plastic footrests!

But the major change was to the power unit. Makoto Suzuki's concept was simple; smaller and lighter than ever before.

Below To reduce unsprung weight, the XR35 rear ventilated disc was drilled as were the titanium fixing screws note the 'Coke' can silencer *Author*

OGBORNE   'It was 7 mm narrower and 10 mm shorter in length than the XR34. The crankshafts were assembled into pairs; one front and one rear which also reduced their overall length. Apart from saving about 3 mm on the crankshafts, another 2 mm each side was saved by shortening the disc valve system; the discs were recessed around the outer main bearings. The 10 mm length saving was gained by reducing the gap between the front and rear cylinders to almost zero—the crankshafts were brought closer together.'

Big Mac even considered the weight of the cylinder head gaskets, replacing them with 'O' rings, one peripheral to seal the water, and a temperature-resistant type around the combustion chamber. The cylinder head was retained by six fixings each with its own small 'O' ring seal. Compression ratio adjustment was achieved by varying base gasket thickness. The boost port, normally of 'loop scavenge' design, was reshaped as an open 'groove' leading up from the crankcase and sealed by the piston skirt. Curiously the piston still incorporated a hole aligning with the boost port.

OGBORNE   'I asked about that and never really received an answer but I suppose it saved a little reciprocating mass and it certainly had no detrimental effect on performance; the XR35s finished 1st and 2nd in the World Championship.'

To increase power, larger $37\frac{1}{2}$ mm Mikuni carburettors were used initially but Mamola reverted to VM36SS versions during the season. The exhausts were brand new, *extremely* light and relied on their inherent three-dimensional form for rigidity.

OGBORNE   'We called them "swan-necks" because they swept down low at the front to bring the bulbous section closer to the front and improve cornering clearance. That was Big Mac's idea. The silencers looked like

Prototype XR34Ms in an annexe off Suzuki's current race shop, where all the XR machines are assembled and tested *Crosby*

"Coke" cans and that's just what they were; they were made of stainless steel by Coca Cola in Japan.'

The re-designed transmission included recessing the clutch into the crankcases, achieved by housing the input shaft bearing inside the clutch itself. Each of the six gear ratios were available in six ratios, a total of 36 matched pairs of gears. The total number of choices available to the riders was thus an incredible 46,656! As before, gear ratios could be changed in under 15 minutes by having a 'spare' gear set and end cover built up ready for insertion. Mamola was able to 'tune' his gearbox to good effect. The 1981 Yugoslav GP for example.

OGBORNE 'Randy's crew did a fantastic job on the gearbox; Randy wanted a *three*-speed gearbox and at first Mitsi thought he was joking. He said "Factory spent many years making six-speed. . . ." But Randy said he could win if he had three speeds. Actually, he used 1st, 2nd and 3rd for the start but not after that. In fact, he rode about two-thirds of the circuit in just one gear!'

The logic was based on the time wasted—and consequent loss of power drive— during gear changes. By deploying clever tactics Mitsi and Randy especially selected 4th, 5th and 6th ratios and ensured that just one gear could be used for most of the race. The plan worked fine; Mamola easily won the Yugoslav GP.

To reduce power losses in the gearbox, oil volumes were carefully chosen.

OGBORNE 'The oil capacity was reduced from 1000 cc to 850 cc after rig-testing a special engine. The test unit had a clear plastic inspection cover so that oil dispersion could be seen with the engine running. I used to think these things were guessed but it's very scientific.'

To shed further weight, all engine covers were shortened and whilst the magneto was similar to the XR34 type, it too was lightened by removing metal from *inside* the steel rotor. Finally, Suzuki and Shiro reduced the length and head sizes of all fixings. These modifications resulted in a 5 bhp

What a mean looking brute! Crosby's 1980 XR69 Formula 1 Suzuki utilised much GP technology in the chassis and suspension areas. Note the cutaway engine cover to optimise cornering clearance
Author

increase and a 9 Kg loss in weight; a 10 per cent boost in power-to-weight ratio. Furthermore, the lower, narrower XR35 wore a new carbon-fibre reinforced fairing with reduced frontal area. All-told, the XR35 made the XR34-M2 seem *antique*. Randy Mamola used his 1980 XR34-M2 for the 1981 Champion Classic race in the USA. How did the XR34 feel after a season astride his XR35?

MAMOLA 'Just getting used to it in training I pulled my back muscle out — because the reach on it was so much bigger; my back and my muscles were so adjusted to riding the XR35. Trying to stretch out and ride it on a bumpy circuit like Laguna Seca was really difficult.'

Even during the 1981 season, Suzuki were still developing the XR35 and during the TT lull, Tadao Mitsui arrived in England with a new lightweight aluminium frame which had been secretly developed at Ryuyo. Suzuki began to test a *round-*tubed aluminium frame in answer to news from Europe in May 1980; at Misano, Roberts had tried an aluminium square-tubed version of the Yamaha OW48. But why was Suzuki's version round-tubed?

OGBORNE 'I believed Suzuki wanted to be different but it was hopeless; it just wobbled and flexed everywhere. I saw this frame in the race shop in October when we were testing the new XR35s.'

Suzuki lacked experience in bending square tubes, and the equipment to do it, but when Ogborne returned to Japan in February 1981, he saw Suzuki's first square section aluminium frame.

OGBORNE 'There on the bench was the frame. They'd run it — I could see that, they said it needed more suspension development and that the front-end was too light.'

The new frame weighed just $7\frac{3}{4}$ lb (3.5 Kg) and in England, Taddy Matsui rebuilt Mamola's 'spare' XR35 using the new frame. Randy then tested it at Oulton

Park and began to set up the new machine during Dutch training.

MAMOLA 'But there wasn't enough time to develop it enough and the motor in the steel frame was a lot better at that time and it wasn't until the San Marino GP that I decided to switch the motors. By that time, the aluminium frame was handling a lot better so I thought, "The hell! I'll stick the good motor in it." From then on we ran the fast motor in that frame and it's handled perfectly.'

In the sixties, Hugh Anderson had noticed the different handling qualities of the aluminium and steel-framed Suzukis, was this difference noticeable on the XR35?

MAMOLA 'The aluminium frame is about 8 lb lighter, maybe a little more, and in handling it's gotta be the biggest difference that I've ever noticed in a bike. It's hard to believe that just 8 lbs would mean so *much* in a chicane, but it's just so much lighter that even now it's hard for me to believe! It's a lot easier for me to throw the thing around, it doesn't tire you out so much. Flexibility? No, I used it at Silverstone and that's a fast course. There's no flexibility. I think we've got it strengthened enough to not even worry about that. One of the biggest problems was it being too *light*, because if you get a bike too light, it won't handle; the suspension just can't handle it.'

Mamola was clearly impressed and used this as his number one machine for the last four 1981 grands prix, and there is no doubt that this development will continue.

Whilst Mamola was solely concerned with XR35 track development, Graeme Crosby's efforts were split between the XR35 and the new Formula One model, the XR69-S, which he and Wes Cooley (mostly in the USA) campaigned in 1981. Croz first rode the new machine at Ryuyo in October 1980 but not until the first samples arrived in the UK early in 1981 did the full extent of Suzuki's efforts become apparent.

The major change was to the rear suspension; the XR69-S sported a new Full-Float system quite different even to that of the XR35 where the rear facing exhausts beneath the saddle prevented the use of the optimum XR69-S system. The triangular swing-arm bracing was now *above* the swing-arm and at its peak, an adjustable horizontal link ran forward to connect to the lower end of an inverted 'L' shaped rocker. The upper end of the 'L' rocker was attached to the top of the near-vertical suspension unit whose lower end was mounted to the swing-arm slightly aft of the swing-arm pivot. This revision of the Full-Float system provided much greater progression and is likely to be seen on Suzuki's future GP hardware. Front suspension differed only in that the anti-dive units were swung outward—into the breeze—at about 45 degrees to the fore-aft line. Brakes and wheels remained unchanged although the chassis inherited some of the lightening features of the XR35, such as plastic footrests. Most weight was shed from the power unit as this was based on the road-going GS1000E model where durability held predominance over mass. Suzuki trimmed down the XR69S engine by many subtle changes; magnesium castings for the clutch, engine and cylinder head covers, for example. That old standby, the electric drill, was used to good effect on the remaining aluminium castings

27 lb (12 Kg) lighter than the XR34M, this XR35 has plastic footrests, aluminium frame, and smaller titanium nuts and bolts. Note the clutch cover recess accommodating the lever (see p 186), and the recessed clutch *Author*

Randy Mamola's XR35. Items of note; the 'swan-neck' exhausts, lightened sprockets, seat fairing extended to obscure the 'full-float' system, plastic shield to promote still air induction, faired-in exhausts and lightened magneto rotor. (See pp 183–188) *Author*

and steel components such as the gear selector mechanism. The clutch bearing hub was first drilled longitudinally then internally bored to leave just a thin lightweight shell. The clutch basket too was lightened whilst the clutch bearing cage housed fewer rollers to lessen frictional drag. To reduce engine width, the ignition system now had the electronic pulser coil housed on the right, whilst the ignition generator coil was on the left of the crankshaft.

Three types of carburettor were used during 1981; 33.4 mm magnesium 'smooth-bore' Mikunis, 31 mm Racing Keihins and, later in the year, a set of modified ex-XR23B Mikuni VM36SSs were successfully adapted for John Newbold's mount. Despite the use of improved cam profiles, the XR69-S retained its remarkable fuel economy, an important asset in long races such as the Isle of Man Formula 1 TT.

The new XR69-S retained its position as the *foremost* Formula 1 machine during 1981, much to Honda's chagrin who, despite the backing and support of a multi-million dollar R & D facility in Japan, invariably finished astern the Suzuki XR69-S of Graeme Crosby, the flying Kiwi.

Makoto Hase's racing involvement spans many years so perhaps it should be he who is best able to predict the future Suzuki racing machines.

HASE 'They will be more light, and more powerful. From the bottom to the top.'

Of this there is no doubt; Suzuki's exploitation of engineering technology will provide many more highly-sophisticated grand prix winners and it is equally certain that their constant search for power will ensure their success in the world's motorcycle markets.

16   Team business: what price success?

When Suzuki entered the grand prix maelstrom in 1960, they knew the path to success would be cheque-strewn; victory would be the result of a no-holds-barred contest.

But president Shunzo Suzuki was a committed believer in racing, and realised that developing the untapped European market would cost a small fortune, and that racing success would promote motorcycle sales. At all times the race team budget was unlimited.

> ISHIKAWA   'Whenever we had trouble, we would telephone or telex Japan and the factory would make new parts for us—even overnight—regardless of the material or labour costs. All parts were flown out to us in Europe; no expense was spared.'

Degner put it another way.

> DEGNER   'I don't know exactly what their racing budget was but they didn't mind whether it was £100,000 or half a million. They wanted to have success for their production business. That was very important, so there was no budget.'

Spares were showered on the Team like confetti, particularly in the early years when the machines were developed on the GP circuits. Whole machines were air-freighted to Europe to replace damaged or suspect models.

> ANDERSON   'I have no real criticism regarding spare parts availability. Trying to get stuff from A to B is always a problem, but they always did their best and certainly, I never missed anything for lack of spares.'

The returns to Suzuki would be immense, but only if their racing efforts were successful. In terms of promoting the Suzuki brand image, grand prix successes would bring more world-wide publicity than any form of specialist advertising. Race reports appear in daily newspapers and GP racing is covered extensively in motorcycle magazines read by potential Suzuki customers throughout the world. As a spin-off Suzuki would benefit from technical advances resulting from classic competition. As war-time stimulates great strides in engineering knowledge, so would racing teach Suzuki in extra short time the problems associated with high-performance two stroke motorcycle engines. This was shown in 1973 when Makoto Hase designed the RG500.

> HASE   'There were two underlying purposes; technical development with feed-back to the production machines, and of course publicity for the market. Even now the purpose is the same.'

Once on the racing merry-go-round, Suzuki became intoxicated and dizzied by its constant movement. Even after Suzuki's disappointing 1960 and 1961 seasons, they couldn't afford *not* to race; having heavily invested in the project, surely success was just around the corner? If Suzuki abandoned racing, they would be remembered only for their failures. Shouldn't the battle be continued to its ultimate conclusion? It is certain these arguments were considered whenever the escalating racing budget was reviewed.

With a racing programme, Suzuki risked a great deal apart from the cold hard cash; they could have lost face when the Degner defection story broke, or if they had failed in their do-or-die 1962 season. Benefits were derived from racing by the riders, but just what were their fees? Anderson, easily the most successful Suzuki rider ever, wouldn't reveal his fee but said that his factory and oil contracts made him the highest paid rider with the exception of Mike Hailwood—reputed to net about £15,000 a year.

ANDERSON 'As far as *total* earnings were concerned, I think Jim Redman

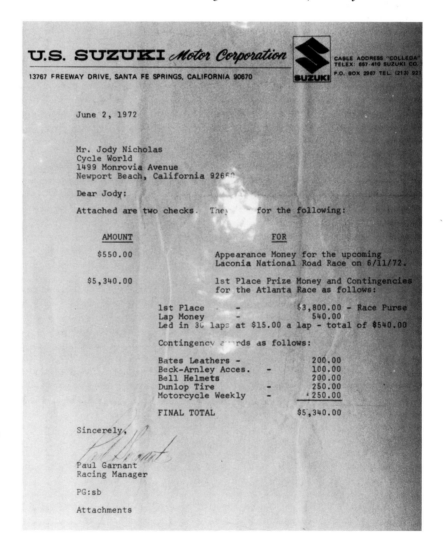

Jody Nicholas' $5340 pay-slip after winning an Atlanta race on his ZR11. Contingency money was payed only if the machine bore the sponsor's decals and the rider declared his interests prior to the race
Author

earned more than I did—I don't really know, we didn't talk much about those matters.'

Perris earned £1100 in 1962, £2600 in 1963 and £7000 in 1966, and Ernst Degner—Suzuki's mentor in the early years—said his earnings varied from DM 60 to 80,000 (about £15,000) each year. Stuart Graham received about £5000 for his 1967 contract. By comparison, how much did Maurice Knight pay Sheene in 1973?

KNIGHT   'When we started racing, I think Barry's first retainer was about £2000. Our *total* budget didn't exceed £30,000.'

A few years later, Sheene's contract—excluding winnings and tyre contract fees—was worth substantially more. In 1980, it was reputed that Honda were offering £20,000 to their riders for F1 events alone! The costs of running a race *team* were phenomenal as Heron Suzuki GB's chairman Peter Agg knew only too well.

AGG   'In the final analysis, when everything is taken account of from directors' time down to the cost of painting the race-shop floor, our racing budget amounts to in excess of £400,000 per annum for a two man team, back-up crew, transport and accommodation. This is just to contest the World Championship and a handful of UK Internationals.
'I was once told by Suzuki Japan that they budgeted £100,000 for each Team machine, which includes their overheads in Japan and the costs of supplying spare parts for each machine. I guess the total annual cost of racing factory Suzukis exceeds one million pounds each year. But that's the cost of success.'

In a 1977 interview, Heron Corporations' chief executive Gerald Ronson, stated that during 1976, Heron Suzuki GB spent £160,000 on motorcycle racing, but that in exchange he'd secured a good return. Without doubt, supporting Team Suzuki is a very, very expensive business. Do the results justify the cost?

KNIGHT   'Racing comes under the heading of advertising; if you don't do it sometimes you feel the pinch: if you do do it, you can never really measure if it's worthwhile. But I've no doubt that the racing scene helped tremendously in getting Suzuki into the bigger bike market.'

A typical Suzuki riders' contract required him to forfeit a proportion of his fee if unable to contest a scheduled event due to injury sustained in a non-scheduled race. If a rider was injured in a scheduled contest, he was covered by an insurance policy, initiated by Ernst Degner.

DEGNER   'Suzuki didn't want a part of the contract that I wanted—that the company would insure me against injury for DM 100,000 (£25,000) at their cost. They said that nobody else wanted it, so why should I have it? I said, "If I don't have it, I don't sign." I wanted to feel safe, and I told them "I'm going to risk a lot to bring your company up, but in return, you have to insure me." And then they agreed and not long afterwards, I had my first real accident when I got burnt and it would have cost me nearly DM 100,000, but for my special contract.'

Signing their 1964 NGK (spark plug) contracts at Nagoya are, L to R: Schneider, Degner, Perris and Anderson. Masazumi Ishikawa concerns himself with the small print
Perris

Barry Sheene and Maurice Knight discuss important business over a buffet lunch
MCW

ANDERSON 'During '62 and '63 I was insured by the factory, but following Degner's accident, the factory paid me the equivalent premium and I insured myself by taking out the usual policy when applying for an ACU international licence—it cost very little—and I ended up having three or four hundred pounds over, which wasn't that bad.'

Bertie Schneider, unlike Degner, was not in a strong bargaining position when he signed his £4000 contract.

SCHNEIDER 'When I first signed with Suzuki, it was on a trial basis of six meetings only. Part of my contract said that I had to lose three stones in weight, because I was signed to ride not only the 250, but also the smaller 125s and 50s. When I signed my contract, no one ever suggested that Degner or Anderson were to be allowed to win the 125 cc World Championship, even if they had, I would still have agreed, because of the money that we received. After all those years of running privately—all the troubles we had living in caravans and tents, sleeping in the car—we were fed up with it all, and didn't mind the fact that the 250 was no good.'

The contracts also contained a rather strange clause.

ANDERSON 'It regarded industrial espionage; we were not to pass on information regarding the design of the engines. Having gone to the expense and trouble of assisting Degner to defect, and divulge his MZ knowledge to Suzuki, they obviously didn't want to lose such hard-won experience to their competitors.'

Another clause stated that all trophies won by Suzuki riders would become the property of Suzuki until two years after the contract expiry. Suzuki were proud of their spoils of war and displayed them in their head-office foyer where many are still to be seen. Regrettably, Japan's humid climate has tarnished them so badly that the inscriptions can scarcely be read.
Until 1964, Mike Ishikawa negotiated the riders' start-money—which the riders could keep—but then Frank Perris took over this role.

ANDERSON 'He did the job well, he was most efficient. However, I received bonus payments direct from several organisers. This was over and above the start-money negotiated by Frank Perris. That's a fact; no one knew about it; there was no need. It was my business. This isn't to say that Frank wasn't doing a good job; they saw fit to give me extra money as they felt that being multi-world Champion at the time, I was worth more.'

Further rider income was derived from contracts signed with NGK, Shell and Avon.
The riders paid their own travelling and accommodation expenses whilst in Europe; the factory picked up the tab for expenses elsewhere. The riders didn't mind paying their own way, most having done so as privateers for many years. Furthermore, they could afford to indulge themselves with fast cars; Perris with a spate of Jaguars, Schneider with Mercedes sports cars, Anderson with some of each. However, unlike many other riders, Anderson did not hold much with the grand prix social life, keeping himself to himself. He was a committed rider; there to race not socialise.

Ten years later, Jaguars gave way to Rolls-Royces, both Sheene and Parrish driving these expensive cars into the paddocks. It must have helped to psyche-out the opposition, even before practice commenced!

The question of Team orders is tricky. They could be used by some riders as an excuse for a poor performance. Conversely, it is unlikely that a rider will admit to winning a race because of Team orders in his favour. Whilst Anderson, Degner, Perris, Graham, Schneider and Anscheidt all recollected Team orders being issued on occasion, there is very little agreement between their recollections.

ANDERSON   'The only time riders finished to a pre-determined pattern was at Daytona '64 and '65, Fuji circuit 1966, and possibly the Argentine 50 cc in '63 when we had to go there to consolidate the 50 cc World Championship, which we did. I'm fairly sure that I won the event.'

DEGNER   'If a Suzuki man was far ahead with Championship points, and was leading a race, the other riders would be told to hold the other riders back so that he could win. The only real orders given were to win. After the first two or three meetings you could see who had the fastest machine, or who had the best condition.'

SCHNEIDER   'In 1963 we had orders for the 125 cc race at Spa. It was for Degner to win, with Anderson, Perris and myself to follow up in that order. In the race, Frank was so slow we left him behind. Degner dropped out and Anderson was going very slow, whilst mine was going like a rocket. I came alongside him and he gave me the sign to carry on, and so this was the only World Championship meeting that I won.'

Anderson disagrees with Schneider's statement.

ANDERSON   'At that time, I was leading the Championship handsomely, though it wasn't as yet settled—Taveri was still hanging about in 3rd place, quite close, quite threatening—and it would be odd if Team orders *were* given, that Degner would be the one to win. That would hardly be good sense, especially when Frank had passed Ernst in both the Isle of Man and Dutch TTs to take 2nd place from him.

'At the Belgian GP in '63, the bike wasn't going particularly well—I didn't handle Francorchamps very well myself—but Bertie did come up beside me, put one finger in the air, pointed at himself and I nodded; I didn't want any rider hanging behind me who could actually ride faster. I hoped they'd see it the same way if they were going slower than I was. I didn't mind that he should win it; I wasn't going quick enough to win it, and I didn't expect favours from other people. Bertie was obviously going faster and deserved to win.'

PERRIS   'I seized whilst in the lead at the end of the first lap. I remember it well because I thought it was going to be my first GP win.'

Other riders recall Team orders.

ANSCHEIDT   'Team orders were spoken of at Barcelona in 1967. They said that the first rider into the first corner should win the race! There were

Above Degner, Perris and Anderson displaying their 1963 victory spoils. Once the publicity photo was taken, the trophies were returned to Suzuki's display cabinets *Archives*

Team orders for the TT race that Katayama should win this because it would be better publicity for the Suzuki factory. He had problems and we were waiting for him at Ramsey on the first lap. I had a slight problem on the third lap—plugs only firing on one cylinder.'

Stuart Graham agrees with Anscheidt's recollection (see page 63).

Tactical talk is one thing, but carrying out the orders on the track was another. Degner said the idea was 'to hold the other riders back.' how was that achieved?

PERRIS   'My job was to try to stay as close to Hughie as possible, *and* ahead of the opposition—not hold them up—and the very fact that you're mixing it with another guy means you can't go as quick as you can by yourself.'

Hugh Anderson says that this idea didn't stand up.

ANDERSON   'The results don't substantiate this. In all the GPs in '63 and '64, Perris finished behind me on two occasions but in front of me twice also. On the two occasions when he finished behind me, he caught and passed Degner to do it—that was the Isle of Man and the Dutch TT of 1963—so no Team orders existed at *that* stage.'

Without doubt, Anderson's statement that Team orders were not the norm is

Below 'I had instructions that I wasn't to win . . . then Georg's bike went sick . . .' Stuart Graham's dilemma at the 1967 West German GP. Both he and Anscheidt are riding the 50 cc RK67 models *Carling*

right. The best man usually won but Mike Ishikawa recalls an occasion when it was decided before the season began who the preferred winner of the Championship should be.

ISHIKAWA 'That was in 1962, when Degner was given priority because of his major contribution toward the Suzuki 125 and 250 GP racers that year.

'In general, orders were given for the purpose of avoiding useless competition amongst our riders, but only after several laps had elapsed and our riders occupied favourable positions. All Team riders were free until the orders were given.

'During the races, we quite frequently showed the positions of team-mates to each rider as information. Some riders may have interpreted this information as a Team order. We never gave Team orders if any opponent was positioned amongst our Team riders.'

Of course, Team orders were used by most successful racing teams in later years. Heron Suzuki GB often supported their riders at critical points in the title chase by fielding additional Suzuki teamsters who, it was hoped, would deprive their rivals of valuable points. Sometimes it worked, but more often it failed. Such a rider must be capable of out-riding the title-*leader* and thus be able to choose his finishing position according to orders. Such riders are usually contracted to rival teams.

Four times World Champion Hugh Anderson was a dedicated GP campaigner and certainly took his racing seriously.

ANDERSON 'I was very much my own man and I did what I wanted to do, which caused a few problems from time to time. I was there to win races basically—the opportunity to win was there—and *I* wanted to win them. In fact I often thought that my ambition was much greater than the factory's at this time. It would often be left for me to win these races and I had some rather strong words to say on this. There were practically no Team tactics at all, and I don't think the factory was ever really in control of the riders at that stage.'

His dedication was matched by his fellow riders and by the Japanese support crew.

ANDERSON 'I saw Frank's TT mechanic stripping his 250 engine for the third time. He'd just put new crankshafts in it and just before he'd finished rebuilding it, a modified set of crankshafts arrived so he stripped it again. Before he'd finished this second rebuilt, yet another set of latest-modified cranks arrived so he stripped it yet again. When they told him to strip it for the third time, his face didn't change—he wasn't upset—it was for the good of the factory of which he was a part. This was one of the reasons for their success; the painstaking work they did, the patience they had.'

This devotion to the racing cause was not a unique 1960s phenomenon; in the Isle of Man 1978, Hailwood's Suzuki engine was also stripped and rebuilt three times—perhaps it's a TT jinx—and Heron Suzuki's Martyn Ogborne and 'Radar' Cullen worked non-stop without sleep for 52 hours! But Hailwood won the Senior.

In the 1960s, with only Japanese mechanics, it was important for riders to strike up a good relationship with their respective crews.

ANDERSON 'Not many of the Japanese could speak English, and my Japanese was never any good—I understood my mechanics and could manage a wee bit—but I mainly got to know them through their mannerisms. I knew what they were talking about even when they were speaking in Japanese. It paid to, and that was the failing of Bertie and Frank; they didn't learn enough about the people and should have been more aware of their value to the company.'

It was not all harmonious, however, Takashi Nakamura, who was with the Team in 1965, recalls that some of the mechanics who doubled as riders were not too happy at having to use 'slower' engines than the European riders. But both Hugh Anderson and Frank Perris agree that in reality, there was little difference between engines. Anderson cites his use of Perris' spare engine at the Ulster GP in 1964, a race which he won, as a perfect example, whilst Frank Perris says that on the track, there was little difference between 250 engines that had shown markedly different power outputs on the dynamometer. So why did the Japanese riders complain?

ANDERSON 'Their main problem was not through having lack of speed—I can well remember getting blown off well and truly in the early laps at Suzuka by Suzuki's Japanese riders—their greatest failing was lack of experience and they couldn't cope with long, hard races.'

The Suzuki Team management went to great pains to convince the riders that all the engines were the same.

ANDERSON 'They believed that sincerely; they didn't feel that a machine could have heart and soul. At one stage they were rather amused with me when I had an engine that was very, very easy to tune. Midway through the season, this engine was deemed worn out and they were going to send it back to the scrap heap in Japan. I spent a lot of time making them promise to save it for me to use as a spare for the Japanese Grand Prix. Their joke, at the time, was that I was having a love-affair with a motorcycle!'

Generally speaking, relationships within the Team during the 1960s were very good and both Perris and Anderson agree that apart from 'their' mechanics, Mike Ishikawa and Masanao Shimizu were the easiest to get along with.

ANDERSON 'Ishikawa was always very good, very patient, and did his best to understand us at all times, and he was a good fellow to be with anyhow. Shimizu was *the* man within the factory development team—there's no doubt about that. He was with us in 1963, then in 1964 he was developing the T20 road-bike engine. In 1965 he was with us again, but a year later was working on the 500 twin roadster. Consequently we were going up and down, up and down. Mr Okano was basically a theory man—a professor—and he and I had a few ups and downs.'

It was sometimes difficult for European riders to accept the Japanese working methods. Total loyalty was demanded and a 100 per cent commitment to Suzuki racing. At least one rider never really came to grips with the problem.

Above 'I sat behind Anscheidt and so earned him a title on the day I could have beaten him easily . . .' Anderson accepted team orders for the 1966 Japanese GP *Anderson*

Left Industrial espionage? Or is the Honda factory mechanic checking the carbs on Croz's XR69-S prior to the rumoured Honda protest at the 1981 British GP? In any case, Crosby's race ended whilst leading the F1 event when his engine (unusually) expired *Author*

SCHNEIDER 'We had very good communications with the Japanese; very friendly, very helpful. But the longer I knew them, the more I realised that I didn't really know them at all. It took me six months or a year before I realised that. They just have a different way of thinking; there is no human feeling—they treat you like a machine—and I complained about it when I signed my second contract.

'They didn't understand that some days you couldn't go as fast as on others, and they would stick out blackboards telling you to go faster. Sometimes I found it difficult to adapt to this kind of pressure. I would dream about getting into trouble in a race—the bike was seizing up—and the next thing I knew, I'd fallen out of bed! I was ashamed even to tell this story, but one night, Frank and I went out for a drink and he told me the same story. So we were both the same.'

Anderson too suffered from nightmares.

ANDERSON 'I woke up screaming many times and my wife was the one that was getting kicked out of bed! Also Tom Arter. I ended up sleeping with him in a double bed at the Isle of Man—I was riding Arter machinery at the time. You don't get any sleep in the Isle of Man—you can just about forget about sleep for a couple of weeks—and Baaregarroo was a nasty spot for me because you go through there at a hell of a speed, and this was *my* nightmare at that time.'

Over the years, the pressures facing Team Suzuki riders changed very little; win at all cost was the dictum, and whether or not the rider had slept the previous night, he was still expected to perform to his limit in the race.

Despite these pressures, the Team survived in many arenas of war. Perhaps because of the loyalty extended by the Japanese, and the loyalty expected in return, the Team was highly successful. But psychological stress was not the only price paid by most of the riders: Degner was severely burned in 1963, Perris injured at Daytona, Schneider injured at Suzuka, Ron Grant and Jody Nicholas in America, Gary Nixon at Ryuyo, Barry Sheene at Daytona, Pat Hennen in the Island, the list is endless. Two Suzuki riders gave their lives; Hiroshi Naito whilst testing an RZ at the Yonezu test course, and Tom Herron in the 1979 North-West 200 race in Northern Ireland. His was the first death of a Team Suzuki rider in competition.

Of all the injuries sustained by the riders, perhaps Sheene's is the most tragic. Peter Agg had a glimpse behind the scenes one race-day morning during the late 1970s.

AGG 'We were staying at the same hotel, and Barry and Stephanie invited me to take breakfast with them in their room. Barry was still in bed when I entered their room and I watched him dress. It took him 20 minutes before he could straighten up enough to finish dressing. I was saddened to see the effect of racing on Barry's health, a side rarely mentioned by him in public.'

But most Team Suzuki riders harbour fond memories of their stay within the Team, and perhaps Frank Perris's summary holds truth for all Suzuki teamsters.

PERRIS 'They were the best years of my life. It really was a lovely Team.'

17 Behind closed doors: secret racing projects

The Suzuki machines that the spectators see racing on the grand prix circuits represent a great deal of development on the part of Suzuki's research department. Their brief is simple; produce the most powerful yet tractable two stroke racing engines possible irrespective of cost.

With time and experienced personnel limited, this policy must have appeared idealistic to the hard-working engineers in Suzuki's race-shop. During the racing season, they were permanently engaged in developing the current hardware, and had no time to dream up new ideas. This constant search for the impossible explains why Suzuki, from the start, split their racing support team into two groups. In this way, more engineers experienced at first hand the problems found on the race-track, and moreover, when they returned to Japan, were able to translate the requirements of the riders into metal.

Nevertheless, there *were* a number of engines, indeed complete machines, that were produced and tested in secret—in some cases without the riders' knowledge. The RS65 is a good example; a 125 cc engine built in 1965 to replace the RT65 for the 1966 season.

Suzuki had learned the benefits of water-cooling whilst testing the RT64A, and also seen the power-bonus of multi-cylinder engines with the RZ63 model. Surely a logical step would be to build a water-cooled 125 cc square-four?

By scaling down the RZ65 motor, Suzuki expected to overcome some of their RZ65 problems. Seichi Suzuki—an engine designer and technican, *not* the rider with the same name—designed the new RS65 motor.

> SUZUKI 'I returned from Europe in the fall of 1965 and immediately commenced work on the RS65 with Yoshihiku Suzuki and Makoto Tajima. Takeharu Okano was in overall charge of the project. The plan was to reduce the stroke and have more cylinders and more power.'

The design soon crystalised—the whole project only took a few weeks from drawing board to dynamometer testing; for the first time four separate crankshafts, each with inboard drive gears, were specified. Thus the two front and two rear cranks were all geared together with power take-off via a primary shaft running above and aft of the rear cranks. The primary shaft also drove the water-pump and tachometer. At its right-hand end, a primary gear drove the clutch and input gears whilst the final drive was via a separate shaft—which also drove the oil-pump—positioned behind the output gearshaft for sprocket alignment reasons. Thus, the crankcase halves sandwiched a total of six shafts. Only two cylinder castings were used, one each for the left and right hand banks, each cylinder incorporating two transfer and the appropriate boost ports. The exhaust layout mirrored the RZ65 as did the intake arrangements; rotary disc valves. The gearbox-mounted Kokusan magneto was driven via the secondary gear.

The engine soon produced the same power as the RT65 machine and more was expected with further development, but it was decided to install it into a chassis for track testing.

SUZUKI 'Both Mitsuo Itoh and Yoshimi Katayama rode the RS65 at Ryuyo but both complained of slow steering response which had been the problem with the RZ63 model. The wheelbase was much longer than the RT65 because the engine was so long in order to install the six shafts. The project was abandoned and we began work on the RJ65, a development of the RS65.'

Makoto Hase joined Suzuki as an engine designer in 1962, and from then until his transfer to the race department in 1966, he had worked on the T250 roadster and a 50 cc motorcycle engine.

HASE 'When I joined the race department, the RS65 was running on the dynamometer and had also been track-tested in Japan but without a good result because of some problem with oil temperature.'

Takashi Nakamura recalls that the RS65 was run in practice for the Japanese GP in 1965 but was not used in the actual race.

The design team considered the means to reduce the engine's length; the crankshaft power take-off was the problem. For maximum durability and lightness, it *had* to be taken from between the cylinders and anyway, it couldn't be taken from a crankshaft extremity because of disc valve obstruction. Their solution was obvious; a three cylinder engine. With the right rear cylinder and crank of the RS65 removed, the left rear crankshaft could be extended across the engine behind the right front cylinder allowing the deletion of a separate primary shaft; the left rear crankshaft extension drove the clutch via a gear. This arrangement produced a more compact crankcase. Thus Suzuki's first three cylinder engine was born. It was thought the three cylinder engine would overcome the narrow power band of the RS65 without sacrificing power per se. But what were Seichi Suzuki's objectives?

SUZUKI 'My purpose was to have more revolutions than the RT65—more power not torque. Power was first. The RK65 had the highest bhp per litre then—about 290—and this was the target but we knew it was impossible to match it with a 125 cc engine.'

In layout, the RJ65 was similar to its forebear, the RS65. A three cylinder 'square-four' housed in a shorter and lighter crankcase. It was running on the test-bed within 12 weeks and immediately produced 30 bhp at 14,500 rpm. Not really enough. After further development, it produced 34 bhp at 15,000 rpm, more than the RT65 and even more than the later RT66. The RJ65, too, was test ridden at Ryuyo and whilst handling was improved, overall performance was not much better than the RT65 and the prototype RT66 which was being tested at the same time. The reason?

SUZUKI 'The RJ65 power unit was heavier than the twin cylinder RT65 and its power band was still too narrow. Adding gears may have solved this

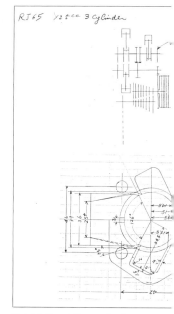

Seichi Suzuki's notebook reveals the layout of the ill-fated RJ65 model: three separate cranks geared together and driving an 8-speed transmission. In its day, the lower porting diagram would have been priceless to a rival company. (See also p 2)

problem but the weight would have increased still further.'

Mike Ishikawa confirms that the RJ65 was track tested and Ernst Degner recalls being told by a Suzuki mechanic that the narrow power band—especially when compared to the torquey Hondas—was the reason for its downfall. Makoto Hase reviews the situation.

> HASE 'We made the RJ65 three cylinder, the RS65 square-four, and a V4—the RS67—which we bench-tested in 1967. After testing, the V4 was best because the square-four had directly-coupled cranks, but even so, was very long. The V4 was more compact even though it had a primary shaft between the crankshafts. This meant that the machine was easier to handle. Also, on the square-four, there were so many crank gears under the oil level rotating at crankshaft rpm and absorbing bhp, that for the V4 we used an oil pump to supply the gearbox because this engine was dry-sump.'

The V4 RS67s which were raced in the 1967 Japanese GP by Stuart Graham and Mitsuo Itoh were also raced in the spring of 1968 when Yoshimi Katayama gave the RS67 its final outing at a race in Singapore. Development of the 1968 model RS68, was halted when Suzuki announced their withdrawal from GP competition. Only one example of the RS67 remains; occasionally exhibited by the factory for publicity purposes.

Suzuki's policy was never to openly inform their riders of new developments, especially if they were apparently satisfied with their current machines. Thus, if a project failed, the riders' confidence in Suzuki's technical abilities never faltered, and they could concentrate their energies on racing.

> SCHNEIDER 'While we were in Europe racing, Suzuki did the engineering in Japan and they decided if it was not good enough, to stop. We saw one or two new machines and Ernst was always complaining about Suzuki wasting their money. Sometimes, the machines were quite good, but if the Japanese didn't think they were, all work was stopped and they were scrapped. I did hear of the 125 three cylinder, but I never saw it; it was just a rumour between the mechanics. When they had something new, they just came out and gave it to you without asking if you wanted it. There was no chance to decide.'

Whilst RJ65 development was shelved, another new 50 cc engine was designed. Like the RJ65, the RP66 was a water-cooled three cylinder unit, and had an identical cylinder and exhaust lay-out. Drawing heavily on the RK66 development, and their square-four experience, Suzuki's engineers achieved their objective; a compact multi-cylinder, multi-gear unit. As with the later RZ engine, the left cylinders were cast in unison—as were the cylinder heads—with an integrally-cast water manifold running the full length of both cylinders, emerging at the front with a hose connection. The right cylinder had a similar manifold and a short 'U' shaped hose connected the two outlets, whilst a centrally-positioned 'T' piece took another hose rearward to the water-pump. The cylinders were four port types; a 'bridged' exhaust port, two scavenge—or transfer—ports and the customary 'boost' port positioned opposite the exhaust.

Each crankshaft was fully independent and geared together directly as on the much later 500 cc square-fours, and on the RS and RT65s. The rear crankshaft

Above Four shafts run within the upper crankcase half of the 50 cc RP68. The oil jets (see p 202) number 19 in total and ensured positive lubrication of the watch-like gearbox. Crankcase material was magnesium *Author*

Above left The RJ65 (left) had three vertical cylinders; two can be seen here, the 3rd fits over the 4 studs. The later RP68 (right) had two horizontal cylinders and one vertical. Small castings sandwiched the crankshafts. Both engines used disc valves *Author*

Left There are no known photographs of the one-off RP68 model, so Suzuki designer S. Masayoshi produced this sketch. Chassis components were similar to the RK67 model *Archives*

gear drove the clutch via an idler gear and the twelve-speed transmission included the normal underslung rotary selector drum. To allow sprocket alignment, the gearbox sprocket was mounted on a separate output shaft which also drove the water-pump via skew gears. Thus, the water-pump was positioned, as on the later Suzuki twins, at the rear of the power-unit.

The deletion of a primary shaft resulted in overlapping rotary disc valves—a feature seen on the RZ65 engine—and a shorter power unit. Indeed, it appears that this engine was barely longer than the twin cylinder engine it was intended to replace. The magnesium crankcases were very heavily finned—up to 65 mm ($2\frac{1}{2}$ inches) deep—and incorporated a transmission gear lubrication gallery in the upper half; the cast-in 'tube' drilled with jets in line with each pair of gears. An oil pump fed the gallery, picking up oil from the gearbox sump—the gears ran above the oil level thus reducing frictional losses—and was bevel gear driven from an idler gear meshing with the gearbox input shaft.

The Kokusan racing magneto featured two sets of points, and was gear-driven from behind the clutch and mounted above the crankcase behind the right-hand side front cylinder.

The engine was fed by three Mikuni M20 carburettors and when tested on a dynamometer, the little 28 mm × 26.5 mm produced about 18 bhp at 19,000 rpm! Unfortunately, the power band was extremely narrow—as with the RS/RJ65—and project RP66 was shelved after a few weeks of bench-testing.

During 1967, it became increasingly apparent, after rumours of a three cylinder Honda 50 cc racer began circulating, that the RP66 design should be re-vamped. The new engine was coded RP68.

The bare technical specifications were identical to those of its RP66 predecessor; three cylinder, water-cooled, 28 mm × 26.5 mm bore and stroke, with a 14-speed gearbox, but the physical form of the engine was unique and unsurpassed in ingenuity; a 90 degree V3!

The intricate magnesium crankcase castings were in four pieces; the lower and upper halves sandwiched the gear-shafts and formed the lower half of the two crankshaft housings. The upper cylinder was vertical, whilst the lower pair were horizontal, and once the crankshafts had been assembled in their relative crankcase lower halves, the upper-half castings were then bolted down followed by the cylinders and heads. Maintenance was thus vastly improved over the twin cylinder models which required a complete engine strip to replace the vulnerable and delicate crankshafts. Like the RP66, the RP68 crankshafts were totally independent and ran almost vertically, one above the other with a primary shaft sandwiched slightly behind the upper crankshaft, but meshing with all three. Apart from transmitting the power to the transmission, this primary shaft drove the auxiliaries; a water-pump mounted alongside the vertical single cylinder, and a lubrication pump externally mounted just behind the same cylinder. Both were skew gear driven. The oil pump drew oil from the dry-sump—as on the RP66—but had ten outlet hoses for bearing and transmission gear lubrication (via a gallery and oil jets.)

Crankshaft lubrication was handled by a diaphragm-operated plunger-type pump, powered from the crankcase depressions of the lower left-hand cylinder. The lubrication system was complex!

The gear-driven Kokusan magneto was located behind the water-pump and directly above the clutch, mounted on the right-hand side. Special 10 mm

Nippon-Denso spark plugs were made to ignite the mixture which was provided by the very latest integral-float VM20 Mikuni instruments. As with the RP66, each cylinder was fed via rotary valves.

Only one complete RP68 was ever built, and was ridden at Ryuyo by Suzuki's development riders and, just prior to the Japanese GP, by Anscheidt and Graham.

> ANSCHEIDT 'On the test-bed, the RP68 had about 2 bhp more than the 50 cc twin—about 20 bhp. However, the lap time of the twin on the circuit was better because the maximum torque and maximum power were too close together on the RP68. 14 gears were not enough; 16 or 18 were needed.'

> ISHIKAWA 'The RP68 was never raced and became known as the "phantom racer". Rumours of the fantastic power developed by Suzuki machines was because a flash reading on the dynamometer would give high readings. If allowed to stabilise for a few minutes, more realistic readings would be obtained. The RK67 twin cylinder 50 cc engine produced 19 or 20 bhp during flash readings, but really produced 17.5 bhp over sustained periods of operation.'

Although the RP68 *machine* was never raced, the RP68 chassis—fitted with a conventional RK67 engine—was ridden by Kawasaki San, a Suzuki test rider, at the Japanese GP of 1967.

The RP68 was doomed to failure when the FIM announced their intention to ban multi-cylinder 50 cc engines; the new rules permitted only single cylinder engines, a maximum of six gears, and a minimum weight of 60 Kg—a limit already broken by the Suzuki twins! With the incentive to improve the 50 cc models destroyed by bureaucratic meddling, the fate of the RP68 was sealed forever. . . .

Only one power-unit remains to testify its existence, together with a crankcase set. The batches of sub-miniature pistons made during the RP68 development, are frequently given to visitors of the race-shop as souvenirs!

Very little is known of Suzuki's experimental racing machines during the early 1970s, but it is known that a 350 cc version of the XR14 square-four was designed and completely detailed during 1975 for a planned attack on the 350 cc World Championship in 1976. It is certain that the budgetry cut-backs of 1976, when the factory's technical expertise was concentrated on the new GS four stroke roadster series, caused the project to be cancelled. Towards the end of 1975, however, it was becoming increasingly obvious that the ageing XR11 TR750 water-cooled triple would need replacement if Suzuki were to continue racing against the Yamaha TZ750s.

Shoji Yanaka, a race department technician from 1970 to 1975, was involved in the XR11 development and remembers working on the project coded XR20. Why was it made?

> TANAKA 'The TR750 had transfer ports that were too small and we couldn't get more than about 120 bhp. The Yamaha had more than this *and* four cylinders so it was easy to get horsepower and rpm.'

The XR20 was a completely new design, not being based on the existing XR11 in

The replacement for the XR11 was the XR20 (RF750). Lay-down shocks confirms dating but note the magneto driven via the primary shaft. The bulky expansion chambers have been moved forward (to increase cornering clearance) by 'swan-necking' the pipes
Crosby

any way. It had three in-line cylinders, each water-cooled and totally independent. Each of the three crankshafts had gears meshing with a primary shaft that ran just behind and below the crankshafts. In this way, maintenance was improved over the XR11; if a piston seized or a crankshaft ran a bearing, the individual units could be replaced more easily. Unfortunately, although individual gear ratios could be changed the crankcases had to be split before extracting the six-speed gear-cluster.

Very little time was spent developing the XR20, probably because of the pressures on the Racing Department; for 1976, the XR14 was modified to 54 × 54 dimensions, a time consuming task.

> TANAKA 'For development work, when we make a multi-cylinder engine, we use a single cylinder. We had two or three development cylinders, each had different exhaust and transfer ports; some had five, others had seven transfer ports. We didn't develop the model, not even as far as determining carburettor size, expansion chambers, or bhp. We spent only three months bench-testing the XR20 before we stopped development. We had a frame for the XR20 but we had a little problem with the engine. Then we broke every machine because it was confidential!'

Makoto Hase, the designer of the XR20—also known as the RF—explained the secrecy surrounding this project.

> HASE 'We make many types of machines for 500 and 750 cc, but we do not always use all that we make so we decided not to use the RF because there was something wrong.'

In an annex off Suzuki's race-shop, the sole surviving XR20 is stored alongside other secret projects, but is rarely seen by outsiders.

In 1977, Suzuki's designers began work on the XR26, a full 750 cc version of the XR14 500 square-four. With the 500 producing around 100 bhp at that time, it did not take much of a mathematician to calculate that the likely output of the 750 would be around 150 bhp! An engine was designed, built, and tested in a slightly modified XR22 chassis. The engine developed no less than 154 bhp on the Suzuki dynamometer and it came as no surprise that track testing at Ryuyo proved the engine power far exceeded the level of chassis development at that time. Had Suzuki the time to develop the chassis in concert with the engine, and had the FIM not abandoned F750, there is no doubt that the XR26 would have proved a world-beater. As it was, the prototype machine, which still exists, could only be put under wraps, classified as 'too fast to race.'

The search at Suzuki has not been one for power per se, but one for more *useable* power. Literally, this really means improving mid-range torque but with the proviso of not diminishing top-end power. Yamaha's 'Power Valve'—a variable exhaust port timing device—provides one solution. Suzuki haven't been inactive in this area either.

> HASE 'We have tested many kinds of special valve which are good as far as performance is concerned. These valves are not the same system as Yamaha's 'Power Valve'. But not now necessary to beat Yamaha—so much complicated. That is why we are not using special valves.'

Suzuki will never be deterred from developing sophisticated machines; for them there is no status quo, the future holds all. Only in searching for the impossible will they possibly stumble upon the key to supremacy on the world's racetracks. That search has taken Suzuki from obscurity in 1960, to domination in 1981. It's a Suzuki trait that will continue and which will sustain them as masters. It is unfortunate, for a public eager to learn of Suzuki's technical developments, that their search must take place in absolute secrecy, behind closed doors.

Suzuki experimental race-engines

Year	1965	1965	1966
Model	RS65	RJ65	RP66
Engine type	W/C sq. 4 2 st.	W/C 3 cyl. 2 st.	W/C 3 cyl. 2 st.
Bore × stroke	35.5 × 31.5 mm	38.5 × 35.75 mm	28 × 26.5 mm
Swept volume	124.71 cc	124.86 cc	48.95 cc
Intake system	(4) Rotary valve	(3) Rotary valve	(3) Rotary valve
Carburettor	(4) Mikuni M22	(3) Mikuni M26	(3) Mikuni M20
Ignition system	Kokusan magneto	Kokusan magneto	Kokusan magneto
Maximum power	36 bhp @ 16,000 rpm	34 bhp @ 15,000 rpm	18 bhp @ 19,000 rpm
Clutch type	Dry multi-plate	Dry multi-plate	Dry multi-plate
Trans. type	Con. mesh 8 speed	Con. mesh 8 speed	Con. mesh 12 speed

Year	1968	1975	1977
Model	RP68	XR20 (RF750)	XR26 (RG750)
Engine type	W/C V3 2 st.	W/C 3 cyl. 2 st.	W/C sq. 4 2 st.
Bore × stroke	28 × 26.5 mm		62 × 62 mm
Swept volume	48.95 cc		748.73 cc
Intake system	(3) Rotary valve	Piston-port	(4) Rotary valve
Carburettor	(3) Mikuni VM20	(3) Mikuni VM	(4) Mikuni VM37SS
Ignition system	Kokusan magneto	ND magneto	ND magneto
Maximum power	19.8 bhp @ 19,000 rpm		154 bhp @ 9500 rpm
Clutch type	Dry multi-plate	Dry multi-plate	Dry multi-plate
Trans. type	Con. mesh 14 speed	Con. mesh 6 speed	Con. mesh 6 speed

PART FOUR   APPENDICES

1   Epilogue: whatever happened to . . .?

It's almost impossible to calculate the total number of Suzuki factory racing machines. In their sixties hey-day, for the Isle of Man TT alone, Suzuki provided in excess of 40 GP motorcycles. The support Team necessary must have exceeded this number. In Japan, the race shop housed further machines as reserves; even more technicians were developing machines for the following season.

After a stint in the race team, many technicians were transferred to road machine work, and were replaced by others drafted direct from college. This Appendix explains the demise of the machines and the progress of the Team Suzuki personnel.

The machines
Very few machines of the 1960s remain.

> BERTIE SCHNEIDER   'If you dig a few holes outside the race-shop door you'll find a few engines and frames. Just digging holes. . . .'

Incredible though that may seem, that's just what happened to the majority of Suzuki's racers. Perris recalls seeing Suzuki employees digging a huge pit outside the race department door and watching as parts and complete machines were dumped ignominiously, prior to being interred.

In later years machines were destroyed in a crusher, but one race mechanic couldn't bear to see the 50 cc machine over which he'd toiled awaiting its fate. At night, he secretly returned and at home, proudly rebuilt it. That mechanic still possesses one of the few surviving factory machines.

> NAKAMURA   'Suzuki were almost over-conscious about the security of their racing machines or spare parts. When we used to leave Holland we would destroy used cylinders, pistons, crankshafts and gearbox parts with a hammer and bury them during the night in fields near the hotel, or throw them into a large river such as the Maas. Yet, after Suzuki lost interest in racing, we destroyed the machines and put them on the factory scrap heap!'

An RT65 and an RK65 were raced in America by Haruo Koshino. The RK65 later became a museum-piece at US Suzuki and was exhibited frequently. In 1980, Rod Coleman obtained that machine and has completely

rebuilt it: the RT65 seems to have disappeared without trace. . . .

Evert Louwman, the Dutch Suzuki concessionnaire, obtained a water-cooled 125 cc twin in the early seventies. This machine, although not completely original, closely resembles an RT66. It is now on display in the Dutch National Motor Museum at Leidschendam.

When Suzuki withdrew from racing in 1968, Anscheidt and Graham obtained some factory machinery with which to continue racing. Anscheidt used an RK67 which he now keeps at his Stuttgart home. He also received a 125 cc RT66 and enough spare parts to build an RT67. He sold the RT66 to Dieter Braun, the West German rider, for about DM35,000 (£8500). In 1970, Braun rode it to victory in the 125 cc World Championship, a remarkable achievement for a four year old machine. In 1971, Braun sold it to the Austrian, Harald Bartol, for DM30,000 (about £7000), who subsequently re-sold it to Maurizio Massimiani. This is probably the machine upon which Malanca based their 1971 125 cc GP racer. Eventually repurchased by Braun, it is now displayed in the Deutsches Zweirad Museum at Neckarsülm, West Germany.

In 1968, the ex-Anscheidt RT67 was sold to the sponsor of Cees van Dongen who raced it with fellow Dutchmen Aalt Toerson and Theo Louwes. Its current location is unknown. A 125 cc Suzuki—possibly the same one—was ridden by Alberto Pagani at the 1971 Dutch TT and again by Pagani—and Francois Moisson—at that year's Belgian GP.

Stuart Graham eventually sold his RT67 and all the spare parts to Barry Sheene shortly after the 1970 TT.

> GRAHAM   'Barry contacted me and asked me how much I wanted for it. I couldn't put a value on it, but shortly after, Barry came up to see me and I liked old Barry so eventually I sold it to him for £2000. He jumped at it. All of a sudden Barry had a bike that was super-competitive and I was glad because it's done for him what it did for me.'

On the Suzuki, Barry was runner-up in the 1971 125 cc World Championship, and it was later sold to an Italian, only to be repurchased by Sheene.

And what of any other early Suzuki racers? A 50 cc machine was stolen from the Hotel d'Orange at

Badhoevedorp and has never been found, and according to rumour, a number of factory 50 cc single cylinder machines were sold to private buyers in Europe.

When Suzuki quit the European racing scene in 1967, they made sure that nobody could pick up the traces.

The factory too has a small collection of machines; an RK67 in poor condition and an RS68 V4 124. This is characterised by its square-section aluminium swing-arm and was raced by Yoshimi Katayama in Far Eastern events during 1968. These 'vintage' racers are stored alongside other archive machines in a dark and dusty storeroom near the current race-shop. Close by, another store houses Suzuki's stock of more recent hard-ware; the XR20 and XR26 replacements for the 750 class, the dainty XR21 and XR24 single cylinder models, and many others that cannot be mentioned here.

In the seventies, the European teams were told to ship old machines back to Japan where the castings were smashed and the frames cut with acetylene torches. Few of the seventies racers therefore exist. Some *were* saved; Heron Suzuki GB successfully retained some of the later machines for display in Peter Agg's museum and for exhibition use by Heron Suzuki GB and Texaco. Barry Sheene too kept hold of a number of his GP machines and was also given an RS67 125 cc V4 engine.

Few remain in the States; as a factory subsidiary, when US Suzuki were instructed to destroy the machines, US Suzuki obeyed. Merv Wright remembers an employee who attempted to save an XR11. En route to the crusher, he dropped one off at his home and was later seen drag-racing the factory bike. He was fired and the XR11 crushed. . . .

The men
Team Suzuki represents more than cold steel and lightweight magnesium. What has happened to all those men who have contributed so much to this story?

Takeharu Okano became one of Suzuki's managing directors whilst Masanao Shimizu is now another director. Yoshichika Maruyama retired from Suzuki but Jimmy Matsumiya left Suzuki to live in Britain, acting as an executive engineering consultant to major international companies. After managing Suzuki's homologation department, Masazumi Ishikawa now liases between Suzuki and General Motors in the USA who are jointly developing an economy car. Still working with motorcycle engines, Hiroyuki Nakano is responsible for Suzuki's four stroke engineering design and development whilst Takashi Nakamura is manager of the European automobile export marketing department. Ex-chief mechanic Yasunori Kamiya now oversees Suzuki's 4-stroke motorcycle laboratory group, whilst mixing riding and engineering, Shunkichi Matsumoto (nee Masuda) is a test and development rider at Ryuyo. Racing and Mitsuo Itoh are synonymous and during 1981 he became manager of Suzuki's European-based endurance racing team. GP rider Yoshimi Katayama still competes and recently became the Japanese Formula Racing Champion *driving*

Nissan (Datsun) factory cars. Having sampled the US open spaces, TR750 technician Shoji Tanaka returned thre and is now a mechanic at Anaheim Suzuki. Tadao Matsui never left the race team and still works with Team Suzuki at most GPs.

Hugh Anderson lives in New Zealand occasionally riding Rod Coleman's RK66 in Classic events whilst Ernst Degner lives and works in Düsseldorf as racing manager for Aral, the giant West German oil company. Chairman of his automotive accessory company, Bertie Schneider, lives in Vienna and recently held high office with the FIM. Hans-George Anscheidt was Kreidler's chief engineer and Frank Perris sells motorcycle riding apparel. Like Katayama, Stuart Graham took to car racing and has been a Ford driver, taking works Capris to many championship victories in saloon car racing. Ron Grant left the USA and now lives in New Zealand — some say he runs a pizza parlour! Following his TT accident, Pat Hennen returned to San Fransisco where his courage and determination shone through and he has taken up kart racing. Just down the coast from Pat, his old race manager Merv Wright runs his own business dealing in classic cars from his Costa Mesa base. Merv's friend Jody Nicholas retired from active racing following a bad accident.

Finally, Dick Hammer. He was last seen by this author knocking hell out of a nail with — a hammer. Now a builder by trade, this swarthy yet serious man exemplifies the character of Team Suzuki.

Hallowed ground! The race shop door of the sixties where many of Suzuki's GP racers were buried. The wooden pallets of the 'dead' machines are stacked up. The site later formed the foundations for Suzuki's engineering block *Perris*

Suzuki factory racers that escaped the crusher

MODEL	YEAR	ENGINE NO.	FRAME NO.	LOCATION	KEEPER/OWNER	COMMENTS
RM63	1963	–	–	Hamamatsu, Japan	Suzuki Motor Company	exhibition model
RK65	1965	–	–	Wanganui, New Zealand	Rod Coleman	ex-Haruo Koshino
RK66	1966	–	–	Hamamatsu, Japan	Suzuki Motor Company	exhibition model
RT66	1966	–	–	Neckarsulm, West Germany	Dieter Braun	ex-Anscheidt
RT66	1966	–	–	Leidschendam, Netherlands	Evert Louwmann	exhibition model
RK67	1967	–	–	Stuttgart, West Germany	Hans-Georg Anscheidt	1967–68 50 cc Classics
RT67	1967	–	–	Donington Museum, UK	Barry Sheene	ex-Graham
RS67	1967	–	–	Charlwood, Surrey, UK	Barry Sheene	power unit only
RS68	1968	–	–	Hamamatsu, Japan	Suzuki Motor Company	ex-Katayama
XR05	1970	–	–	Castletown, Isle of Man	Des Collins	1970 IoM TT model
XR11	1973	–	CS37657	Donington Museum, UK	Barry Sheene	1973 F750 winner (Seeley)
XR05	1974	–	–	Ramsey, Isle of Man	Dennis Brew	ex-Woods
XR05	1974	–	–	New Malden, Surrey, UK	Richard Piers-Jones	ex-Sheene
XR11	1975	–	–	Effingham Park Museum, UK	P. James Agg	ex-Sheene (1975–76)
XR14	1976	1101	1101	Donington Museum, UK	Barry Sheene	ex-Sheene
XR14	1976	–	–	Crawley, West Sussex, UK	Heron Suzuki GB Ltd	exhibition model (not original)
XR14	1977	1202	1202	Donington Museum, UK	Barry Sheene	ex-Sheene
XR14	1977	1201	1201	Effingham Park Museum, UK	P James Agg	ex-Sheene
XR14	1977	1011	1203	Beaulieu, Hampshire, UK	National Motor Museum	ex-Sheene/Hennen
XR22	1978	1001	1006	Donington Museum, UK	Mike Hailwood Trust	1979 IoM TT winner
XR22	1978	1008	1008	Donington Museum, UK	Barry Sheene	ex-Sheene
XR23	1978	1101	1005	London, UK	Texaco	rebuilt to resemble XR22
XR27B	1979	1005	1005	Effingham Park Museum, UK	P. James Agg	ex-Sheene
XR3402H	1980	1101	1101	Effingham Park Museum, UK	P. James Agg	ex-Mamola
XR34M2	1980	1103	1103	Crawley, West Sussex, UK	Heron Suzuki GB Ltd	ex-Mamola (exhibition)
XR69	1980	003	003	Effingham Park Museum, UK	P James Agg	ex-Crosby
XR69	1980	002	002	Southwood Museum, New Zealand	Graeme Crosby	ex-Crosby

2 Suzuki's codes: cryptanalysis

Suzuki have used various code names for their racing motorcycles. Some are logical: others just baffle. For example, the 1962 version of the RT series (Racer, Twin cylinder) was the Degner-inspired *single* cylinder model! Similarly, the prefix RJ was used in 1965 when RP would have been more appropriate.

In 1967, the now-familiar XR series was born. XR has been used by Suzuki ever since for all their eXperimental Racers including off-road machines, which explains the gaps in the XR codes issued for the road-racing motorcycles.

Whilst not complete, this Appendix is included to aid understanding.

Code prefix (2 Alpha characters)
RB—Racing Bike
RF—Racer, F750
RG—Racer, Grand Prix
RJ—Racer, Japan
RK—not known
RM—Racer, Mini
RP—Racer Prototype
RS—not known
RT—Racer, Twin cylinder
RV—not known
RZ—not known
TR—Two stroke Racer
XR—eXperimental Racer

Code body (2/3 Numeric digits)

All except TR, RG and XR prefixes—indicates last 2 digits of year when raced ie 64 = 1964

TR and RG prefixes —indicates nominal engine capacity (cc)

XR —issued sequentially commencing '01' (first issued in 1967)

Code suffix (1 Alpha/Greek character)

1) *All except XR and RG prefixes*
   X—experimental design i.e. RT63X
   A—first modification i.e. RT64A

2) *XR prefixes only*
   A—designed for use in 1978
   B—designed for use in 1979
   H—designed for use in 1980 (conventional rear suspension) Hartog specification
   M—designed for use in 1980 (full-float rear suspension) Mamola specification

3) *RG prefixes only*
   A —as above
   B —as above
   C—designed for use in 1980
   Γ—designed for use in 1981

Suzuki factory codes (alphabetically arranged)

MODEL CODE	ENGINE	TYPE	YEAR USED	COMMENTS
RJ65	125 cc triple	1965	prototype	
RK65	50 cc twin	1965		
RK66	50 cc twin	1966		
RK67	50 cc twin	1967		
RM62	50 cc single	1962		
RM63	50 cc single	1963		
RM64	50 cc single	1964		
RP66	50 cc triple	1966	prototype	
RP68	50 cc triple	1967	prototype	
RS65	125 cc four	1965	prototype	
RS67	125 cc four	1967		
RS68	125 cc four	1968		
RT60	125 cc twin	1960		
RT61	125 cc twin	1961		
RT62	125 cc single	1962		
RT63	125 cc twin	1963		
RT63X	125 cc twin	1962	experimental—twin cylinde	
RT64	125 cc twin	1964		
RT64A	125 cc twin	1964	prototype—water-cooled	
RT65	125 cc twin	1965		
RT66	125 cc twin	1966		
RT67	125 cc twin	1967		
RV61	250 cc twin	1961		
RV62	250 cc twin	1962		
RZ63	250 cc four	1963		
RZ64	250 cc four	1964		
RZ65	250 cc four	1965		
TR250	250 cc twin	1968/70		
X6	250 cc twin	1966/67	also known as Super 6	
XR05	500 cc twin	1968/75	also known as TR500	
XR11	750 cc triple	1972/75	also known as TR750	
XR14	500 cc four	1974/77	also known as RG500	
XR20	750 cc triple	1975	prototype—also known as RF750	
XR21	100 cc single	1977	also known as TR100	
XR22	500 cc four	1978	also known as RG500	
XR23	650 cc four	1977	also known as RG700	
XR23A	650 cc four	1978	also known as RG700A	
XR23B	650 cc four	1979	also known as RG700B	
XR24	125 cc single	1977	also known as TR125	
XR26	750 cc four	1977	prototype	
XR27B	500 cc four	1979	also known as RG500B	
XR29	100 cc single	1978	also known as RJ100	
XR34H	500 cc four	1980	also known as RG500C	
XR34M	500 cc four	1980	also known as RG500C	
XR35Γ	500 cc four	1981	also known as RG500Γ	
XR69	1000 cc four	1980	also known as GS1000R	
XR69–S	1000 cc four	1981	also known as GS1000R	

3   Power graphics: plotting the horsepower path

Power output is in itself, not a satisfactory measure of engine 'technology'. Specific bhp is a more useful yard-stick for comparison purposes, although Suzuki's engineers were well aware that higher specific outputs were yielded with multi-cylinder engines. Another factor concerns the individual cylinder capacity; the smaller the cylinder, the higher the specific output.

It can be seen that progress between 1953 and 1961 was slow, and the graph reflects the 'Degner influence'; the RT62 specific power output was 60 per cent greater than the RT61.

One could speculate on the specific power outputs that would have been achieved had the FIM not introduced restrictive regulations in 1968. As it was, Suzuki's 50 cc three cylinder RP68, which produced 19.8 bhp, gave Suzuki an unofficial world record; 395 bhp per litre. By comparison a grand prix-winning Formula 1 racing car produces no more than about 180 bhp per litre!

The falling trend in specific power output following Suzuki's GP withdrawal is clearly indicated, as is the development trends of their 500 cc four cylinder racers of today.

SUZUKI RACE ENGINE DEVELOPMENT

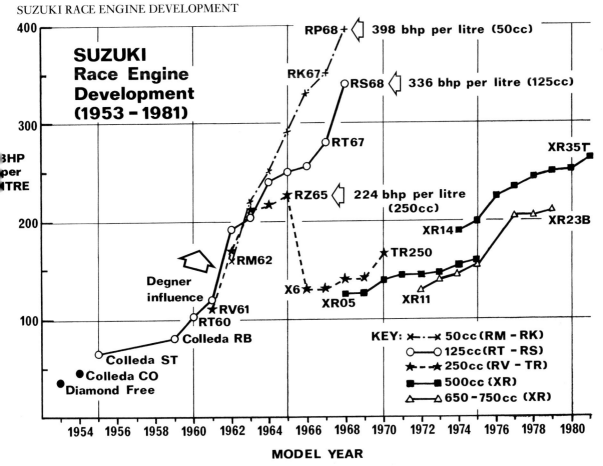

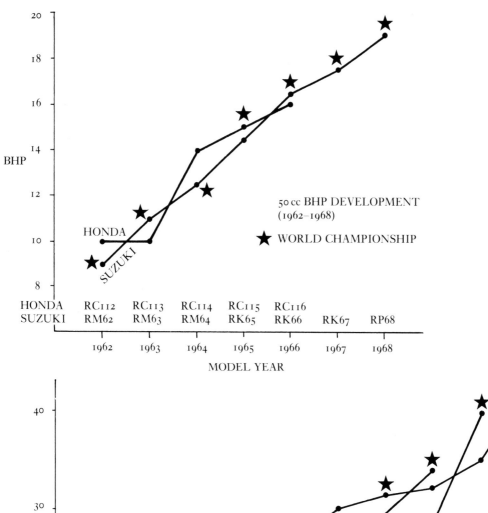

50 cc BHP DEVELOPMENT
(1962–1968)

★ WORLD CHAMPIONSHIP

| HONDA | RC112 | RC113 | RC114 | RC115 | RC116 | | |
| SUZUKI | RM62 | RM63 | RM64 | RK65 | RK66 | RK67 | RP68 |

| 1962 | 1963 | 1964 | 1965 | 1966 | 1967 | 1968 |

MODEL YEAR

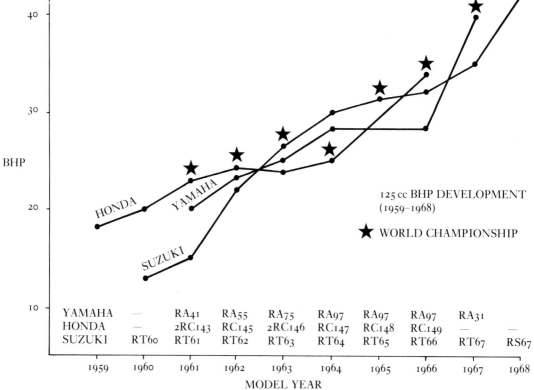

125 cc BHP DEVELOPMENT
(1959–1968)

★ WORLD CHAMPIONSHIP

YAMAHA	—	RA41	RA55	RA75	RA97	RA97	RA97	RA31	
HONDA	—	2RC143	RC145	2RC146	RC147	RC148	RC149	—	—
SUZUKI	RT60	RT61	RT62	RT63	RT64	RT65	RT66	RT67	RS67

| 1959 | 1960 | 1961 | 1962 | 1963 | 1964 | 1965 | 1966 | 1967 | 1968 |

MODEL YEAR

4 Machine specifications and race results

Specifications
The technical specifications of Suzuki's machines changed
frequently as new ideas were tried out on the track. The
specs listed do not relate to any actual point in time but
are intended to give a broad picture for a particular
machine in a particular year.

Results
It would be impossible to list each result of every Team
Suzuki rider. The results that follow are as complete as
possible but tend to ignore races other than the Grands
Prix themselves, and the major International events. *Team
Suzuki* is concerned only with the Team's performances
and it has not been possible to include the results of the
Team's rivals.

  In general, results are shown beneath the machine to
which they relate. However, there are cases where this
principal has been abandoned in order to integrate the
Team's results for a particular year into a composite
whole. In all cases, notes are shown indicating the actual
machine in use.

Illustrations
In most cases, the machine illustrated depicts that to
which the technical specification refers, but in isolated
examples—where one technical specification refers to two
similar though not *identical* machines—the illustration
used shows a typical example of the machine in question.

1953 Diamond Free *Archives*

Diamond Free 1953
Engine type *air cooled single cylinder 2-stroke*
Bore × stroke (mm) 43 × 40
Swept volume (cc) 58
Intake system *piston port*
Carburettor *not available*
Compression ratio (to 1) 7.0
Ignition system *flywheel magneto*
Maximum power (bhp) 2.0 @ 4000
Maximum speed mph (Km/h) *approx.* 20 (32)
Clutch type *free-wheel system*
Transmission type *2-speed*
Tyre size (F) (in.) 1.375–24
Tyre size (R) (in.) 1.375–24
Brake system (F) (in.) *none*
Brake system (R) (in.) *drum*
Chassis type *diamond type bicycle*
Suspension system (F) *coil-sprung telescopic fork*
Suspension system (R) *none*
Dry weight lb (Kg) 104 (47)

1953 Japanese National Races *Mount Fuji* (12.7.53)
Yamashita rode the first cycle-based machine to finish in
under one hour

Colleda Co 1954
Engine type *air-cooled single cylinder 4-stroke*
Bore × stroke (mm) 48 × 50
Swept volume (cc) 90.48

1954 Colleda CO *Archives*

1955 Colleda ST *Archives*

1959 Colleda RB *Archives*

1960 RT60 *Archives*

Intake system   *side valve*
Carburettor   *n/a*
Compression ratio (to 1)   *n/a*
Ignition system   *magneto*
Maximum power (bhp @ rpm)   4 @ 5000
Maximum speed mph (Km/h)   30 (48)
Clutch type   *wet multi-plate*
Transmission type   *constant mesh 3-speed*
Tyre size (F) (in.)   *n/a*
Tyre size (R) (in.)   *n/a*
Brake system (F) (in.)   *1 × drum, single leading shoe*
Brake system (R) (in.)   *1 × drum, single leading shoe*
Chassis type   *tubular cradle*
Suspension system (F)   *coil sprung telescopic fork*
Suspension system (R)   *plunger type*
Dry weight lb (Kg)   188 (85)

1954 Japanese National Races   *Mount Fuji* (8.7.54)
90 cc class — 1st Yamashita

Colleda ST   1955
Engine type   *air cooled single cylinder 2-stroke*
Bore × stroke (mm)   52 × 58
Swept volume (cc)   123.17
Intake system   *piston port*
Carburettor   *Mikuni*
Compression ratio (to 1)   *n/a*
Ignition system   *coil ignition*
Maximum power (bhp)   8–9
Maximum speed mph (Km/h)   55 (90)
Clutch type   *wet multi-plate*
Transmission type   *constant mesh 4-speed*
Tyre size (F) (in.)   3.00–18
Tyre size (R) (in.)   3.25–18
Brake system (F)   *1 × drum, single leading shoe*
Brake system (R)   *1 × drum, single leading shoe*
Chassis type   *tubular cradle*
Suspension system (F)   *coil sprung telescopic fork*
Suspension system (R)   *swing arm*
Dry weight lb (Kg)   165 (75)

1955 Japanese National Races   *Asama Plains*
(5/6.11.55) 125 cc class — 5th Yamashita, 6th Suzuki, 7th Kamiya

Colleda RB   1959
Engine type   *air cooled single cylinder 2-stroke*
Bore × stroke (mm)   56 × 50.6
Swept volume (cc)   124.63
Intake system   *piston port*
Carburettor   *Mikuni M22*
Compression ratio (to 1)   8.0
Ignition system   *magneto*
Maximum power (bhp @ rpm)   10 @ 9500
Maximum speed mph (Km/h)   77 (124)
Clutch type   *wet multi-plate*
Transmission type   *constant mesh 4-speed*
Tyre size (F) (in.)   2.75–18
Tyre size (R) (in.)   2.75–18

Brake system (F)   *1 × drum, single leading shoe*
Brake system (R)   *1 × drum, single leading shoe*
Chassis type   *duplex tubular cradle*
Suspension system (F)   *coil spring telescopic fork*
Suspension system (R)   *swing arm*
Dry weight lb (Kg)   176 (80)

1959 Japanese National Races   *Asama Plains*
(22/24.8.59) 125 cc class—5th Ichino

RT60   1960
Engine type   *air-cooled parallel twin cylinder 2-stroke*
Bore × stroke (mm)   44 × 41
Swept volume (cc)   124.68
Intake system   *piston port*
Carburettor   *2 × Mikuni M20*
Compression ratio (to 1)   8.8
Ignition system   *magneto*
Maximum power (bhp @ rpm)   13 @ 11,000
Maximum speed mph (Km/h)   87 (140)
Clutch type   *dry multi-plate*
Transmission type   *constant mesh 6-speed*
Tyre size (F) (in.)   2.50–18
Tyre size (R) (in.)   2.50–18
Brake system (F)   *1 × drum, twin leading shoe*
Brake system (R)   *1 × drum, single leading shoe*
Chassis type   *duplex tubular cradle*
Suspension system (F)   *coil sprung telescopic fork*
Suspension system (R)   *swing arm*
Dry weight lb (Kg)   180 (82)

1960 125 cc World Championship   *Isle of Man TT*
(13/17.6.60) 15th Matsumoto[1], 16th Ichino, 18th Fay

[1]Received Bronze Replica

RT61   1961
Engine type   *air-cooled parallel twin cylinder 2-stroke*
Bore × stroke (mm)   44 × 41
Swept volume (cc)   124.68
Intake system   *2 × rotary valve*
Carburettor   *2 × Mikuni M22*
Compression ratio (to 1)   8.8
Ignition system   *magneto*
Maximum power (bhp @ rpm)   15 @ 10,000
Maximum speed mph (Km/h)   93 (150)
Clutch type   *dry multi-plate*
Transmission type   *constant mesh 6-speed*
Tyre size (F) (in.)   2.50–18
Tyre size (R) (in.)   2.50–18
Brake system (F)   *1 × drum, twin leading shoe*
Brake system (R)   *1 × drum, single leading shoe*
Chassis type   *duplex tubular cradle*
Suspension system (F)   *coil sprung telescopic fork*
Suspension system (R)   *swing arm*
Dry weight lb (Kg)   172 (78)

1961 125 cc World Championship   *Dutch TT*
(24.6.61) 14th Ichino, 16th Itoh, 17th Matsumoto.

Belgian GP (2.7.61) 14th Ichino
Singapore GP[1] (16/17.9.61) 2nd Suzuki, 3rd Morishita

[1]Non-classic event

RV61   1961
Engine type   *air-cooled parallel twin cylinder 2-stroke*
Bore × stroke (mm)   56 × 50.5
Swept volume (cc)   248.63
Intake system   *2 × rotary valve*
Carburettor   *2 × Mikuni M30*
Compression ratio (to 1)   8.8
Ignition system   *Kokusan magneto*
Maximum power (bhp @ rpm)   28 @ 11,000
Maximum speed mph (Km/h)   118 (190)
Clutch type   *dry multi-plate*
Transmission type   *constant mesh 6-speed*
Tyre size (F) (in.)   2.75–18
Tyre size (R) (in.)   2.75–18
Brake system (F)   *1 × drum, twin leading shoe*
Brake system (R)   *1 × drum, single leading shoe*
Chassis type   *duplex tubular cradle*
Suspension system (F)   *coil sprung telescopic fork*
Suspension system (R)   *swing arm*
Dry weight lb (Kg)   198 (90)

1961 250 cc World Championship   *Isle of Man TT*
(12/16.6.61) 10th Anderson, 12th Ichino.   *Belgian GP*
(2.7.61) 7th Driver.   *Singapore GP*[1] (16/17.9.61) 3rd
Suzuki, 4th Morishita, 5th Kubo[2]

[1]Non-classic event
[2]Local rider recruited in Singapore

RM62   1962
Engine type   *air-cooled inclined single cylinder 2-stroke*
Bore × stroke (mm)   40 × 39.5
Swept volume (cc)   49.64
Intake system   *rotary valve*
Carburettor   *Mikuni M20*[1]
Compression ratio (to 1)   9.0
Ignition system   *Kokusan magneto*
Maximum power (bhp @ rpm)   8 @ 10,500[2]
Maximum speed mph (Km/h)   83 (135)[3]
Clutch type   *dry multi-plate*
Transmission type   *constant mesh 8-speed*
Tyre size (F) (in.)   2.00–18
Tyre size (R) (in.)   2.25–18
Brake system (F)   *1 × drum, twin leading shoe*
Brake system (R)   *1 × drum, single leading shoe*
Chassis type   *duplex tubular cradle*
Suspension system (F)   *coil sprung telescopic fork*
Suspension system (R)   *swing arm*
Dry weight lb (Kg)   132 (60)

1962 50 cc World Championship   *Spanish GP* (6.5.62)
7th Ichino.   *French GP* (13.5.62) 5th Suzuki, 6th Itoh, 7th
Degner.   *Isle of Man TT* (4/8.6.62) 1st Degner, 5th Itoh,
6th Ichino, 8th Suzuki.   *Dutch TT* (30.6.62) 1st Degner,

4th Suzuki, 5th Itoh, 8th Ichino. *Belgian GP* (8.7.62) 1st Degner, 4th Suzuki, 7th Ichino, 9th Itoh, 14th Perris. *West German GP* (15.7.62) 1st Degner, 3rd Itoh, 5th Suzuki, 6th Ichino. *East German GP* (19.8.62) 2nd Itoh, 3rd Anderson. *Italian GP* (9.9.62) 2nd Itoh, 4th Anderson, 5th Morishita. *Finnish GP* (23.9.62) 4th Degner, 6th Anderson. *Argentine GP* (14.10.62) 1st Anderson, 2nd Degner, 4th Itoh. *Japanese GP[4]* (3/4.11.62) 2nd Anderson, 3rd Morishita, 4th Suzuki. *1962 Individual Championship* 1st Degner, 5th Itoh, 7th Anderson, 8th Suzuki, 11th = Ichino/Morishita. *1962 Manufacturer's Championship* 1st Suzuki.

1963 50 cc World Championship   *US GP[4]* (9/10.2.63)
1st Itoh, 2nd Degner, 3rd Anderson, 4th Morishita

[1] Increased to 'M22' mid-season
[2] Increased to 10 bhp @ 12,000 rpm mid-season
[3] Increased to 90 mph (145 km/h) mid-season
[4] Non-classic event

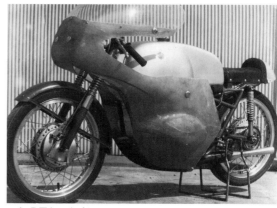

1961 RT61   *Archives*

1961 RV61   *Grüber*

RT62   1962
Engine type   *air-cooled inclined single cylinder 2-stroke*
Bore × stroke (mm)   54 × 54
Swept volume (cc)   123.67
Intake system   *rotary valve*
Carburettor   *Mikuni M29*
Compression ratio (to 1)   9.0
Ignition system   *Kokusan magneto*
Maximum power (bhp @ rpm)   20 @ 10,500, 23 @ 11,000, [24 @ 11,000][1]
Maximum speed mph (Km/h)   102–106 (165–172)
Clutch type   *dry multi-plate*
Transmission type   *constant mesh 7-speed*
Tyre size (F) (in)   2.50–19
Tyre Size (R) (in)   2.50–19
Brake system (F)   *1 × drum, twin leading shoe*
Brake system (R)   *1 × drum, single leading shoe*
Chassis type   *duplex tubular cradle*
Suspension system (F)   *coil sprung telescopic fork*
Suspension system (R)   *swing arm*
Dry weight lb (Kg)   165 (75)

1962 RM62   *MCN*

1962 125 cc World Championship   *French GP* (13.5.62) 5th
Degner. *Isle of Man TT* (4/8.6.62) 8th Degner. *Dutch TT* (30.6.62) 4th Degner, 9th Itoh. *West German GP* (15.7.62) 6th Anderson. *Ulster GP* (11.8.62) 5th Anderson, 7th Perris. *Italian GP* (9.9.62) 7th Perris, 8th Anderson. *Finnish GP* (23.9.62) 5th Perris. *Argentine GP* (14.10.62) 1st Anderson, 3rd Itoh. *Japanese GP[2]* (3/4.11.62) 2nd Perris, 6th Koshino, 10th Anderson.[3] *1962 Individual Championship[4]* 6th Anderson, 11th Degner, 13th Itoh, 19th Perris. *1962 Manufacturer's Championship* 2nd Suzuki

[1] Details as per front-exhaust model. Where different, rear-exhaust figures in brackets [].   [2] Non-classic event.
[3] Riding an RT63X
[4] Degner used a rear-exhaust model throughout 1962; other riders commencing with the Ulster GP

1962 RT62   *Archives*

RV62 1962

Engine type *air-cooled parallel twin cylinder 2-stroke*
Bore × stroke (mm) 54 × 54
Swept volume (cc) 247.34
Intake system *2 × rotary valve*
Carburettor *2 × Mikuni M29*
Compression ratio (to 1) 9.0
Ignition system *Kokusan magneto*
Maximum power (bhp @ rpm) 42 @ 10,500
Maximum speed mph (Km/h) 131 (210)
Clutch type *dry multi-plate*
Transmission type *constant mesh 6-speed*
Tyre size (F) (in) 2.75–18
Tyre size (R) (in) 3.00–18
Brake system (F) *2 × drum, single leading shoe*
Brake system (R) *1 × drum, single leading shoe*
Chassis type *duplex tubular cradle*
Suspension system (F) *coil-spring telescopic fork*
Suspension system (R) *swing arm*
Dry weight lb (Kg) 237 (108)

1962 250 cc World Championship *Dutch TT* (30.6.62)
Perris. *1962 Individual Championship* 20th Perris. *1962
Manufacturer's Championship* 8th Suzuki

RM63 1963

Engine type *air-cooled inclined single cylinder 2-stroke*
Bore × stroke (mm) 40 × 39.5
Swept volume (cc) 49.64
Intake system *rotary valve*
Carburettor *Mikuni M24*
Compression ratio (to 1) 8.8
Ignition system *Kokusan magneto*
Maximum power (bhp @ rpm) 11 @ 13,000
Maximum speed mph (Km/h) 93 (150)
Clutch type *dry multi-plate*
Transmission type *constant mesh 9-speed*
Tyre size (F) (in) 2.00–18
Tyre size (R) (in) 2.25–18
Brake system (F) *1 × drum, twin leading shoe*
Brake system (R) *1 × drum, single leading shoe*
Chassis type *duplex tubular cradle*
Suspension system (F) *coil sprung telescopic fork*
Suspension system (R) *swing arm*
Dry weight lb (Kg) 132 (60)

1963 50 cc World Championship *Spanish GP* (5.5.63) 2nd
Anderson, 4th Morishita. *West German GP* (26.5.63) 1st
Anderson, 2nd Morishita, 3rd Degner, 5th Itoh, 6th
Ichino. *French GP* (2.6.63) 2nd Degner, 3rd
Ichino. *Isle of Man TT* (10/14.6.63) 1st Itoh, 2nd
Anderson, 4th Morishita, 5th Ichino. *Dutch TT*
(29.6.63) 1st Degner, 2nd Anderson, 3rd Ichino, 4th
Morishita, 5th Itoh. *Belgian GP* (7.7.63) 1st Morishita,
2nd Degner, 4th Anderson, 5th Itoh, 8th
Ichino. *Finnish GP* (1.9.63) 2nd Itoh, 3rd Anderson, 4th
Morishita. *Argentine GP* (13.10.63) 1st Anderson, 2nd
Degner. *Japanese GP* (10.11.63) 2nd Anderson, 3rd

Masuda,[1] 4th Ichino, 6th Itoh, 7th Degner. *1963
Individual Championship* 1st Anderson, 3rd Degner, 4th
Morishita, 5th Itoh, 6th Ichino, 10th Masuda.
1963 Manufacturer's Championship 1st Suzuki

[1] After marriage adopted surname 'Matsumoto'

RT63/RT63X 1963

Engine type *air cooled parallel twin cylinder 2-stroke*
Bore × stroke (mm) 43 × 42.6
Swept volume (cc) 123.7
Intake system *2 × rotary valve*
Carburettor *2 × Mikuni M24*
Compression ratio (to 1) 8.8
Ignition system *Kokusan magneto*
Maximum power (bhp @ rpm) 25.5 @ 12,000, [24 @
12,000]
Maximum speed mph (Km/h) 114 (184) [108 (175)][1]
Clutch type *dry multi-plate*
Transmission type *constant mesh 8-speed*
Tyre size (F) (in) 2.50–18
Tyre size (R) (in) 2.50–18
Brake system (F) *2 × drum, single leading shoe*
Brake system (R) *1 × drum, single leading shoe*
Chassis type *duplex tubular cradle*
Suspension system (F) *coil sprung telescopic fork*
Suspension system (R) *swing arm*
Dry weight lb (Kg) 207 (94)

1963 125 cc World Championship *USA GP*[2]
(9/10.2.63) 1st Degner, 2nd Koshino, 5th Anderson.
Spanish GP (5.5.63) 7th Schneider. *West German GP*
(26.5.63) 1st Degner, 2nd Anderson. *French GP* (2.6.63)
1st Anderson, 4th Perris, 6th Degner. *Isle of Man TT*
(10/14.6.63) 1st Anderson, 2nd Perris, 3rd Degner, 5th
Schneider. *Dutch TT* (29.6.63) 1st Anderson, 2nd
Perris, 4th Schneider. *Belgian GP* (7.7.63) 1st
Schneider, 2nd Anderson. *Ulster GP* (10.8.63) 1st
Anderson, 2nd Schneider, 6th Perris. *East German GP*
(18.8.63) 1st Anderson, 3rd Schneider. *Finnish GP*
(1.9.63) 1st Anderson. *Japanese GP* (10.11.63) 1st
Perris, 3rd Degner, 5th Anderson, 6th Itoh, 10th
Koshino. *1963 Individual Championship* 1st Anderson,
4th Perris, 5th Schneider, 6th Degner, 20th Itoh. *1963
Manufacturer's Championship* 1st Suzuki

[1] Details as per rear-exhaust model. RT63X front-exhaust
figures in brackets []
[2] Non-classic event (riding RT63X machines)

RZ63 1963

Engine type *water cooled square four cylinder 2-stroke*[1]
Bore × stroke (mm) 43 × 42.6
Swept volume (cc) 247.32
Intake system *4 × rotary valve*
Carburettor *4 × Mikuni M24*
Compression ratio (to 1) 8.8

1962 RV62 *MCW*

1963 RM63 *MCW*

1963 RT63 *Archives*

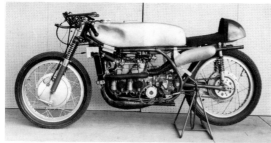

1963 RZ63 *Archives*

Ignition system *Kokusan magneto*
Maximum power (bhp @ rpm) 52 @ 12,500
Maximum speed mph (Km/h) 140 (225)
Clutch type *dry multi-plate*
Transmission type *constant mesh 6-speed*
Tyre size (F) (in) 2.75–18
Tyre size (R) (in) 3.00–18
Brake system (F) *2 × drum, single leading shoe*
Brake system (R) *1 × drum, single leading shoe*
Chassis type *duplex tubular cradle*
Suspension system (F) *coil sprung telescopic fork*
Suspension system (R) *swing arm*
Dry weight lb (Kg) 330 (150)

1963 250 cc World Championship *Japanese GP*
(10.11.63) 9th Anderson

[1]Thermo-syphon

RM64 1964
Engine type *air cooled inclined single cylinder 2-stroke*
Bore × stroke (mm) 41.5 × 36.8
Swept volume (cc) 49.78
Intake system *rotary valve*
Carburettor *Mikuni M24*
Compression ratio (to 1) 8.8
Ignition system *Kokusan magneto*
Maximum power (bhp @ rpm) 12.5 @ 14,000
Maximum speed mph (Km/h) 100 (160)
Clutch type *dry multi-plate*
Transmission type *constant mesh 9-speed*
Tyre size (F) (in) 2.00–18
Tyre size (R) (in) 2.25–18
Brake system (F) *1 × drum, twin leading shoe*
Brake system (R) *1 × drum, single leading shoe*
Chassis type *duplex tubular cradle*
Suspension system (F) *coil sprung telescopic fork*
Suspension system (R) *swing arm*
Dry weight lb (Kg) 132 (60)

1964 50 cc World Championship *USA GP* (1/2.2.64)
1st Anderson, 2nd Morishita, 3rd Itoh. *Spanish GP*
(10.5.64) 2nd Anderson, 3rd Itoh, 4th Morishita. *French
GP* (17.5.64) 1st Anderson, 5th Morishita. *Isle of Man
TT* (8/12.6.64) 1st Anderson, 3rd Morishita, 5th
Itoh. *Dutch TT* (27.6.64) 2nd Morishita, 3rd
Itoh. *Belgian GP* (5.7.64) 3rd Anderson, 4th Itoh, 5th
Morishita. *West German GP* (18/19.7.64) 2nd Morishita,
3rd Itoh. *Finnish GP* (30.8.64) 1st Anderson, 4th
Morishita. *1964 Individual Championship* 1st Anderson,
4th Morishita, 5th Itoh. *1964 Manufacturer's
Championship* 1st Suzuki

RT64 1964
Engine type *air cooled parallel twin cylinder 2-stroke*
Bore × stroke (mm) 43 × 42.6
Swept volume (cc) 123.7
Intake system *2 × rotary valve*

Carburettor   *2 × Mikuni M26*
Compression ratio (to 1)   8.8
Ignition system   *Kokusan magneto*
Maximum power (bhp @ rpm)   30 @ 13,000
Maximum speed mph (Km/h)   118 (190)
Clutch type   *dry multi-plate*
Transmission type   *constant mesh 8-speed*
Tyre size (F) (in)   2.50–18
Tyre size (R) (in)   2.50–18
Brake system (F)   *2 × drum, single leading shoe*
Brake system (R)   *1 × drum, single leading shoe*
Chassis type   *duplex tubular cradle*
Suspension system (F)   *coil sprung telescopic fork*
Suspension system (R)   *swing arm*
Dry weight lb (Kg)   199 (90)

1964 125 cc World Championship   *USA GP (1/2.2.64)*
1st Anderson, 2nd Itoh, 3rd Schneider, 4th
Morishita.   *Spanish GP (10.5.64)* 4th Schneider, 5th
Anderson, 9th Perris.   *French GP (17.5.64)* 2nd
Schneider, 3rd Perris.   *Dutch TT (27.6.64)* 4th
Schneider, 5th Anderson, 6th Perris.   *West German GP*
(18/19.7.64) 4th Schneider.   *East German GP (26.7.64)*
1st Anderson.   *Ulster GP (8.8.64)* 1st Anderson, 4th
Perris, 5th Schneider.   *Finnish GP (30.8.64)* 4th
Schneider.   *Italian GP (13.9.64)* 2nd Anderson, 3rd
Degner, 5th Perris.   *Japanese GP (1.11.64)* 1st Degner[1],
3rd Katayama.   *1964 Individual Championship* 3rd
Anderson, 4th Schneider, 6th Degner, 7th Perris, 8th
Itoh, 11th Katayama, 14th Morishita.
1964 Manufacturer's Championship 2nd Suzuki

[1] Using RT64A prototype water-cooled twin

RZ64   1964
Engine type   *water cooled square four cylinder 2-stroke[1]*
Bore × stroke (mm)   43 × 42.6
Swept volume (cc)   247.32
Intake system   *4 × rotary valve*
Carburettor   *4 × Mikuni M26*
Compression ratio (to 1)   8.8
Ignition system   *Kokusan magneto*
Maximum power (bhp @ rpm)   54 @ 12,500
Maximum speed mph (Km/h)   142 (230)
Clutch type   *dry multi-plate*
Transmission type   *constant mesh 6-speed*
Tyre size (F) (in)   2.75–18
Tyre size (R) (in)   3.00–18
Brake system (F)   *2 × drum twin leading shoe*
Brake system (R)   *1 × drum twin leading shoe*
Chassis type   *duplex tubular cradle*
Suspension system (F)   *coil sprung telescopic fork*
Suspension system (R)   *swing arm*
Dry weight lb (Kg)   308 (140)

1964 250 cc World Championship   *Spanish GP*
(10.5.64) 5th Anderson, 8th Schneider.   *French GP*
(17.5.64) 3rd Schneider.   *Ulster GP (8.8.64)* 6th
Schneider.   *1964 Individual Championship* 13th

1964 RM64   *Archives*

1964 RT64   *Archives*

1964 RZ64   *Grüber*

1965 RK65   *MCN*

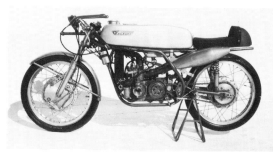

1965 RT65 *Archives*

1965 RZ65 *Grüber*

1966 RK66 (with Degner) *Grüber*

Schneider, 20th Anderson. *1964 Manufacturer's Championship* Suzuki un-placed

[1] Thermo-syphon

RK65 1965
Engine type *water cooled parallel twin cylinder 2-stroke*[1]
Bore × stroke (mm) 32.5×30
Swept volume (cc) 49.75
Intake system *2 × rotary valve*
Carburettor *2 × Mikuni M18*
Compression ratio (to 1) 8.6
Ignition system *Kokusan magneto*
Maximum power (bhp @ rpm) 14.5 @ 16,500
Maximum speed mph (Km/h) 102 (165)
Clutch type *dry multi-plate*
Transmission type *constant mesh 12-speed*
Tyre size (F) (in) 2.00–18
Tyre size (R) (in) 2.25–18
Brake system (F) *2 × drum, single leading shoe*
Brake system (R) *1 × drum, single leading shoe*
Chassis type *duralumin duplex tubular 'open'*
Suspension system (F) *coil sprung telescopic fork*
Suspension system (R) *duralumin swing arm*
Dry weight lb (Kg) 132 (60)

1965 50 cc World Championship *USA GP* (20.3.65)
1st Degner, 2nd Anderson, 3rd Ichino, 4th Koshino.
West German GP (25.4.65) 3rd Anderson, 4th
Itoh. *Spanish GP* (9.5.65) 1st Anderson, 7th
Itoh. *French GP* (16.5.65) 3rd Degner, 4th Itoh, 6th
Anderson. *Isle of Man TT* (14/18.6.65) 2nd Anderson,
3rd Degner, 8th Ichino. *Dutch TT* (26.6.65) 2nd
Anderson, 4th Itoh, 5th Degner. *Belgian GP* (4.7.65) 1st
Degner, 2nd Anderson, 4th Itoh. *Japanese GP*
(23/24.10.65) 3rd Itoh, 4th Anscheidt, 5th Ichino, 8th
Anderson. *1965 Individual Championship* 3rd Anderson,
4th Degner, 5th Itoh, 6th Ichino, 10th Koshino. *1965
Manufacturer's Championship* 2nd Suzuki

[1] Thermo-syphon

RT65
Engine type *water cooled parallel twin cylinder 2-stroke*[1]
Bore × stroke (mm) 43×42.6
Swept volume (cc) 123.7
Intake system *2 × rotary valve*
Carburettor *2 × Mikuni M29*
Compression ratio (to 1) 8.6
Ignition system *Kokusan magneto*
Maximum power (bhp @ rpm) 31 @ 13,650
Maximum speed mph (Km/h) 119 (193)
Clutch type *dry multi-plate*
Transmission type *constant mesh 9-speed*
Tyre size (F) (in) 2.50–18
Tyre size (R) (in) 2.50–18
Brake system (F) *2 × drum, twin leading shoe*
Brake system (R) *1 × drum, single leading shoe*

Chassis type *duplex tubular cradle*
Suspension system (F) *coil sprung telescopic fork*
Suspension system (R) *swing arm*
Dry weight lb (Kg) 198 (90)

1965 125 cc World Championship *USA GP* (20.3.65)
1st Anderson, 2nd Degner, 3rd Perris. *West German GP*
(25.4.65) 1st Anderson, 2nd Perris, 4th Degner. *Spanish GP* (9.5.65) 1st Anderson, 2nd Perris. *French GP*
(16.5.65) 1st Anderson, 2nd Degner, 3rd Perris. *Isle of Man TT* (14/18.6.65) 5th Anderson, 8th Degner. *Dutch TT* (26.6.65) 2nd Katayama, 3rd Anderson. *East German GP* (17/18.7.65) 1st Perris. *Czechoslovakian GP* (25.7.65) 1st Perris. *Ulster GP* (7.8.65) 1st Degner. *Finnish GP* (22.8.65) 1st Anderson, 2nd Perris. *Italian GP* (5.9.65) 1st Anderson, 2nd Perris. *Japanese GP* (23/24.10.65) 1st Anderson, 7th Perris. *1965 Individual Championship* 1st Anderson, 2nd Perris, 4th Degner, 11th Katayama. *1965 Manufacturer's Championship* 1st Suzuki

[1]Thermo-syphon

RZ65 1965
Engine type *water cooled square four cylinder 2-stroke*[1]
Bore × stroke (mm) 43 × 42.6
Swept volume (cc) 247.32
Intake system *4 × rotary valve*
Carburettor *4 × Mikuni M29*
Compression ratio (to 1) 8.8
Ignition system *Kokusan magneto*
Maximum power (bhp @ rpm) 56 @ 12,850
Maximum speed mph (Km/h) 148 (238)
Clutch type *dry multi-plate*
Transmission type *constant mesh 8-speed*
Tyre size (F) (in) 2.75–18
Tyre size (R) (in) 3.00–18
Brake system (F) *2 × drum, twin leading shoe*
Brake system (R) *1 × drum, twin leading shoe*
Chassis type *duplex tubular cradle*
Suspension system (F) *coil sprung telescopic fork*
Suspension system (R) *swing arm*
Dry weight lb (Kg) 286 (130)

1965 250 cc World Championship *USA GP* (20.3.65)
4th Perris. *Isle of Man TT* (14/18.6.65) 3rd Perris.
Dutch TT (26.6.65) 4th Katayama. *Belgian GP* (4.7.65)
4th Katayama, 5th Perris. *1965 Individual Championship*
10th Perris, 12th Katayama. *1965 Manufacturer's Championship* 5th Suzuki

[1]Forced circulation via water pump

RK66 1966
Engine type *water cooled parallel twin cylinder 2-stroke*[1]
Bore × stroke (mm) 32.5 × 30
Swept volume (cc) 49.75

Intake system *2 × rotary valve*
Carburettor *2 × Mikuni M20*
Compression ratio (to 1) 8.5
Ignition system *Kokusan magneto*
Maximum power (bhp @ rpm) 16.5 @ 17,000
Maximum speed mph (Km/h) 106 (172)
Clutch type *dry multi-plate*
Transmission type *constant mesh 12–14 speed*
Tyre size (F) (in) 2.00–18
Tyre size (R) (in) 2.25–18
Brake system (F) *2 × drum, single leading shoe*
Brake system (R) *1 × drum, single leading shoe*
Chassis type *duralumin duplex tubular 'open'*
Suspension system (F) *coil sprung telescopic fork*
Suspension system (R) *duralumin swing arm*
Dry weight lb/Kg 130 (59)

1966 50 cc World Championship *Spanish GP* (8.5.66)
2nd Anscheidt, 4th Anderson. *West German GP*
(22.5.66) 1st Anscheidt, 3rd Anderson. *Dutch TT*
(25.6.66) 3rd Anderson, 4th Anscheidt, 5th Katayama, 7th
Degner. *Isle of Man TT* (28.8–2.9.66) 3rd Anderson,
4th Degner. *Italian GP* (11.9.66) 1st Anscheidt, 4th
Anderson. *Japanese GP* (15/16.10.66) 1st Katayama,
2nd Anscheidt, 3rd Anderson, 4th Itoh. *1966 Individual Championship* 1st Anscheidt, 4th Anderson, 5th
Katayama, 6th Degner, 7th Itoh. *1966 Manufacturer's Championship* 2nd Suzuki

[1]Thermo-syphon

RT66 1966
Engine type *water cooled parallel twin cylinder 2-stroke*[1]
Bore × stroke (mm) 43 × 42.6
Swept volume (cc) 123.7
Intake system *2 × rotary valve*
Carburettor *2 × Mikuni M29*
Compression ratio (to 1) 8.6
Ignition system *Kokusan magneto*
Maximum power (bhp @ rpm) 32 @ 13,800
Maximum speed mph (Km/h) 123 (197)
Clutch type *dry multi-plate*
Transmission type *constant mesh 9-speed*
Tyre size (F) (in) 2.50–18
Tyre size (R) (in) 2.50–18
Brake system (F) *2 × drum, twin leading shoe*
Brake system (R) *1 × drum, single leading shoe*
Chassis type *duralumin duplex tubular 'open'*
Suspension system (F) *coil sprung telescopic fork*
Suspension system (R) *duralumin swing arm*
Dry weight lb (Kg) 196 (89)

1966 125 cc World Championship *West German GP*
(22.5.66) 4th Perris, 5th Anscheidt. *Dutch TT* (25.6.66)
4th Anderson. *East German GP* (17.7.66) 2nd
Katayama, 5th Perris. *Czechoslovakian GP* (24.7.66) 4th
Anderson, 5th Perris. *Finnish GP* (7.8.66) 4th Anderson,
5th Katayama. *Ulster GP* (20.8.66) 5th Anderson, 6th

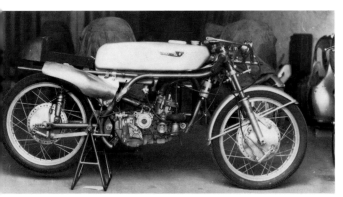

1966 RT66 *Grüber*

1967 RK67 (with Matsui) *Grüber*

1967 RT67 *Anscheidt*   1967 RT67 *Anscheidt*

Perris. *Isle of Man TT* (28.8.66–2.9.66) 3rd Anderson, 5th Perris. *Japanese GP* (15/16.10.66) 2nd Katayama, 3rd Itoh, 9th Anderson. *1966 Individual Championship* 5th Anderson, 6th Katayama, 7th Perris, 9th Itoh, 12th Anscheidt. *1966 Manufacturer's Championship* 3rd Suzuki

[1]Thermo-syphon

RK67 1967
Engine type   *water cooled parallel twin cylinder 2-stroke*[1]
Bore × stroke (mm)   32.5 × 30
Swept volume (cc)   49.75
Intake system   *2 × rotary valve*
Carburettor   *2 × Mikuni M22*
Compression ratio (to 1)   8.5
Ignition system   *Kokusan magneto*
Maximum power (bhp @ rpm)   17.5 @ 17,300
Maximum speed mph (Km/h)   109 (176)
Clutch type   *dry multi-plate*
Transmission type   *constant mesh 14-speed*
Tyre size (F) (in)   2.00–18
Tyre size (R) (in)   2.25–18
Brake system (F)   *2 × drum, single leading shoe*
Brake system (R)   *1 × drum, single leading shoe*
Chassis type   *duralumin duplex tubular 'open'*
Suspension system (F)   *coil sprung telescopic fork*
Suspension system (R)   *duralumin swing arm*
Dry weight lb (Kg)   128 (58)

1967 50 cc World Championship   *Spanish GP* (30.4.67) 1st Anscheidt, 2nd Katayama. *West German GP* (7.5.67) 1st Anscheidt. *French GP* (21.5.67) 1st Katayama, 2nd Anscheidt, 3rd Graham. *Isle of Man TT* (12/16.6.67) 1st Graham, 2nd Anscheidt. *Dutch TT* (24.6.67) 1st Katayama, 4th Anscheidt. *Belgian GP* (2.7.67) 1st Anscheidt, 2nd Katayama, 3rd Graham. *Japanese GP* (15.10.67) 1st Itoh[2], 2nd Graham, 4th Anscheidt. *1967 Individual Championship* 1st Anscheidt, 2nd Katayama, 3rd Graham, 6th Itoh.[2] *1967 Manufacturer's Championship* 1st Suzuki

[1]Forced circulation via water pump
[2]Official FIM race documents show Itoh as winner of the Japanese GP. For reasons now unknown to the FIM, he was omitted from the overall Individual Championship results.
The 8 points that should have been awarded to Itoh would have placed him 6th in the Individual Championship

---

RT67 1967
Engine type   *water cooled parallel twin cylinder 2-stroke*[1]
Bore × stroke (mm)   43 × 42.6
Swept volume (cc)   123.7
Intake system   *2 × rotary valve*
Carburettor   *2 × Mikuni M29*

Compression ratio (to 1) 8.5
Ignition system *Kokusan magneto*
Maximum power (bhp @ rpm) 35 @ 14,000
Maximum speed mph (Km/h) 129 (208)
Clutch type *dry multi-plate*
Transmission type *constant mesh 10-speed*
Tyre size (F) (in) 2.50–18
Tyre size (R) (in) 2.50–18
Brake system (F) *2 × drum, twin leading shoe*
Brake system (R) *1 × drum, twin leading shoe*
Chassis type *duralumin duplex tubular 'open'*
Suspension system (F) *coil sprung telescopic fork*
Suspension system (R): *duralumin swing arm*
Dry weight lb (Kg) 196 (89)

1967 125 cc World Championship *Spanish GP*
(30.4.67) 3rd Katayama, 4th Graham. *West German GP*
(7.5.67) 1st Katayama, 2nd Anscheidt. *French GP*
(21.5.67) 3rd Katayama, 4th Graham. *Isle of Man TT*
(12/16.6.67) 2nd Graham. *Dutch TT* (24.6.67) 3rd
Graham, 4th Katayama. *East German GP* (14.7.67) 3rd
Graham. *Czechoslovakian GP* (23.7.67) 2nd
Graham. *Finnish GP* (6.8.67) 1st Graham. *Ulster GP*
(19.8.67) 3rd Graham. *Italian GP* (3.9.67) 2nd
Anscheidt. *Japanese GP* (15.10.67) 2nd
Graham.[2] *1967 Individual Championship* 3rd Graham,
4th Katayama, 6th Anscheidt. *1967 Manufacturer's
Championship* 2nd Suzuki

[1]Forced circulation via water pump
[2]Riding an RS67

RS67/68 1967
Engine type *water cooled 90° V-4 cylinder 2-stroke*[1]
Bore × stroke (mm) 35.5 × 31.5
Swept volume (cc) 124.7
Intake system *4 × rotary valve*
Carburettor *4 × Mikuni VM24*
Compression ratio (to 1) 8.4
Ignition system *2 × Kokusan magneto*
Maximum power (bhp @ rpm) 42 @ 16,500
Maximum speed mph (Km/h) 137 (220)
Clutch type *dry multi-plate*
Transmission type *constant mesh 12-speed*
Tyre size (F) (in) 2.50–18
Tyre size (R) (in) 2.75–18
Brake system (F) *2 × drum, twin leading shoe*
Brake system (R) *1 × drum, twin leading shoe*
Chassis type *duralumin duplex tubular 'open'*
Suspension system (F) *coil-sprung telescopic fork*
Suspension system (R) *duralumin swing arm*
Dry weight lb (Kg) 209 (95)

1967 125 cc World Championship[2] *Japanese GP*
(15.10.67) 2nd Graham

[1]Forced circulation via water pump
[2]For full Championship results refer to model RT67

X6[1] **Racer** 1966–67
Engine type *air cooled parallel twin cylinder 2-stroke*
Bore × stroke (mm) 54 × 54
Swept volume (cc) 247.34
Intake system *piston port*
Carburettor *2 × Mikuni VM26*[2]
Compression ratio (to 1) 7.61
Ignition system *magneto*[3]
Maximum power (bhp @ rpm) 33 @ 10,500
Maximum speed mph (Km/h) 118 (190)
Clutch type *wet, multi-plate*
Transmission type *constant mesh 6-speed*
Tyre size (F) (in) 2.75–18
Tyre size (R) (in) 3.00–18
Brake system (F) *1 × drum, twin leading shoe*
Brake system (R) *1 × drum, single leading shoe*
Chassis type *duplex tubular cradle*
Suspension system (F) *coil-sprung telescopic fork*
Suspension system (R) *swing arm*
Dry weight lb (Kg) 260 (118)

1966–67 US National Races *Daytona* (20.3.66) 2nd
Hammer. *Carlsbad* (18.9.66) 2nd Mann, 3rd Grant, 8th
Hammer *Indianapolis* (6.8.66) 2nd Grant, 3rd Hammer

[1]US model name. Otherwise known as T20 or 'Super 6'
[2](2) Mikuni VM27 for 1967 X6
[3]'ARD' type for 1967 X6

TR250 1968–69
Engine type *air cooled parallel twin cylinder 2-stroke*
Bore × stroke (mm) 54 × 54
Swept volume (cc) 247.34
Intake system *piston port*
Carburettor *2 × Mikuni VM29*
Compression ratio (to 1) 7.0
Ignition system *Kokusan magneto*
Maximum power (bhp @ rpm) 35 @ 9000
Maximum speed mph (Km/h) 117 (190)
Clutch type *wet, multi-plate*
Transmission type *constant mesh 6-speed*
Tyre size (F) (in) 2.75–18
Tyre size (R) (in) 2.75–18
Brake system (F) *2 × drum, twin leading shoe*
Brake system (R) *1 × drum, single leading shoe*
Chassis type *duplex tubular cradle*
Suspension system (F) *coil-sprung telescopic fork*
Suspension system (R) *swing arm*
Dry weight lb (Kg) 253 (115)

1968–69 US National Races *Loudon* (16.6.68) 4th
Grant. *Sears Point* (7.9.69) 7th Grant

XR05 (TR500) 1968–69
Engine type *air cooled parallel twin cylinder 2-stroke*
Bore × stroke (mm) 70 × 64

Swept volume (cc)   492.6
Intake system   *piston port*
Carburettor   *2 × Mikuni VM32SC*
Compression ratio (to 1)   7.2
Ignition system   *Kokusan magneto*
Maximum power (bhp @ rpm)   63.5 @ 8000[1]
Maximum speed mph (Km/h)   135 (219)[2]
Clutch type   *wet multi-plate*
Transmission type   *constant mesh 5-speed*
Tyre size (F) (in)   3.00–18
Tyre size (R) (in)   3.50–18
Brake system (F)   *Fontana 2 × drum twin leading shoe*
Brake system (R)   *Fontana 1 × drum twin leading shoe*
Chassis type   *duplex tubular cradle*
Suspension system (F)   *Ceriani coil-sprung telescopic fork*
Suspension system (R)   *swing arm, Ceriani units*
Dry weight lb (Kg)   297 (135)

1968–69 US National Championship   *Daytona*
(17.3.68) 5th Grant, 9th Itoh.   *Loudon* (16.6.68) 7th
Grant.   *Indianapolis* (4.8.68) 7th Grant.   *Daytona*
(23.3.69) 2nd Grant, 13th Baumann.   *Loudon* (15.6.69)
15th Baumann.   *Indianapolis* (3.8.69) 2nd Grant, 3rd
Baumann.   *Sears Point* (7.9.69) 1st Baumann

[1]64.5 bhp @ 8000 rpm for 1969 model
[2]147 mph (238 Km/h) for 1969 model

TR250   1970

Engine type   *air cooled parallel twin cylinder 2-stroke*
Bore × stroke (mm)   54 × 54
Swept volume (cc)   247.34
Intake system   *piston port*
Carburettor   *2 × Mikuni VM30*
Compression ratio (to 1)   7.03
Ignition system   *Kokusan magneto*
Maximum power (bhp @ rpm)   41 @ 9000
Maximum speed mph (Km/h)   122 (197)
Clutch type   *wet multi-plate*
Transmission type   *constant mesh 6-speed*[1]
Tyre size (F) (in)   2.75–18
Tyre size (R) (in)   2.75–18[2]
Brake system (F)   *Ceriani (CFW225) 9 in. dia, 2 × drum*
                  twin leading shoe
Brake system (R)   *Ceriani (CFW170) 8 in. dia, 1 × drum*
                  twin leading shoe
Chassis type   *duplex tubular cradle*
Suspension system (F)   *Ceriani (CS1207-3G) coil sprung*
                       telescopic fork
Suspension system (R)   *Ceriani-damped (2404–325)*
                       swing arm
Dry weight lb (Kg)   248 (113)[3]

1970 US National Races   *Daytona* (15.3.70) 8th Grant,
9th Nicholas

[1]5-Speed for AMA events
[2]3.00–18 inch for Daytona
[3]Dry weight distribution 48% front, 52% rear. Weight
distribution (with rider) 40% front, 60% rear

1967 RS67 (with Itoh)   *Archives*

1966 X6 Racer   *Cycle World*

1968 TR250   *MCW*

1969 XR05 (TR500)   *MCN*

XR05 (TR500) 1970

Engine type *air cooled parallel twin cylinder 2-stroke*
Bore × stroke (mm) *70 × 64*
Swept volume (cc) *492.6*
Intake system *piston port*
Carburettor *2 × Mikuni VM34SC*
Compression ratio (to 1) *7.34*
Ignition system *Kokusan magneto*
Maximum power (bhp @ rpm) *70.5 @ 8000*
Maximum speed mph (Km/h) *152 (246)*
Clutch type *wet multi-plate*
Transmission type *constant mesh 5-speed*
Tyre size (F) (in) *3.00–18*
Tyre size (R) (in) *3.50–18*
Brake system (F) *Ceriani (CFW225) 9 in. dia, 2 × drum twin leading shoe*
Brake system (R) *Ceriani (CFW170) 8 in. dia, 1 × drum twin leading shoe*
Chassis type *duplex tubular cradle*
Suspension system (F) *Ceriani (CS1207-3G) coil sprung telescopic fork*
Suspension system (R) *Cerinai-damped (2404-325) swing arm*

Dry weight lb (Kg) *298 (135.5)[1]*

1970 US Grand National Championship *Kent*
(6.4.70) 1st Grant, 5th Baumann. *Talladega (17.5.70)*
2nd Nicholas, 4th Baumann

[1]Dry weight distribution 50% front, 50% rear. Weight distribution (with rider) 43% front, 57% rear

1970 TR250 (with Nicholas) *MCN*

1970 XR05 (TR500) *White*

XR05 (TR500)[1] 1971–2

Engine type *air cooled parallel twin cylinder 2-stroke*
Bore × stroke (mm) *70 × 64*
Swept volume (cc) *492.64*
Intake system *piston port*
Carburettor *2 × Mikuni VM34SC*
Compression ratio (to 1) *7.2*
Ignition system *Kokusan PEI magneto*
Maximum power (bhp @ rpm) *71.5 @ 8000*
Maximum speed mph (Km/h) *154 (250)*
Clutch type *wet multi-plate*
Transmission type *constant mesh 5-speed*
Tyre size (F) (in) *3.00–18*
Tyre size (R) (in) *3.50–18*
Brake system (F) *Fontana 2 × drum, twin leading shoe 250 dia*
Brake system (R) *Fontana 1 × drum, twin leading shoe 210 dia*
Chassis type *duplex tubular cradle*
Suspension system (F) *Ceriani (SC1207-3G) coil sprung telescopic fork*
Suspension system (R) *Ceriani-damped (2404-325) swing arm*

Dry weight lb (Kg) *287 (130.6)[2]*

1971–72 US Grand National Championship *Kent*
(11.7.71) 7th Nicholas. 8th Baumann. *Pocono (22.8.71)*

1971 XR05 (TR500) *MCW*

1972 XR11 (TR750) *MCW*

5th Nicholas, 9th Pierce. *Talladega* (5.9.71) 2nd Nicholas, 6th Grant, 18th Baumann. *Ontario* (17.10.71) 3rd Grant, 4th Baumann.

1971 500 cc World Championship *Austrian GP* (2.5.71) 2nd Turner, 4th Findlay. *West German GP* (16.5.71) 2nd Bron. *Isle of Man TT* (5/11.6.71) 3rd Perris[3]. *Dutch TT* (26.6.71) 2nd Bron, 4th Turner. *Belgian GP* (4.7.71) 3rd Findlay, 4th Bron. *East German GP* (10/11.7.71) 2nd Turner, 8th Bron. *Swedish GP* (24/25.7.71) 2nd Turner, 10th Findlay. *Finnish GP* (31.7–1.8.71) 3rd Bron, 4th Turner, 5th Findlay. *Ulster GP* (14.8.71) 1st Findlay, 2nd Bron. *Italian GP* (12.9.71) 5th Findlay, 6th Turner. *Spanish GP* (25/26.9.71) 5th Turner, 6th Findlay. *1971 Individual Championship* 2nd Turner, 3rd Bron, 5th Findlay, 11th Perris. *1971 Manufacturer's Championship* 2nd Suzuki.

1972 500 cc World Championship *French GP* (7.5.72) 3rd Bron, 8th Mandracchi. *Austrian GP* (14.5.72) 2nd Mandracchi, 4th Bron. *Yugoslavian GP* (18.6.72) 4th Mandracchi. *Dutch TT* (24.6.72) 10th Mandracchi. *1972 Individual Championship* 11th Mandracchi, 13th Bron. *1972 Manufacturer's Championship* 5th Suzuki

1973 UK International races *1973 Shellsport Championship* 1st Sheene[4], 2nd Woods[4]

[1]Became TR500II for 1972
[2]Dry weight distribution 49% front, 51% rear
[3]Using 1970 TR500 engine in a Seeley chassis
[4]Using 1972 TR500 II engine in a Seeley chassis

XR11 (TR750) 1972

Engine type *water-cooled three cylinder in-line 2-stroke*
Bore × stroke (mm) 70 × 64
Swept volume (cc) 738.9
Intake system *piston port*
Carburettor *3 × Mikuni VM34SC*[1]
Compression ratio (to 1) 7.0
Ignition system *Nippon-Denso CDI magneto*
Maximum power (bhp @ rpm) 100 @ 8000
Maximum speed mph (Km/h) 170 (275)
Clutch type *dry multi-plate*
Transmission type *constant mesh 5-speed*
Tyre size (F) (in) 3.25–18
Tyre size (R) (in) 3.50–18
Brake system (F) *twin discs 270 mm dia*
Brake system (R) *single disc 250 mm dia*
Chassis type *duplex tubular cradle*
Suspension system (F) *coil-sprung telescopic fork*
Suspension system (R) *swing arm*[2]
Dry weight lb (Kg) 367 (167)

US Grand National Championship *Atlanta*[3] (16.4.72) 1st Nicholas, 4th Grant. *Talladega* (3.9.72) 3rd Baumann. *Ontario* (1.10.72) 2nd Perry.

UK International Races *Isle of Man TT* (5.6.72) 3rd Findlay (750 cc race).
Italian International Races *Imola 200* (23.4.72) 17th Grant

[1]Mikuni VM32 SC carburettors used at Daytona only
[2]Rear suspension units mounted vertically
[3]This result disallowed after AMA inquiry decided that engine castings were 'illegal'

XR05 (TR500 III) 1973

Engine type *water-cooled parallel twin cylinder 2-stroke*
Bore × stroke (mm) 70 × 64
Swept volume (cc) 492.6
Intake system *piston port*
Carburettor *2 × Mikuni VM36SS*
Compression ratio (to 1) 7.0
Ignition system *Kokusan PEI magneto*
Maximum power (bhp @ rpm) 73 @ 8000
Maximum speed mph (Km/h) 157 (254)
Clutch type *dry multi-plate*
Transmission type *constant mesh 5-speed*[1]
Tyre size (F) (in) 3.25–18
Tyre size (R) (in) 3.50–18
Brake system (F) *twin discs 270 mm dia*
Brake system (R) *single disc 250 mm dia*
Chassis type *duplex tubular cradle*
Suspension system (F) *coil-sprung telescopic fork*
Suspension system (R) *swing arm*[2]
Dry weight lb (Kg) 308 (140)

1973 500 cc World Championship *French GP* (22.4.73) 6th Mandracchi, 10th Findlay. *Austrian GP* (6.5.73) 4th Mandracchi. *Isle of Man TT* (2/8.6.73) 1st Findlay. *Dutch TT* (23.6.73) 5th Findlay. *Belgian GP* (1.7.73) 3rd Findlay. *Czechoslovakian GP* (15.7.73) 5th Findlay. *1973 Individual Championship* 5th Findlay, 14th Mandracchi. *1973 Manufacturer's Championship* 4th Suzuki

[1]6-speed for some events
[2]Rear suspension units mounted vertically

XR11 (TR750) 1973

Engine type *water-cooled three cylinder in-line 2-stroke*
Bore × stroke (mm) 70 × 64
Swept volume (cc) 738.9
Intake system *piston port*
Carburettor *3 × Mikuni VM38SS*
Compression ratio (to 1) 7.0
Ignition system *Nippon-Denso CDI magneto*
Maximum power (bhp @ rpm) 107 @ 8000
Maximum speed mph (Km/h) 174 (282)
Clutch type *dry multi-plate*
Transmission type *constant mesh 5-speed*
Tyre size (F) (in) 3.25–18
Tyre size (R) (in) 3.50–18

Brake system (F)   *twin discs 270 dia*[1]
Brake system (R)   *single disc 200 dia*
Chassis type   *duplex tubular cradle*
Suspension system (F)   *Showa coil-sprung telescopic fork*
Suspension system (R)   *swing arm*[2]
Dry weight lb (Kg)   352 (160)

1973 US Grand National Championship   *Daytona* (11.3.73) 7th Emde.   *Dallas* (1.4.73) 1st Smart.   *Atlanta* (3.6.73) 1st Perry.   *Loudon* (17.6.73) 5th Perry.   *Laguna Seca* (29.7.73) 4th Smart.   *Pocono* (19.8.73) 6th Grant. *Talladega* (2.9.73) 6th Grant.   *Charlotte* (16.9.73) 4th Grant.   *Ontario* (30.9.73) 5th Smart, 10th Grant.

1973 FIM F750 Cup Series   *Italy* (15.4.73) 6th Findlay, 13th Woods.   *France* (27.5.73) 1st Sheene[3], 4th Woods.   *Sweden* (22.7.73) 1st Findlay, 2nd Woods, 3rd Sheene[3], 4th Mandracchi.   *Finland* (1.8.73) 2nd Sheene[4], 3rd Findlay, 4th Mandracchi, 5th Woods.   *Britain* (12.8.73) 1st Smart, 2nd Findlay.   *West Germany* (30.9.73) 1st Woods, 2nd Sheene[3], 5th Findlay.   *Spain* (7.10.73) 2nd Sheene[3], 3rd Mandracchi, 4th Findlay, 6th Woods. *1973 Individual Championship* 1st Sheene, 3rd Findlay, 4th Woods, 5th Mandracchi, 7th Smart.   *1973 Manufacturer's Championship* 1st Suzuki.

1973 UK International Races   *Isle of Man TT* 5th Woods (750 cc race).   *MCN Superbike Championship* 1st Sheene, 4th Woods

[1]Lockheed calipers fitted
[2]Rear suspension units mounted vertically
[3]Using a 1972 TR750 engine in a Seeley chassis
[4]Using a 1972 TR500 II engine in a Seeley chassis

XR05 (TR500 III)   1974

Engine type   *water-cooled parallel twin cylinder 2-stroke*
Bore × stroke (mm)   70 × 64
Swept volume (cc)   492.6
Intake system   *piston port*
Carburettor   2 × Mikuni VM38SS
Compression ratio (to 1)   7.2/7.4
Ignition system   *Kokusan PEI magneto*
Maximum power (bhp @ rpm)   78 @ 8700
Maximum speed mph (Km/h)   160 (260)
Clutch type   *dry multi-plate*
Transmission type   *constant mesh 6-speed*
Tyre size (F) (in)   3.25–18
Tyre size (R) (in)   3.50–18
Brake system (F)   *twin discs 270 mm dia*
Brake system (R)   *single disc 250 mm dia*
Chassis type   *duplex tubular cradle*
Suspension system (F)   *coil-sprung telescopic fork*
Suspension system (R)   *swing arm*[1]
Dry weight lb (Kg)   308 (140)

1974 UK International Races   *Shellsport Championship* 1st Sheene, 4th Woods

[1]Suspension units mounted vertically

1973 XR05 (TR500III) *Grüber*

1973 XR11 (TR750) *Archives*

1974 XR05 (TR500III) with Sheene *MCW*

1974 XR14 (RG500) with full-loop frame *Grüber*

XR14 (RG500) 1974

Engine type   *water-cooled square four cylinder 2-stroke*
Bore × stroke (mm)   *56 × 50.5*
Swept volume (cc)   *497.52*
Intake system   *4 × rotary valve*
Carburettor   *4 × Mikuni single-float VM34SS*
Compression ratio (to 1)   *8.0*
Ignition system   *Nippon-Denso CDI magneto*
Maximum power (bhp @ rpm)   *95 @ 11,200*
Maximum speed mph (Km/h)   *170 (275)*
Clutch type   *dry multi-plate*
Transmission type   *constant mesh 6-speed*
Tyre size (F) (in)   *variable (rim size 2.5–18)*
Tyre size (R) (in)   *variable (rim size : 3.5–18)*
Brake system (F)   *twin discs 280 mm dia*
Brake system (R)   *single ventilated disc 250 mm dia*
Chassis type   *duplex tubular 'open'[1]*
Suspension system (F)   *Kayaba coil-sprung telescopic fork*
Suspension system (R)   *Kayaba-damped swing arm[2]*
Dry weight lb (Kg)   *290 (137)[3]*

1974 500 cc World Championship   *French GP (21.4.74)*
2nd Sheene.   *Austrian GP (5.5.74)* 3rd Sheene, 4th
Findlay.   *Italian GP (19.5.74)* 4th Findlay.   *Belgian GP*
(7.7.74) 5th Findlay.   *Finnish GP (27/28.7.74)* 4th
Findlay.   *Czechoslovakian GP (25.8.74)* 4th Sheene, 7th
Findlay.   *1974 Individual Championship* 5th Findlay, 6th
Sheene.   *1974 Manufacturer's Championship* 3rd Suzuki

[1]Lower rails temporarily used mid-season. Duplex
tubular cradle frame used later
[2]Rear suspension units mounted in 'lay-down' position on
tubular steel swing-arm
[3]301 lb (137 Kg) after chassis changes (see note 1)

XR11 (TR750) 1974

Engine type   *water-cooled three cylinder in-line 2-stroke*
Bore × stroke (mm)   *70 × 64*
Swept volume (cc)   *738.9*
Intake system   *piston port*
Carburettor   *3 × Mikuni VM38SS*
Compression ratio (to 1)   *7.1*
Ignition system   *Nippon-Denso CDI magneto*
Maximum power (bhp @ rpm)   *110 @ 8000*
Maximum speed mph (Km/h)   *178 (288)*
Clutch type   *dry multi-plate*
Transmission type   *constant mesh 5-speed*
Tyre size (F) (in)   *3.50–18*
Tyre size R) (in)   *4.50–18*
Brake system (F)   *twin discs 270 mm dia[1]*
Brake system (R)   *single disc 250 mm dia*
Chassis type   *duplex tubular cradle*
Suspension system (F)   *Showa coil-sprung telescopic fork*
Suspension system (R)   *swing arm[2]*
Dry weight lb (Kg)   *339 (154)*

1974 US Grand National Championship   *Daytona*
(10.3.74) 9th Smart, 11th Carr.   *Atlanta (2.6.74)* 3rd

Nixon.   *Loudon (16.6.74)* 1st Nixon, 13th
Smart.   *Laguna Seca (28.7.74)* 4th Smart.   *Talladega*
(1.9.74) 4th Sheene, 5th Carr.   *Ontario (6.10.74)* 4th
Sheene.

1974 FIM F750 Cup Series   *Spain (26.5.74)* 2nd
Findlay, 6th Mandracchi.   *Britain (10/11.8.74)* 1st
Smart, 4th Woods[3], 7th Findlay.   *1974 Individual*
Championship 3rd Findlay, 4th Smart, 9th Woods, 13th
Mandracchi.   *1974 Manufacturer's Championship* 2nd Suzuki

1974 UK International Races   *MCN Superbike*
Series 1st Sheene, 2nd Woods[3]

[1]Double-piston calipers used
[2]Rear suspension units mounted vertically
[3]Using a 1973 TR750 engine in a Seeley chassis

XR05 (TR500 III) 1975

Engine type   *water-cooled parallel twin cylinder 2-stroke*
Bore × stroke (mm)   *70 × 64*
Swept volume (cc)   *492.6*
Intake system   *piston port*
Carburettor   *2 × Mikuni VM38SS*
Compression ratio (to 1)   *7.4*
Ignition system   *Kokusan PEI magneto*
Maximum power (bhp @ rpm)   *80 @ 8900*
Maximum speed mph (Km/h)   *160 (260)*
Clutch type   *dry multi-plate*
Transmission type   *constant mesh 6-speed*
Tyre size (F) (in)   *3.25–18*
Tyre size (R) (in)   *3.50–18*
Brake system (F)   *twin discs 270 mm dia*
Brake system (R)   *single disc 250 mm dia*
Chassis type   *duplex tubular cradle*
Suspension system (F)   *coil-sprung telescopic fork*
Suspension system (R)   *swing arm[1]*
Dry weight lb (Kg)   *308 (140)*

1975 UK International Races   *Shellsport Championship*
8th Newbold
[1]Rear suspension units mounted in lay-down position

XR14 (RG500) 1975

Engine type   *water-cooled square four cylinder 2-stroke*
Bore × stroke (mm)   *56 × 50.5*
Swept volume (cc)   *497.52*
Intake system   *4 × rotary valve*
Carburettor   *4 × Mikuni single-float VM34SS*
Compression ratio   *8.0*
Ignition system   *Nippon-Denso CDI magneto*
Maximum power (bhp @ rpm)   *100 @ 11,200*
Maximum speed mph (Km/h)   *175 (284)*
Clutch type   *dry multi-plate*
Transmission type   *constant mesh 6-speed*
Tyre size (F) (in)   *variable (rim size: 2.5–18)*
Tyre size (R) (in)   *variable (rim size: 3.5–18)*

Brake system (F)   *twin floating discs 270 mm dia*[1]
Brake system (R)   *single ventilated disc 250 mm dia*
Chassis type   *duplex tubular cradle*
Suspension system (F)   *Kayaba coil-sprung telescopic fork*
Suspension system (R)   *Kayaba-damped aluminium swing arm*[2]
Dry weight lb (Kg)   298 (135)

1975 500 cc World Championship   *Austrian GP* (4.5.75) 2nd Lansivuori.   *West German GP* (11.5.75) 3rd Lansivuori, 5th Woods.   *Italian GP* (18.5.75) 4th Toracca, 5th Woods, 7th Newbold[3].   *Dutch TT* (28.6.75) 1st Sheene, 4th Newbold, 5th Lansivuori.   *Belgian GP* (6.7.75) 2nd Newbold.   *Swedish GP* (20.7.75) 1st Sheene.   *Finnish GP* (27.7.75) 2nd Lansivuori.   *1975 Individual Championship* 4th Lansivuori, 6th Sheene, 8th = Toracca[4], 8th = Newbold, 16th Woods.   *1975 Manufacturer's Championship* 3rd Suzuki.

1975 UK International Races   *Shellsport Championship* 2nd Sheene.

1976 500 cc World Championship[5]   *Isle of Man TT* (7/12.6.76) 7th Williams.   *Dutch TT* (27.6.76) (27.6.76) 6th Williams.   *Belgian GP* (4.7.76) 1st Williams, 9th Newbold.   *Swedish GP* (25.7.76) 10th Newbold   *Finnish GP* (1.8.76) 4th Newbold.   *Czechoslovakian GP* (22.8.76) 1st Newbold.   *West German GP* (29.8.76) 4th Newbold.   *1975 Individual Championship* 5th Newbold, 9th Williams.   *1975 Manufacturer's Championship* 1st Suzuki.

1976 UK International Races   *Shellsport Championship*[5] 4th Williams, 5th Newbold.

1977 New Zealand International Races   *Marlboro Series* 1st Hennen[6].

1977 UK International Races   *Isle of Man TT* (11/17.6.77) 1st Read[6] (Senior race)

[1]Plasma-sprayed aluminium (1975 only)
[2] Rear suspension units (with *remote* reservoirs) mounted in 'lay-down' position
[3]Using a 1975 TR500 III
[4]Includes points scored whilst riding MV Agustas
[5]Barry Sheene's 1976 results detailed under RG500 (XR14), 1976
[6]Using engine only (engine no. 1011) mounted in production RG500 chassis

XR11 (TR750)   1975

Engine type   *water-cooled three cylinder in-line 2-stroke*
Bore × stroke (mm)   70 × 64
Swept volume   (cc) 738.9
Intake system   *piston port*
Carburettor   *3 × Mikuni VM38SS*
Compression ratio (to 1)   7.4
Ignition system   *Nippon-Denso CDI magneto*
Maximum power (bhp @ rpm)   116 @ 8250

Maximum speed mph (Km/h)   180 (292)
Clutch type   *dry multi-plate*
Transmission type   *constant mesh 6-speed*
Tyre size (F) (in)   *variable (rim size: 2.50–18)*
Tyre size (R) (in)   *variable (rim size: 3.50–18)*
Brake system (F)   *twin floating discs 270 mm dia*[1]
Brake system (R)   *single ventilated disc 250 mm dia*
Chassis type   *duplex tubular cradle*
Suspension system (F)   *Kayaba coil-sprung telescopic fork*
Suspension system (R)   *Kayaba-damped aluminium swing arm*[2]
Dry weight lb (Kg)   326 (148)

1975 US Grand National Championship   *Daytona* (9.3.75) 10th Aldana.   *Laguna Seca* (3.8.75) 5th Hennen.   *Ontario* (5.10.75) 12th Hennen.

1975 FIM F750 Cup Series   *Italy* (6.4.75) 15th Newbold.   *Belgium* (15.6.75) 6th Newbold.   *France* (22.6.75) 1st Sheene, 5th Newbold.   *Sweden* (19/20.7.75) 1st Sheene.   *Finland* (3.8.75) 3rd Lansivuori.   *Britain* (9/10.8.75) 1st Sheene, 2nd Lansivuori.   *Holland* (7.9.75) 3rd Newbold.   *Germany* (27/28.9.75) 2nd Williams, 5th Newbold.   *1975 Individual Championship* 2nd Sheene, 5th Newbold, 7th Lansivuori.   *1975 Manufacturer's Championship* 2nd Suzuki.

1975 UK International Races   *MCN Superbike Championship* 3rd Sheene, 4th Newbold, 8th Woods[3].

1976 FIM F750 Cup Series   *Venezuela* (21.3.76)[4] 3rd Newbold.   *Italy* (4.4.76) 3rd Sheene, 6th Newbold.   *Belgium* (23.5.76) 4th Newbold.   *Britain* (14/15.8.76) 4th Newbold.   *Holland* (5.9.76) 4th Newbold, 13th Williams.   *Germany* (26.9.76) 4th Newbold, 7th Williams.   *1976 Individual Championship* 3rd Newbold, 18th Sheene, 31st Williams.

1976 UK International Races   *Isle of Man TT* (7/12.6.76) 1st Williams (Classic race).   *MCN Superbike Championship* 1st Sheene[5], 5th Williams, 10th Newbold

[1]Plasma-sprayed aluminium
[2]Rear suspension units mounted in 'lay-down' position
[3]Using a 1974 TR750 (XR11)
[4]This result disallowed after FIM inquiry deleted the Venezuelan round
[5]Sheene occasionally used an enlarged 532 cc 1976 XR14

XR14 (RG500)   1976

Engine type   *water-cooled square four cylinder 2-stroke*
Bore × stroke (mm)   54 × 54
Swept volume (cc)   494.69
Intake system   *4 × rotary valve*
Carburettor   *4 × Mikuni single-float VM34SS*
Compression ratio (to 1)   8.2
Ignition system   *Nippon-Denso CDI magneto*
Maximum power (bhp @ rpm)   114 @ 11,000
Maximum speed mph (Km/h)   183 (296)

1975 XR11 (TR750) *Gruber*

1976 XR14 (RG500) *Author*

1977 XR21 (TR100) *Archives*

1977 XR24 (TR125) *Archives*

Clutch type *dry multi-plate*
Transmission type *constant mesh 6-speed*
Tyre size (F) (in) *variable (rim size: 2.50–18)*
Tyre size (R) (in) *variable (rim size: 3.50–18)*
Brake system (F) *twin floating discs 290 mm dia*
Brake system (R) *single ventilated disc 240 mm dia*
Chassis type *duplex tubular cradle*
Suspension system (F) *Kayaba pneumatic telescopic fork[1]*
Suspension system (R) *Kayaba-damped aluminium swing arm[2]*
Dry weight lb (Kg) 290 (132)

1976 500 cc World Championship[3] *French GP* (25.4.76) 1st Sheene. *Austrian GP* (2.5.76) 1st Sheene. *Italian GP* (16.5.76) 1st Sheene. *Dutch TT* (27.6.76) 1st Sheene. *Belgian GP* (4.7.76) 2nd Sheene. *Swedish GP* (25.7.76) 1st Sheene. *1976 Individual Championship* 1st Sheene. *1976 Manufacturer's Championship* 1st Suzuki.

1976 UK International Races *Shellsport Championship[3]* 1st Sheene

[1] Leg diameter: 35 mm, stroke: 150 mm, nitrogen-charged
[2] Kayaba units gas-charged with remote reservoirs
[3] Other 1976 results detailed under RG500 (XR14), 1975

XR21 (TR100) 1977

Engine type *air-cooled inclined single cylinder 2-stroke*
Bore × stroke (mm) 52 × 47
Swept volume (cc).81
Intake system *rotary valve*
Carburettor *Mikuni single-float VM32SS*
Compression ratio (to 1) 8.4
Ignition system *Nippon-Denso CDI magneto*
Maximum power (bhp @ rpm) 24 @ 11,500
Maximum speed mph (Km/h) 111 (180)
Clutch type *dry multi-plate*
Transmission type *constant mesh 6-speed*
Tyre size (F) (in) 2.50–18
Tyre size (R) (in) 2.75–18
Brake system (F) *single floating disc 250 mm dia*
Brake system (R) *single leading shoe drum-type 150 mm dia*
Chassis type *duplex tubular cradle*
Suspension system (F) *Kayaba pneumatic telescopic fork[1]*
Suspension system (R) *Kayaba-damped swing arm*
Dry weight lb (Kg) 147 (67)

[1] Nitrogen-charged

XR24 (TR125) 1977

Engine type *air-cooled inclined single cylinder 2-stroke*
Bore × stroke (mm) 54 × 54
Swept volume (cc) 123.67
Intake system *rotary valve*
Carburettor *Mikuni single-float VM34SS*
Compression ratio (to 1) 8.2

Ignition system *Nippon-Denso CDI magneto*
Maximum power (bhp @ rpm) 28.6 @ 11,250
Maximum speed mph (Km/h) 124 (200)
Clutch type *dry multi-plate*
Transmission type *constant mesh 6-speed*
Tyre size (F) (in) 2.50–18
Tyre size (R) (in) 2.75–18
Brake system (F) *single floating disc 250 mm dia*
Brake system (R) *single leading shoe drum-type 150 mm dia*
Chassis type *duplex tubular cradle*
Suspension system (F) *Kayaba pneumatic telescopic fork[1]*
Suspension system (R) *Kayaba-damped swing arm*
Dry weight lb (Kg) 147 (67)

[1] Nitrogen-charged

XR14 (RG500) 1977

Engine type *water-cooled square four cylinder 2-stroke*
Bore × stroke (mm) 54 × 54
Swept volume (cc) 494.69
Intake system *4 × rotary valve*
Carburettor *4 × Mikuni single-float VM34SS*
Compression ratio (to 1) 8.3
Ignition system *Nippon-Denso CDI magneto*
Maximum power (bhp @ rpm) 119 @ 10,800
Maximum speed mph (Km/h) 183 (296)
Clutch type *dry multi-plate*
Transmission type *constant mesh 6-speed*
Tyre size (F) (in) *variable (rim size: 2.50–18)*
Tyre size (R) (in) *variable (rim size: 4.00–18)*
Brake system (F) *twin floating discs 295 mm dia*
Brake system (R) *single ventilated disc 240 mm dia*
Chassis type *duplex tubular cradle*
Suspension system (F) *Kayaba pneumatic telescopic fork[1]*
Suspension system (R) *Kayaba 'Golden shock'[2]*
    with braced aluminium swing arm
Dry weight lb (Kg) 298 (135)

1977 500 cc World Championship *Venezuelan GP*
(20.3.77) 1st Sheene, 3rd Hennen, 9th Parrish. *West German GP* (8.5.77) 1st Sheene, 2nd Hennen, 4th Parrish. *Italian GP* (15.5.77) 1st Sheene, 11th Parrish. *French GP* (29.5.77) 1st Sheene, 6th Parrish, 10th Hennen. *Dutch TT* (25.6.77) 2nd Sheene, 3rd Hennen. *Belgian GP* (3.7.77) 1st Sheene, 3rd Hennen, 5th Parrish. *Swedish GP* (23/24.7.77) 1st Sheene, 4th Parrish, 10th Hennen. *Finnish GP* (31.7.77) 5th Parrish, 6th Sheene. *Czechoslovakian GP* (7.8.77) 4th Hennen, 7th Parrish. *British GP* (13/14.8.77) 1st Hennen. *1977 Individual Championship* 1st Sheene, 3rd Hennen, 5th Parrish. *1977 Manufacturer's Championship* 1st Suzuki.

1977 UK International Races *Isle of Man TT*
(11/17.6.77) 5th Hennen, 16th Parrish (Senior race), 9th Parrish (Classic race).

1977 UK International Races *Shellsport Championship*
1st Sheene, 2nd Hennen, 3rd Parrish

[1] Leg diameter: 36 mm, stroke: 140 mm, nitrogen-charged
[2] Nitrogen-charged, with adjustable pre-load, rate and damping

XR23 (RG700) 1977

Engine type *water-cooled square four cylinder 2-stroke*
Bore × stroke (mm) 62 × 54
Swept volume (cc) 652.12
Intake system *4 × rotary valve*
Carburettor *4 × Mikuni single-float VM36SS*
Compression ratio (to 1) 8.1
Ignition system *Nippon-Denso CDI magneto*
Maximum power (bhp @ rpm) 135 @ 10,800
Maximum speed mph (Km/h) 187 (303)
Clutch type *dry multi-plate*
Transmission type *constant mesh 6-speed[1]*
Tyre size (F) (in) *variable (rim size: 2.50–18)*
Tyre size (R) (in) *variable (rim size: 4.00–18)*
Brake system (F) *twin floating discs 295 mm dia*
Brake system (R) *single ventilated disc 240 mm dia*
Chassis type *duplex tubulas cradle*
Suspension system (F) *Kayaba pneumatic telescopic fork[2]*
Suspension system (R) *Kayaba 'golden shock'[3] with*
    braced aluminium swing arm
Dry weight lb (Kg) 299 (136)

1977 UK International Races *MCN Superbike Championship* 1st Sheene, 3rd Hennen, 5th Parrish

[1] With side-loading gear cluster
[2] Leg diameter: 37 mm, stroke: 140 mm, nitrogen-charged
[3] Nitrogen-charged, with adjustable pre-load, rate and damping

XR29 (RJ100) 1978

Engine type *water-cooled inclined single cylinder 2-stroke*
Bore × stroke (mm) 52 × 47
Swept volume (cc) 99.81
Intake system *rotary valve*
Carburettor *Mikuni single float VM32SS*
Compression ratio (to 1) 8.1
Ignition system *Nippon-Denso CDI magneto*
Maximum power (bhp @ rpm) 25 @ 11,500
Maximum speed mph (Km/h) 113 (183)
Clutch type *dry multi-plate*
Transmission type *constant mesh 6-speed*
Tyre size (F) (in) 2.50–18
Tyre size (R) (in) 2.75–18
Brake system (F) *single floating disc 285 mm dia*
Brake system (R) *single disc 200 mm dia*
Chassis type *duplex tubular cradle*
Suspension type (F) *Kayaba pneumatic telescopic fork[1]*
Suspension type (R) *Kayaba-damped aluminium swing arm[2]*
Dry weight lb (Kg) 152 (69)

[1] Nitrogen-charged
[2] Kayaba units gas-charged with remote reservoirs

XR22 (RGA500) 1978

Engine type *water-cooled square four cylinder 2-stroke*
Bore × stroke (mm) 54 × 54
Swept volume (cc) 494.69
Intake system *4 × rotary valve*
Carburettor *4 × Mikuni single-float VM34SS*
Compression ratio (to 1) *8.3*
Ignition system *Nippon-Denso CDI magneto*
Maximum power (bhp @ rpm) 122 @ 11,000
Maximum speed mph (Km/h) 185 (300)
Clutch type *dry multi-plate*
Transmission type *constant mesh 6-speed*[1]
Tyre size (F) (in) *variable (rim size: 2.50–18)*
Tyre size (R) (in) *variable (rim size: 4.00–18)*
Brake system (F) *twin floating discs 300 mm dia*
Brake system (R) *single ventilated disc 230 mm dia*
Chassis type *duplex tubular cradle*
Suspension system (F) *Kayaba pneumatic telescopic fork*[2]
Suspension system (R) *Kayaba 'golden shock'*[3] *with braced aluminium swing arm*
Dry weight lb (Kg) 299 (136)

1978 500 cc World Championship *Venezuelan GP*
(19.3.78) 1st Sheene, 2nd Hennen, 3rd Baker[4]. *Spanish GP* (16.4.78) 1st Hennen, 5th Sheene, 6th
Baker[4]. *Austrian GP* (30.4.78) 3rd Sheene. *French GP* (7.5.78) 2nd Hennen, 3rd Sheene. *Italian GP*
(13/14.5.78) 2nd Hennen, 4th Baker, 5th Sheene. *Dutch TT* (24.6.78) 3rd Sheene, 5th Hartog, 9th
Baker. *Belgian GP* (2.7.78) 1st Hartog, 3rd Sheene, 4th Rougerie. *Swedish GP* (23.7.78) 1st Sheene, 2nd
Hartog. *Finnish GP* (30.7.78) 1st Hartog. *British GP* (5/6.8.78) 3rd Sheene, 11th Rougerie. *West German GP*
(20.8.78) 1st Ferrari, 4th Sheene, 6th Rougerie. *1978 Individual Championship* 2nd Sheene, 4th Hartog, 6th
Hennen, 7th Baker[5], 10th Rougerie[5].
1978 Manufacturer's Championship 1st Suzuki.

1978 UK International Races Isle of Man TT
(3/9.6.78) 2nd Williams (Classic race).

1978 UK International Races *Shellsport Championship*
1st Sheene, 3rd Hennen.

1979 UK International Races *Isle of Man TT* (2/8.6.79)
1st Hailwood (Senior race), 2nd Hailwood (Classic race).

[1] With side-loading gear cluster
[2] Leg diameter: 37 mm, stroke: 130 mm, nitrogen-charged
[3] Nitrogen-charged, with adjustable pre-load, rate and damping
[4] Using a 1977 RG500 (XR14)
[5] Includes points scored whilst riding production RG500 III

XR23A (RGA700) 1978

Engine type *water-cooled square four cylinder 2-stroke*
Bore × stroke (mm) 62 × 54
Swept volume (cc) 652.12

1977 XR14 (RG500) *Author*

1978 XR29 (RJ100) *Archives*

1978 XR22 (RGA500) *Gruber*

1978 XR23A (RGA700) *Author*

Intake system   *4 × rotary valve*
Carburettor   *4 × Mikuni 'funnel type' twin-float VM36SS*
Compression ratio (to 1)   8.1
Ignition system   *Nippon-Denso CDI magneto*
Maximum power (bhp @ rpm)   135 @ 10,800
Maximum speed mph (Km/h)   191 (309)
Clutch type   *dry multi-plate*[1]
Transmission type   *constant mesh 6-speed*[2]
Tyre size (F) (in)   *variable (rim size: 2.50–18)*
Tyre size (R) (in)   *variable (rim size: 4.00–18)*
Brake system (F)   *twin floating discs 300 mm dia*
Brake system (R)   *single ventilated disc 230 mm dia*
Chassis type   *duplex tubular cradle*
Suspension system (F)   *Kayaba pneumatic telescopic fork*[3]
Suspension system (R)   *Kayaba 'golden shock'*[4] *with braced aluminium swing arm*
Dry weight lb (Kg)   299 (136)

1978 UK International Races   *MCN Superbike Championship* 1st Sheene, 5th Hartog, 9th Hennen

[1] Incorporating 'pull-type' clutch operating mechanism.
[2] With side-loading gear cluster.
[3] Leg diameter: 37 mm, stroke: 130 mm, nitrogen-charged.
[4] Nitrogen-charged, with adjustable pre-load, rate and damping.

XR27B (RGB500)   1979

Engine type   *water-cooled square four cylinder 2-stroke*
Bore × stroke (mm)   54 × 54
Swept volume (cc)   494.69
Intake system   *4 × rotary valve*
Carburettor   *4 × Mikuni 'funnel type' twin-float VM34SS*
Compression ratio (to 1)   8.3
Ignition system   *Nippon-Denso CDI magneto*
Maximum power (bhp @ rpm)   124 @ 11,000
Maximum speed mph (Km/h)   185 (300)
Clutch type   *dry multi-plate*[1]
Transmission type   *constant mesh 6-speed*[2]
Tyre size (F) (in)   *variable (rim size: 2.50–18)*
Tyre size (R) (in)   *variable (rim size: 4.00–18)*
Brake system (F)   *twin floating discs 310 mm dia*
Brake system (R)   *single ventilated disc 220 mm dia*
Chassis type   *duplex tubular cradle*
Suspension system (F)   *Kayaba pneumatic telescopic fork*[3]
Suspension system (R)   *Kayaba 'golden shock'*[4] *with braced aluminium swing arm*
Dry weight lb (Kg)   299 (136)

1979 500 cc World Championship   *Venezuelan GP* (18.3.79) 1st Sheene, 2nd Ferrari, 3rd Herron. *Austrian GP* (29.4.79) 2nd Ferrari, 3rd Hartog, 4th Herron, 5th Kawasaki, 7th Parrish, 12th Sheene. *West German GP* (6.5.79) 1st Hartog, 3rd Ferrari, 9th Parrish. *Italian GP* (13.5.79) 2nd Ferrari, 3rd Herron, 4th Sheene, 11th Parrish. *Spanish GP* (20.5.79) 2nd Hartog, 4th Ferrari, 11th Parrish. *Yugoslavian GP* (17.6.79) 2nd Ferrari, 4th Hartog, 9th Parrish. *Dutch TT* (23.6.79) 1st Ferrari, 2nd

Sheene, 3rd Hartog, 10th Parrish. *Swedish GP* (20.7.79) 1st Sheene, 5th Parrish. *Finnish GP* (28.7.79) 3rd Sheene, 10th Hartog, 11th Parrish, 15th Ferrari. *British GP* (12.8.79) 2nd Sheene, 3rd Hartog, 4th Ferrari. *French GP* (2.9.79) 1st Sheene, 7th Parrish. *1979 Individual Championship* 2nd Ferrari, 3rd Sheene, 4th Hartog, 10th Herron, 12th Parrish. *1979 Manufacturer's Championship* 1st Suzuki.

1979 UK International Races   *Shellsport Championship*[5] 1st Parrish.

[1] Incorporating 'pull-type' clutch operating mechanism.
[2] With side-loading gear cluster.
[3] Leg diameter: 37 mm, stroke: 130 mm, nitrogen-charged. With anti-dive mechanism
[4] Nitrogen-charged, with adjustable pre-load, rate and damping
[5] Sheene did not contest the Shellsport Championship

XR23B (RGB700)   1979

Engine type   *water-cooled square four cylinder 2-stroke*
Bore × stroke (mm)   62 × 54
Swept volume (cc)   652.12
Intake system   *4 × rotary valve*
Carburettor   *4 × Mikuni 'funnel type' twin-float VM36SS*
Compression ratio (to 1)   8.1
Ignition system   *Nippon-Denso CDI magneto*
Maximum power (bhp @ rpm)   138 @ 10,800
Maximum speed mph (Km/h)   191 (309)
Clutch type   *dry multi-plate*[1]
Transmission type   *constant mesh 6-speed*[2]
Tyre size (F) (in)   *variable (rim size: 2.50–18)*
Tyre size (R) (in)   *variable (rim size: 4.00–18)*
Brake system (F)   *twin floating discs 310 mm dia*
Brake system (R)   *single ventilated disc 220 mm dia*
Chassis type   *duplex tubular cradle*
Suspension system (F)   *Kayaba Pneumatic telescopic fork*[3]
Suspension system (R)   *Kayaba 'golden shock'*[4] *with braced aluminium swing arm*
Dry weight lb (Kg)   299 (136)

1979[5] UK International Races   *MCN Superbike Championship* 5th Parrish, 6th Sheene.

[1] Incorporating 'pull-type' clutch operating mechanism
[2] With side-loading gear cluster
[3] Leg diameter: 37 mm, stroke: 130 mm, nitrogen-charged. With anit-dive mechanism
[4] Nitrogen-charged, with adjustable pre-load, rate and damping
[5] These machines were occasionally raced in 1980

XR34M and XR34H (RGC500)   1980

Engine type   *water-cooled square four cylinder 2-stroke*
Bore × stroke (mm)   54 × 54

1979 XR27BFR (RGB500) front radiator version *Author*

1979 XR23B (RGB700) *Author*

1980 XR34M2 (RGC500) *Author*

1980 XR69 (GS1000R) *Author*

Swept volume (cc)   494.69
Intake system   *4 × rotary valve*
Carburettor   *4 × Mikuni 'funnel type' twin-float VM36Ss*[10]
Compression ratio (to 1)   8.5
Ignition system   *Nippon-Denso CDI magneto*
Maximum power (bhp @ rpm)   125 @ 10,800
Maximum speed mph (Km/h)   191 (309)
Clutch type   *dry multi-plate*[1]
Transmission type   *constant mesh 6-speed*[2]
Tyre size (F) (in)   *variable (rim size: 2.50–18)*[3]
Tyre size (R) (in)   *variable (rim size: 4.00–18)*
Brake system (F)   *twin floating discs 310 mm dia*
Brake system (R)   *single ventilated disc 220 mm dia*
Chassis type   *duplex tubular cradle*
Suspension system (F)   *Kayaba pneumatic telescopic fork*[4]
Suspension system (R)   *Suzuki-Kayaba 'full-float' monoshock*[5]
Dry weight lb (Kg)   317 (144)

1980 500 cc World Championship   *Italian Gp* (11.5.80) 3rd Rossi[6,7]. *Spanish GP* (18.5.80) 2nd Lucchinelli[6,7], 3rd Mamola, 12th Crosby[6]. *French GP* (25.5.80) 2nd Mamola, 3rd Lucchinelli[6,7], 4th Rossi[7], 5th Crosby[6]. *Dutch TT* (28/29.6.80 2nd Rossi[7], 5th Mamola, 8th Crosby[6]. *Belgian GP* (6.7.80) 1st Mamola, 2nd Lucchinelli[6,7], 4th Crosby[6], 5th Hartog[6]. *Finnish GP* (27.7.80) 1st Hartog[7], 4th Mamola. *British GP* (10.8.80) 1st Mamola, 3rd Lucchinelli[7], 4th Rossi[7], 13th Crosby[6]. *West German GP* (24.8.80) 1st Lucchinelli[7], 2nd Crosby[6], 3rd Hartog[7], 5th Mamola. *1980 Individual Championship* 2nd Mamola, 3rd Lucchinelli, 5th Rossi, 6th Hartog, 8th Crosby. *1980 Manufacturer's Championship* 1st Suzuki.

1980 UK International Races   *Isle of Man TT* (31.5/6.6.80) 1st Crosby (Senior race). *Shellsport Championship* 1st Mamola, 2nd Crosby[6]. *MCN Superbike Championship* 5th Mamola, 12th Crosby[6,8].

1981 500 cc World Championship   *Austrian GP* (26.4.81) 9th Hartog[9]. *West German GP* (3.5.81) 14th Hartog[9]. *British GP* (2.8.81) 16th Uncini. *Swedish GP* (16.8.81) 4th Uncini. *1981 Individual Championship* 13th Uncini.

1981 UK International Races   *Isle of Man TT* (6.6.81) 1st Grant (Senior race), 2nd Grant (Classic race).

US International Races   *Laguna Seca* (19.7.81) 1st Mamola (both legs).

[1] Incorporating 'pull-type' clutch operating mechanism
[2] With side-loading gear cluster
[3] Optional wheel sizes, 2.50–16 inch, and 2.25–16 inch
[4] Leg diameter: 40 mm, stroke: 120 mm, nitrogen-charged. With anti-dive mechanism
[5] XR34H models feature conventional rear suspension; XR3403H has steering-head positioned 20 mm rearwards, and swing-arm length increased by 20 mm
[6] Using XR34H model
[7] Using 16 inch diameter front wheel

[8]Using GS1000R for Brands Hatch round
[9]Using XR34 engine in Niko Bakker/Mike Sinclair chassis
[10]Lucchinelli and Rossi sometimes used 37.3 mm Mikunis in the latter half of season.

XR69 (GS1000R) 1980

Engine type *air-cooled dohc four cylinder in-line 4-stroke*[1]
Bore × stroke (mm) 70 × 64.8
Swept volume (cc) 997.52
Intake system *poppet valve (2 per cylinder)*
Carburettor *4 × Mikuni VM29SS 'smooth-bores'*
Compression ratio (to 1) 11.0
Ignition system *Nippon-Denso CDI*
Maximum power (bhp @ rpm) 130 @ 9500
Maximum speed mph (Km/h) 186 (301)
Clutch type *wet multi-plate*
Transmission type *constant mesh 5-speed*
Tyre size (F) (in) *variable (rim size: 2.50–18)*
Tyre size (R) (in) *variable (rim size: 4.00–18)*
Brake system (R) *twin floating discs 310 mm dia*
Brake system (R) *single ventilated disc 240 mm dia*
Chassis type *duplex tubular cradle*
Suspension system (F) *Kayaba pneumatic telescopic fork*[2]
Suspension system (R) *Kayaba-damped braced aluminium swing arm*[3]
Dry weight lb (Kg) 367 (167)

1980 TT F1 World Championship *Isle of Man TT*
(31.5/6.6.80) 2nd Crosby. *Ulster GP* (16.8.80) 1st Crosby, 2nd Dunlop. *1980 Individual Championship* 1st Crosby, 3rd Dunlop. *1980 Manufacturer's Championship* 1st Suzuki.

1980 UK International Races *Forward Trust TT F1 Championship* 2nd Crosby, 7th Dunlop.

1980 US International Races *Daytona* (9.3.80) 1st Crosby (100 mile Superbike race).

1980 Australian International Races *Swann series* 1st Crosby.

1980 Japanese International Races *Suzuka* (27.7.80) 1st Crosby[4] (8 hour race)

[1]Engine development by 'Pops' Yoshimura
[2]Leg diameter: 40 mm, stroke: 130 mm, nitrogen-charged. With anti-drive mechanism
[3]Kayaba units gas-charged with remote reservoirs
[4]Partnered by American rider, Wes Cooley

XR35 (RG500 Gamma) 1981

Engine type *water-cooled square four cylinder 2-stroke*
Bore × stroke (mm) 54 × 54
Swept volume (cc) 494.69
Intake system *4 × rotary valve*
Carburettor *4 × Mikuni 'funnel type' twin-float VM37½SS*[1]
Compression ratio (to 1) 8.5

Ignition system *Nippon-Denso CDI magneto*
Maximum power (bhp @ rpm) 130 @ 11,000
Maximum speed mph (Km/h) 194 (313)
Clutch type *dry multi-plate*[2]
Transmission type *constant mesh 6-speed*[3]
Tyre size (F) (in.) *variable (rim size: 3.00–16)*[4]
Tyre size (R) (in.) *variable (rim size: 4.00–18)*[5]
Brake system (F) *twin floating discs 310 mm dia*
Brake system (R) *single ventilated disc 220 mm dia*
Chassis type *duplex tubular cradle*[6]
Suspension system (F) *Kayaba telescopic fork*[7]
Suspension system (R) *Suzuki-Kayaba 'full-float' monoshock*
Dry weight lb (Kg) 297 (135)

1981 500 cc World Championship[10] *Austrian GP* (26.4.81) 1st Mamola, 2nd Crosby, 3rd Kawasaki. *West German GP* (3.5.81) 2nd Mamola, 3rd Lucchinelli, 7th Kawasaki, 13th Crosby. *Italian GP* (10.5.81) 2nd Crosby, 5th Lucchinelli[9]. *French GP* (17.5.81) 1st Lucchinelli[9], 2nd Mamola, 3rd Crosby, 6th Kawasaki. *Yugoslavian GP* (31.5.81) 1st Mamola[9], 2nd Lucchinelli[9], 4th Crosby[9]. *Dutch TT* (28.6.81) 1st Lucchinelli[9]. *Belgian GP* (5.7.81) 1st Lucchinelli[9], 3rd Mamola[8], 7th Crosby. *San Marino GP* (12.7.81) 1st Lucchinelli[9], 3rd Crosby[9], 4th Mamola.[9] *British GP* (2.8.81) 3rd Mamola[8], 19th Lucchinelli[9]. *Finnish GP* (9.8.81) 1st Lucchinelli[9], 2nd Mamola[8], 5th Crosby. *Swedish GP* (16.8.81) 5th Crosby[9], 9th Lucchinelli[9], 13th Mamola.[9] *1981 Individual Championship* 1st Lucchinelli, 2nd Mamola, 5th Crosby, 10th Kawasaki. *1981 Manufacturer's Championship* 1st Suzuki.

1981 UK International Races *Shellsport Championship* 1st Crosby

[1]Mikuni VM36SS type sometimes used
[2]Incorporating 'pull-type' clutch operating mechanism
[3]With side-loading gear cluster. Choice of 6 ratios for each gear position. (46,656 combinations)
[4]3.50–16 inch and 3.00–18 inch sometimes used
[5]4.50–18 inch used on aluminium frame only
[6]Normally circular steel tube but square-section aluminium alloy frame also available from June onwards (Mamola only.)
[7]Leg diameter: 40 mm, stroke: 120 mm, helically-sprung with anti-dive system, and adjustable pre-load. Variable fork leg off-set: 27 mm, 32 mm or 37 mm for trail adjustment
[8]Using square-section aluminium alloy frame
[9]Using Mikuni VM36SS carburetters
[10]Other 1981 results detailed under RG500 (XR34M and XR34H) 1980

XR69–S (GS100R) 1981

Engine type *air-cooled dohc four cylinder in-line 4-stroke*[1]
Bore × Stroke (mm) 70 × 64.8
Swept volume (cc) 997.52
Intake system *Poppet valve (2 per cylinder)*
Carburettor *4 × Mikuni VM33.4SS*[2]
Compression ratio (to 1) 11.0
Ignition system *Nippon-Denso CDI*
Maximum power (bhp @ rpm) 134 @ 9500
Maximum speed mph (Km/h) 189 (305)
Clutch type *wet multi-plate*
Transmission type *constant mesh 5-speed*
Tyre size (F) (in) *variable (rim size: 2.50–18)*
Tyre size (R) (in) *variable (rim size: 4.00–18)*
Brake system (F) (mm) *twin floating discs 310 mm dia*
Brake system (R) (mm) *single ventilated disc 240 mm dia*
Chassis type *duplex tubular cradle*
Suspension system (F) *Kayaba pneumatic telescopic fork*[3]
Suspension system (R) *Suzuki-Kayaba 'full-float'
monoshock*
Dry weight lb (Kg) 350 (159)

1981 TT F1 World Championship *Isle of Man TT*
(6.6.81) 1st Crosby, 4th Newbold[4]. *Ulster GP* (24.8.81)
2nd Crosby, 3rd Grant, 4th Newbold. *1981 Individual
Championship* 1st Crosby, 4th Newbold, 5th Grant. *1981
Manufacturer's Championship* 1st Suzuki

1981 UK International Races *Forward Trust/Motor
Cycle Weekly F1 Championship* 1st Crosby, 3rd
Newbold. *Isle of Man TT* (6.6.81) 1st Crosby, 2nd
Grant, 4th Newbold[4] (Classic race).

1981 US International Races *Daytona* (7/8.3.81) 100
Mile: 2nd Crosby.

[1] Engine development by Pops Yoshimura
[2] 31MM Keihin racing carburetters sometimes used
[3] Leg diameter: 40 mm, stroke: 130 mm, nitrogen-charged.
With anti-drive mechanism.
[4] Using 1980 GS1000R (XR69)

1981 XR35 (RG500 Gamma)
aluminium-framed version
Author

1981 XR69-S
(GS1000R) *Author*

Index

What they say about

Technicians

Team Suzuki is a good read and a great work of reference including two special chapters on Suzuki's US racing. Ray's attention to detail is second to none.
George Vukmanovich
Crew Chief to:
Warren Willing, Australian 750cc Champion 1976
Randy Mamola, US 250cc Champion 1978; 2nd 500cc World Championship 1980, 1981
Freddie Spencer, Double 500cc World Champion 1983, 1985
Luca Cadalora, Double 250cc World Champion 1991, 1992
Max Biaggi, 250cc World Champion 1997

From the moment I arrived at Beddington Lane in 1980, Ray was talking to me about the book he was writing, photographing and noting all that George (Vukmanovich) and I were doing to improve Randy's machines. I've had a copy of the resulting masterpiece on my bookshelves ever since.
Jerry Burgess
Mechanic to:
Randy Mamola 1980–82
Ron Haslam 1983–84
Freddie Spencer, 500cc World Champion 1985
Crew Chief to:
Wayne Gardner 1986-88, 500cc World Champion 1987
Mick Doohan, 5 times 500cc World Champion 1989–99
Valentino Rossi, 5 times 500cc and MotoGP World Champion 2000–08

Ray was the fly on the wall and he got all the info from all sides of the operation so he probably gathered a better picture of what was happening than many of us in the team had done. This is the straight scoop and shows Team Suzuki during some of its best years.
Mike Sinclair
Crew Chief to:
Pat Hennen 1977–78
Wil Hartog 1979–81
Virginio Ferrari 1982
Randy Mamola 1983–84, 1986–87
Rob McElnea 1985
Mike Baldwin 1986–87
Wayne Rainey, Triple 500cc World Champion 1988–93
Darryl Beattie 1994
Norifumi Abe 1995–96
Jean-Michel Bayle 1997–98
Max Biaggi 1999–2000